Aging: An Apprenticeship

Aging
An Apprenticeship

Nan Narboe, Editor

Red Notebook Press
PORTLAND, OREGON

First edition

Individual essay copyrights
are listed on pages 280-284.

Cover design by Ed Conn
Book design by Richard Warren

ISBN 978-0-692-75399-6 (print)
978-0-692-75400-9 (ebook)

Published by Red Notebook Press
Portland, Oregon

The force that through the green fuse drives the flower

Drives my green age.

— DYLAN THOMAS

Contents

Informed Aging

Nan Narboe

People who see me for therapy regularly ask if I can recommend a book on turning fifty. Or sixty or sixty-five: different ages resonate for different people. I generally have one to suggest, since a characteristic of my own aging has been to seek out what those a decade ahead of me have to say about their fifties, their sixties, their seventies (where I now reside), their eighties, and their nineties.

I think of such reading as an apprenticeship. Little kids imitate the way big kids walk and talk and chew gum. Adults of a certain age grow curious about who they will become, suspecting that the faded photos in their family albums don't foretell their own futures. In my forties, I pinned photos of older women whose faces I liked to the corkboard that held my jewelry, the better to study them. I see now that I was orienting myself in relation to an imagined future: gathering images in an attempt to envision myself, older.

Age is a state of being as much as it is a fact, something that fascinates both me and my clients, particularly when the clock runs backwards. A cycle of grief comes to an end, a thyroid supplement works, a client sheds a bullying boss or a controlling spouse and suddenly they are "younger." More energetic, more assured. They feel like themselves again, which is one of the challenges that growing older presents. If aging is the issue, adjustment is called for, whereas submitting to circumstances that can be improved is just plain dumb.

Much human misery, as Allen Wheelis pointed out, comes from mistaking problems for circumstances and vice versa. Problems have solutions. Circumstances, we have to live with—hence the attraction to informed aging, particularly as it is described in detail-rich essays like the ones in this volume.

Medical and sociological works on the life cycle have their place, but people in transition need stories as much as they need information. Stories reassure us that we are not alone. A client of mine once wailed, "No one warned me that my pubic hair was going to go gray!" He wasn't complaining about going gray; he was saying he would have liked a heads-up. Comments like his—along with my own ambition to age well—led to the creation of this collection.

Reading thousands of pieces to select the fifty-six that follow confirmed my original intuition. There are choices to be made: lives and attitudes to emulate, and ones to reject. Exemplars help. Hearing the least whiff of nostalgia in his speech, my dad would mutter, "I sound like an old fart," and change the subject. A ninety-one-year-old I know answers honestly when asked about his failing health, and then focuses on something he appreciates about the present moment, a pivot anyone can make, at any age.

Aging brings constraints. You know that and I know that. What we want to know is how to live well within those constraints. At my daughter's request, I no longer climb ladders unless someone else is present. Am I enlarged by her protectiveness or diminished by my lack of freedom? Were the sixty-eight years I clambered up ladders enough? Is anything ever enough?

Subjective Age: *I am vaguely forty, and have thought of myself as forty for thirty years. The longer this slippage continues, the more I wish I knew what was going on.*

This puzzling disjunction—no one who was born in 1945 is forty years old—led me to ask others to describe the age they are to themselves, despite what mirrors and calendars have to say. Two-thirds of the authors responded; their takes on this loosey-goosey, rarely discussed aspect of aging follow their essays.

It appears that some of us live in the tension between our actual age and our subjective, internal age, while others experience themselves as either ageless or all over the place.

NEARING

50

Middles

Jane Hamilton

I'm here in praise of middles. As much as the amorphous middle can be praised. That long beige corridor, but with doors, doors on every side. Door number one, door number two, door number three. And behind each one could there be—is there—an argument, a dining room set, a secret garden, a marriage, a box of Tide, the big emptiness, a moment of love? Could it be that in our life, this real life, the corridor goes on forever, generation after generation, world without end, end without end? For every action there is a reaction, reaction, reaction, the ripple out and out and out.

In storytelling the endings have an awful job, to pretend to hold that interminable middle, to bring all of the middleness to a screeching halt. No ending is nearly always a bad ending, and no good ending truly ends. It might be that there's no finality we can get a glimmer of except presumably and eventually our own, that greatest of mysteries to ourselves. How and when, and will we have dignity or make a mess of it? Will there be anyone at our side? Will it matter once we are in that final bubble of our own aloneness? Will we have one instant of firm knowledge that this then is what an ending actually is? The real ending of the story of our lives is that someone, somewhere, has the privilege of doing the difficult job of getting up the next morning, taking the walk down the hall—the intelligent body one hopes will do its work—and through the next door. Is there enough coffee? Daylight has come again.

If not endings, what? Shifts, transformations, the caterpillar to butterfly. Pauses, illuminations, and moments, briefest moments of conclusion. The slipperiest of moments, proved from the diploma, the divorce papers, the eviction notice. The Berlin Wall comes down, concluding fifty years of visible separation. Monica's book hits the remainders table, concluding two years of national insanity. Elvis is dead and yet he lives. In black ink, the bard says three hundred years later, "My love may still shine bright." Death is an end, so they say, but how does this simple story come to be?

In the overwhelming middle of giving birth I look around: a husband, midwife, doctor, nurse—no one there who can help me. "Father," I cry to my own father, ten years dead, "where are you? Can't you please come here just for a minute? Oh, where are you?" And there he is, as always at the ready, his dear face before mine. How has this happened to a matter-of-fact Midwestern woman of Puritan stock, about to give birth to a daughter? How is it that I am telling this to you tonight, years and years later? What has possessed me? These are sorts of questions of the overlooked middle, the unsung middle, the essential middle, the forever-ticking heart of the story, the place where characters do their mysterious work of living.

JANE HAMILTON, b. 1957, is an American novelist based in Wisconsin, where she lives in a farmhouse on an apple orchard. She has written seven novels, including the international best seller, *A Map of the World*. Her first novel, *The Book of Ruth*, won the PEN/Ernest Hemingway Foundation Award for best first novel, and was an Oprah's Book Club selection.

Subjective Age: *I have no idea how old I am. Anywhere from three-and-a-half to the aged, poor, good people in the dementia lockup. That is to say, it depends on the day.*

Thoughts on Aging

Germaine Koh

I turn forty-five tomorrow. I'm the oldest player in my roller derby league, and twice as old as some of my league-mates. I'm by no means the oldest person in the sport, but I'm definitely on the far right-hand side of the sport's bell curve.

I'm an Olympics junkie, and it was tough for me to listen to commentators discuss how improbable it would be for this or that mid-thirties athlete to medal, how they should be content just to have a respectable showing. It makes me think: that's what those athletes' years and years of training comes to, is it?

A lifelong jock, I do know what it's like to do awesome and extreme things with my body, and it hurts my pride each time I encounter something I can no longer excel at—but those moments are happening more and more often, so I need to come to terms with them.

Roller derby is my first contact sport, and I took it up at age forty-one, three years after blowing out my ACL and a year after rupturing my Achilles tendon. Those were my first major injuries, and despite diligent physio- and other therapy, it's been a challenge to return to top form. Instead, as the derby-related injuries accumulate, I'm starting to realize that I may need to learn to compromise and adjust.

I play with a great bunch of women, most of them ten or fifteen or more years younger than me, and I marvel at some of their skills improving literally by leaps and bounds. I doubt many of them dwell on it, but I am acutely aware of my age, especially at those practices when, against my own best advice, I skate hurt. I recognize that it's pointless and counterproductive, but I swallow my pride and grit through the pain of lap after lap. For someone with competitive habits, the fear of falling behind is more compelling than almost anything.

It's not for lack of training or effort, but I'm struggling to match my own personal bests. My league knows me as a champion of fitness and a student of training methods who leads by example. Although I can still out-pushup most of them, I'm starting to accept that there are real processes of decline that come with age. I'm not under-training, I start to realize; I'm…just…old.

Still, although my abilities are waning on some fronts, I do recognize that maturity gives me an advantage on others. Here's what I've figured out so far about being an aging athlete—though some of these insights really aren't age-specific.

TRAIN SMARTER, NOT HARDER

The small traumas produced by training take longer to clear as you get older, and it's silly to deny that fact by punishing the same muscles day after day. When it comes to repetitive practice, everyone has a point of diminishing return, and I reach mine sooner than I did when I was younger. Taking rest days, or alternating your focus, is just smart. And training while injured is just plain dumb.

CROSS-TRAIN

Overuse injuries are a real concern in roller derby, especially if you don't have the resiliency of young tissue. It has become clear to me that I'm much better off doing yoga or going for a run—anything, really, that uses my whole body in a balanced way—than attending a third day of practice in a row.

BALANCE

Not only do overused muscles ache to be balanced by cross-training, you're more useful on the track if you have personal balance. Unlike some of my most eager league-mates, I don't mind admitting that derby is not my entire life. Instead, on non-practice days, I decompress, I have a life, I cross-train, and I honestly think I'm a more focused and productive player because of it.

BE REALISTIC, BE INFORMED

There are real physiological changes associated with age: the fast-twitch muscles that give speed and power decline significantly, plus there's "declining VO2 max, reduced strength, increased body fat, reduced lactic acid clearance, declining bone density and more" (*Running Times*, November 2009). But in my case, with age also comes enough wisdom to research the facts and modify my training in a practical way.

SELF-KNOWLEDGE

I've always been focused on becoming Faster, Higher, Stronger, etc. However, as I've begun to accept that I may not be as naturally fast as I once was, I have to assess pragmatically what I should focus on. I now think strategically about optimizing my particular strengths and developing new ones, doing what I can to minimize weaknesses, and recognizing the difference between productive aches and injuring myself. Visualization can be a great tool for athletes, but my problem lately has been that I keep imagining myself doing things that my aging body contradicts. I'm still working out how to reconcile the optimism of visualization with the reality of corporeal limits, but I think the answer may lie in self-awareness.

EVOLVING STRENGTHS

Okay, so my fast-twitch muscles are disappearing. Other strengths have emerged that I never had before: endurance, for one. I used to be a sprinter, with all power and no stamina, but somewhere along the line I developed a capacity and a taste for the long haul. My viewpoint has also emerged from a tunnel to encompass much more, and I'm more self-directed because I'm taking responsibility for finding the right way for me to train. There's value in these skills; they're just different.

FIND THE RIGHT ROLE FOR YOU

When I started derby, I assumed I'd be a jammer. My mental self-image was still of a fast, agile, and offensive-minded athlete. But something hadn't yet sunk in: I'm getting old. I still jam when needed, but I'm learning to love the craft of defense and the synergy of teamwork, and I've become a strategy nerd. I crunch numbers as well as abs. I'm seeing patterns and potential plays on the track (the bigger picture?) that I was totally unaware of when I wore the jammer blinders. Over this past year, my team has really been learning to work together, and I've contributed to that. I'm not in this sport for the glory, so I'm okay with being the kind of player that most fans won't notice. My coaches and teammates know—and the statistics bear out—that there is a unique role for me, even if it's beneath the radar.

TRUST YOUR EXPERIENCE

I've played sports all my life, some quite competitively. Sometimes I feel a kind of instinctive knowledge, accumulated through years of being in competitive situations, kick in. My body knows how to bear down in a crunch, remembers how to find my reserves. I think practice and experience not only build muscle memory, they must also build strategic instincts and a kind of mental strength.

PATIENCE AND MATURITY

Two more characteristics I didn't have before. I'm not sure where they came from, but one day I realized that I was a de facto leader on my team, one of the people others looked to for constancy and stability. I may not be the fastest, but my team knows that I'll be there for them. And realistically, as much as I agonize over my performance, I do know that I'm doing pretty okay for an Ancient One. I may be better at rational self-assessment than I ever was.

GRACE AND HUMILITY

I realize I am not aging easily, but I am trying to find new ways for me to be an athlete. Yes, I wish I could be young again. I wish this amazing sport had existed in my physical prime. I realize that I'm not on the path to the Olympics. Still, I am going to forgive myself for having limits.

CARPE DIEM, BUT HAVE AN EXIT PLAN

I love roller derby, but this is probably my last year playing. Fate willing, I hope this time next year to be part of my league's first team to go to regional playoffs. This sport, which is on an accelerated evolutionary path that has barely even started recruiting hockey players or training youth, is going to pass me by before long. So I've already started looking around for my next sport, to soften my eventual retirement from this one. I'm not just going to let that river of time take me where it will. If you know of a sport that welcomes wily old folk who can throw a hip check, hit me up.

GERMAINE KOH, b. 1967, is a visual artist, independent curator, and lifelong athlete based in Vancouver, BC. "Thoughts on Aging" first appeared as a Facebook status under Koh's roller derby name, PLAYER1. More can be found on her website, germainekoh.com.

Subjective Age: *I am perhaps 35.*

Mouth

Pablo Tanguay

I got old all of a sudden. My mouth went first. I was at the Kroger, in the tooth aisle, comparing Orajels. The night before, in Novelties, I wavered, hands in pockets, body rocking for minutes, heel-toe, toe-heel, between the Cool Whip Extra Creamy and the Cool Whip Fat Free. I do love a brownie, and the picture on the white plastic tub of Extra Creamy featured just that: a thick chocolate brownie luxuriating in a frothy Cool Whip bath. But I felt almost equally called to the Fat Free, which sported not only enticing healthy alphabetic text—Fat Free—but also the image of, indulging in its own Cool Whip bath, a mound of plump blueberries. The Cool Whip Original, meanwhile, was content to display on its plastic lid some strawberries, a fruit which has moved me only once, on a night while working third-shift room service at the Luxor, in Las Vegas. But the strawberries on that night were mere addendum to the crux of a glorious, unexpectedly moving experience, and so for the Original, a little past midnight, I had no desire whatsoever.

In the early 2000s, a gum man in Nashville, a good one, if the early Internet was to be believed, my blood all over his smock, scolded me for my smoking.

"That's why you're here," he said. He wore yellow pants. "That's why this. Do you see?"

And I remember a dentist on Santa Monica Boulevard in the very late '80s setting out on her desk, after my exam, a clean glass ashtray. We smoked her Pall Malls or Carltons as she reviewed various payment options for the work my mouth required. She wore a light blue outfit, maybe a jumper of some sort, was older, slender, definitely a longtime smoker. I say Santa Monica Boulevard but her office was tiny, and to get to it I climbed two or three flights of stairs. The stairwell and her office, even the interior office into which she'd invited me to talk and smoke, as if we'd been cast in a revival of *Marcus Welby, M.D.*, smelled of cat piss. Still, I felt important: never before (and not since, actually) had a medical person invited me behind a closed door to discuss, across a desk in serious tones, my condition. There I was, smoking long cigarettes with a Hollywood dentist in her Hollywood office, discussing financial packages.

In many regards, my mother was terrible about mothering. She did, though, for almost a half-decade in the '70s, refuse me all candy and made sure I got to the dentist regularly. The dentist was Dr. DalPorto, who had a full head of wavy, decade-appropriate hair. I remember him as perfectly decent but his son, Todd, though only a couple years older than me and so only thirteen or so when I last knew him, had already achieved the affect of what I would come to know as Cruel Frat Boy. They lived in The New Homes, on the other side of the orchard. Though I wouldn't have been aware of it at the time, I'm sure, thinking about it in retrospect, Dr. DalPorto maintained my mouth pro bono. My mother, despite addictions and the general lack of good will toward others that forever kept her from achieving what ordinary Americans might call success, was good at making deals that made sure our needs got met. The route manager for *The Chronicle*—the shleppy, middle-aged guy who oversaw all the paperboys—was named Mr. Chiotti. I can still hear, breaking the silence of the midnight hours, my mother shouting, from behind her bedroom door, "Chiotti! Chiotti! Ah, damn, that's right, Chiotti!" What I mean is, my mother wasn't above putting out if it meant, say, we got the paper free everyday.

. . . .

Of my pleasures, the sweetest might be waking with my children. When I was maybe twenty-one, I read *The Clown*, by Heinrich Boll. For a long time, I kept a copy of it. When my then-wife broke things off and took up with another, I went hard at the book with a red pen, underlining and circling and exclamation-pointing what I thought were relevant passages, passages, really, in my distress, I knew were meant for me. (Books could overwhelm me then.) I haven't read *The Clown* since and don't recall the specifics of what I marked up, but I do recall that the hero's girl had left him for a more proper soul and so the hero was distraught and confused and angry. So I splashed the relevant passages with red ink and mailed the book to my ex. And then I think I forgot about it because I remember being startled, some time after we'd reconciled, when she said, half-jokingly, that what I'd done was the act of a lunatic. What must I have been thinking, she wondered, to do such a thing? No matter that the act was actually rather tame, in comparison anyway to a thousand other acts I'd committed or would commit, but the answer, of course, was that I wasn't thinking at all: I was feeling and I was acting. My twenties were spent that way, almost exclusively. But what I remember most about Boll's book now, what has remained with me, oddly, over several decades, has nothing to do with humiliating, inexplicable loss. Rather, what I remember is a description of a small sleeping child's breath as being "sweet."

At some point in my early twenties I bragged to a roomful of people at a party that I hadn't brushed my teeth in a year. An artist asked a few minutes later if I would pose as David. He'd won a commission, he said, to paint the slaying of Goliath on the ceiling of some church on the Lower East Side. He'd pay $10 an hour and feed me. A week or so later, there I was in the artist's Brooklyn apartment, naked, doing slow motion somersaults on a blue gymnastics mat he'd unrolled in his front room. He stood a few feet away, sketching what he saw by the light from a small desk lamp. From what looked to me like a large, stand-up toolbox, he'd opened, earlier, when I'd first arrived, a couple drawers and removed from them dozens of sketches, many of which he spread on the floor. They were sketches of bodies in motion. He was proving his bona fides to me, me, who knew nothing of art. The sketches reminded me of da Vinci drawings I'd seen in textbooks. After tumbling a while, I stopped for dinner. He'd made macaroni and cheese. I warned him that my belly distended when I ate, that, after eating, I'd look a little less like David. I don't remember if I ate in the nude or whether I sat or stood, and I don't remember the plate I ate off or the cup I drank from. Surely I washed the mac and cheese down with something. Then, after eating, I went back to my slo-mo tumbling.

Later that night, on the platform at 59th Street, waiting for the local, I was frisked by a pair of cops who said I looked just like a guy they were looking for. As they were frisking me, a woman came running down the steps screaming that someone was getting beat upstairs. One of the officers told me to stay put until they got back. They were big New York cops. One of them waved a big fat finger at me. Then they went lumbering up the stairs. After a couple minutes, the local came and I was on my way again. I saw the artist at another party some time later and when he tried to speak to me I pretended I didn't know him. I'd started brushing my teeth again, which may have been why he didn't press it. I kept up the brushing, too, regularly, until some next catastrophe struck. By thirty-three, I was brushing two, three times a day, no matter what. I was a real go-getter. By forty, I was full on into the floss.

My companion is not romantic about the morning breath of our children. She prides herself on calling a spade a spade.

"They stink," she says, of all three of them. "Their mouths stink. Their asses stink."

Me, I like to crawl into bed with them in the early morning. I snuggle my nose up as close as possible to their little mouths. They are seven, five, and five. Sometimes, if one of them is still sleeping soundly, I'll rest my hand on their chest and feel, simultaneously, their heartbeat and their breath. I just read a Cortazar story in which it's difficult to tell the past from the future, the real from a dream. Who knows why we remember what we do.

PABLO TANGUAY, b. 1963, lives in Columbus, Ohio, and works in the English Department at Ohio State University. He is the Associate Poetry Editor for the Ohio State Press' Journal Prize series. He blogs at *The Kenyon Review*, where "Mouth" originally appeared.

Subjective Age: *My subjective age depends on what's going in and coming out of my mouth, on any given day.*

Aging

Paulina Porizkova

"Old age is the revenge of the ugly ones," is a French proverb; one that I first heard at the very advanced age of fifteen upon my arrival in Paris. I had spent five years in the ugly bin at school in Sweden, and had only recently been upgraded to beautiful. My ego was still fragile and my mind still pumped full of highbrow arty self-education and nerdy jokes, which is how one gets by when one is ugly. Which of course, I promptly realized, is exactly what will pay off as one ages: beauty fades, but a mind constantly energized will shine even brighter with age. I immediately took the proverb as my own personal motto and patted myself on the back with satisfaction. I will continue to be intelligent, I vowed, no matter how beautiful I become. And then, at, like, the old age of thirty-five, I'll be an incredibly smart and kinda attractive old lady. In interviews I gave at the wise age of seventeen and eighteen, I pontificated about the beauty of age and wisdom, and blabbered on about how I look forward to my first wrinkle. What an idiot I was.

My first recognition of age setting in was exactly on my thirty-sixth birthday. I have no idea why, on this day of all days, I looked in the mirror and realized my face no longer looked young. I didn't look bad: only, the freshness had somehow disappeared. I immediately became hyper-conscious of my looks and went out and bought the most expensive cream on the market. (For your information, it did nothing.) And I began the battle of acceptance, something I have to do now almost every time I face a mirror.

"Oh sure, Miss Supermodel, it must be hard for you," you may think, pityingly. (I have also heard it spoken aloud more than once, although, oddly enough, the tone wasn't so much pitying as sarcastic.) "You have always been more beautiful than the average," the conversation goes, "so it goes without saying, you still are. At least, in your age category." Hmm, I know it's a compliment, so why do I not fluff up with delight?

Maybe because nothing ages as poorly as a beautiful woman's ego.

When you're used to one sort of treatment, it's really hard to get demoted, even if that new treatment is still better than the average. Boo-hoo. I know. My life sucks. Now, I don't actually know the exact cut-off age where beautiful ceases and "must-have-once-been-beautiful" begins. It's true it's not forty-five. I can still get attention when I try really hard, even if it's greatly reduced. But would I ever have dreamed that I would miss the time I couldn't walk past a construction site unmolested? These days when someone whistles at me, it's mostly a bike messenger about to mow me down.

Having been confident with the way my looks affected others, I was used to using them as extra cash. True, this worked mostly with the male population, but that little extra I could get out of them—as I begged them not to give poor-little-me a ticket, or keep that door open just a second longer or try just a little harder to find an empty seat on that plane— I took for granted.

Like everything else in life, there is always payback and it's a bitch. Beauty, unlike the rest of the gifts handed out at birth, does not require dedication, patience and hard work to pay off. But it's also the only gift that does NOT keep on giving. It usually blossoms at an age where you're least equipped to handle its benefits and rewards and instead take it all for granted, and by the time you start understanding the value of it, it slowly trickles away. How's that for revenge of the ugly ones?

To me, to let yourself age means that you're comfortable with who you are. Yes, sorry, I do believe that all the little shots here and there, and the pulling of skin here and there and the removal of fat here and there, means you still have something to prove; you're still not comfortable in your skin. The beauty of age was supposed to be about the wisdom acquired and with it, an acceptance and celebration of who you are. Now all we want for people to see is that we have not yet attained that wisdom. Aging has become something to fight, not something to accept. Aging is a matter of control and control of matter. We can call injections of foreign stuff under our skin "having nothing done" since it doesn't actually involve surgery. So what if Botox makes you look like a poorly dubbed movie, or worse, human sock puppet where there is no match-up between what you say and how you feel, and you're turning all your family and friends slightly Asperger-ish.

What if you chose the fillers instead? Then you can proudly say "no Botox here" and forget to mention the rest of the stuff that now inhabits your epidermis. The problem there seems to be that the minute you fix those frown lines, your forehead looks tremendously wrinkled. And the moment you fix that, your eyes are so hollowed, you need just a touch of extra cheekbone. And suddenly, you look really great as long as you don't move a single facial muscle. Because once you do, a single twitch will reveal a whole landscape of matter under your skin that really shouldn't be there. So you may use a little Botox to fix that and…and gray is much easier to blend with blonde and…before you know it, you have joined the cult of the Scandinavian Stepfords. The members of this clan, like the once hairy-brunette-Italian Madonna and the once freckled-redhead-Aussie Nicole Kidman, now resemble no one as much as the blonde American Barbara Walters, who could, in turn, not only be their mother but also the sister of Linda Evans. They are all now high-cheekboned, smooth-skinned Scandinavian blondes. But only one of them started out that way.

Now, let me state once and for all that I am not against plastic surgery. In many cases, it is something that can so vastly improve the quality of life it actually saves it. And even in the more frivolous cases, I do not have a problem with a woman who chooses a teensy bit of this or that to make herself feel better, as long as she admits to it. Nothing galls me as much as age-defying celebrities who achieve their looks by "healthy food and yoga." I know this is bullshit. You may not. But I can guarantee we will both feel bad about the way we look, the way we have let ourselves go, when Michelle Pfeiffer and Demi Moore look not a day over thirty.

I recently saw a comment posted on to one of the blogs I had written by a woman who stated that my problem is that I'm obviously jealous of these women I criticize, because they are not only beautiful but successful, something I'm clearly not. That gave me pause. Am I just jealous? Is my entire creative output completely reliant on this baser of emotions? It's true I'm trying to find a new place in the world that would rather

I had just shut up and stayed beautiful (dying young is a terrific way to achieve this, by the way), which makes me a tad resentful. It's also true I'm still very insecure and want attention and universal love and have not a friggin' clue on how to achieve it. And likewise, it is true that I am jealous, and envious, and covetous of things I don't have. Which are, or is, rather—surprise, surprise—not an unlined forehead or puffy lips, nor a hot career, but confidence. True confidence: the kind that should come with age and that I keep glimpsing off in the distance, the kind I tell myself I would have developed already had I relied on wit rather than looks.

I keep a list of my "heroines," the women who have dared to age, and I'm always stupidly grateful to see these women highlighted in the media. I just found out that Jamie Lee Curtis, one of the women on my list, and Madonna are the same age. Looking at photos of them side by side is a revelation. One looks no older than thirty, hard-edged, determined and hungry. The other looks like she's old enough to be her mother, but radiant, confident and content. I already know I'm too vain and too insecure to follow her footsteps. This is what and whom I'm jealous of. But even as I struggle with the choices—age, age a little, age not at all—I realize I'm blessed to even be in the position to age. To age is a privilege, not a birthright, even though most of us in the civilized world seem to forget this. This choice of "not-aging" is actually reserved for well-off women with lots of time and money. I've met a lot of these women at parties and social gatherings, and they were all lovely, gracious, generous and often way smarter than me. So when I asked them all who they would elect as their symbol of graceful aging, the overwhelmingly popular choice, Madonna, was disheartening. With all the choices we have, with all those beautiful and strong and powerful women in their forties and fifties (Oprah? Arianna Huffington? Kathryn Bigelow? Christiane Amanpour?), the choice was the one woman who has elected to NOT age. Of course, the kicker is: artificial youth takes a lot of maintenance. Maintenance takes a lot of time.

So, the more time you chase—the more time you waste.

PAULINA PORIZKOVA, b. 1965, is a Czech model, actress, and writer. As a supermodel in the 1980s and 1990s, she appeared on the covers of *Sports Illustrated*, *Vogue*, and *Cosmopolitan*. She is the author of the novel *A Model Summer* and is a regular contributor to *Modelinia* and *The Huffington Post*. Porizkova is also featured in the documentary *About Face: Supermodels, Then and Now*.

Passing for Young-ish

Christian M. Lyons

Some years ago I was laid off from a government position. As my career was well established, I didn't think I'd have any difficulty finding another job. I took a week to update my résumé and then, freshly printed documents in hand, natty tie around my neck, I went in search of a new career.

I dutifully researched prospective companies, staff, and markets for months. And months. And months. True, this was after an economic downturn and unemployment rates were high, but I behaved as if I had plenty of time before my money ran out. Before I knew it, a year had passed. I was getting interviews, but once I met with the team of potential employers, I never heard from them again. With funds running dangerously low, I turned to staffing agencies and fared much better.

The need for short-term, non-benefitted, non-permanent staff is a thriving business. What I didn't know—and what I learned quickly—is that having a staffing agency place you into a temporary position rarely results in being hired full-time and permanent. In fact, staffing agencies are a red flag to serious employers who look at potential candidates' stability, marketability, and longevity. While workers might imagine businesses would focus on the fact that we at least maintained employment in some form, many employers do not. They instead see instability, and perhaps an undesirable candidate.

I continued to send out résumés while working contract positions, and landed interviews time and again. But nothing I did led to a job offer. I began to examine some of the subtle ways employers harvest information about potential employees, as I believed age and experience were behind me not landing a position.

When filling out online applications, employers request your educational background, and ask when you attended school or which year you graduated. They would like you to believe that it's so they can assess your background and suitability for the position offered. So we, proud of our achievements, willingly comply and fill in those boxes. Instead, I learned it was a "legal" way to determine the age of an applicant without coming right out and asking. So I stopped completing those boxes, listing simply the school and the degree and nothing else. That increased my marketability, it seemed, for then the phone rang daily with invitations to interview. Perhaps age, among other factors, *did* have something to do with the hiring process.

I didn't believe I was what anyone would call "old." Many times, those in the interview room with me were the same age. A few times the interviewer was considerably younger, which made me noticeably uncomfortable, like being put on the spot by a grandchild, or worse. A younger person might be more marketable, but I had maturity, experience, and now, a wide range of diverse skills in my background. I had only to market *around* my age, which proved to be a challenge.

I couldn't very well hide how old I was, especially in person. Instead, I strived to present my age as strength. As a former people pleaser, I often apologized for mundane things, projecting an attitude of subservience. Borrowing a stanza from a seventies song, I took the unrepentant mental stance of, *I am forty ... hear me roar!* I wanted to make employers see forty as the new twenty.

I met with increased success, now getting second and sometimes third callbacks. But still no solid offers. That's when, in a stroke of genius— *I am forty, hear me roar!*—I called random corporate human resource departments and staffing agencies, requesting interviews, claiming I was writing a paper on career hunting. Several agreed to meet with me on the basis of anonymity. Then I asked the questions that no one seemed to be asking:

What demographic is the bulk of your employee base?

Is there bias when considering age?

How do age, gender, and cultural determinants impact your decision, based on the public image your company is trying to present?

The answers were surprising. The people I spoke with admitted that they were afraid of hiring someone too old or too experienced, who would expect a higher salary and more benefits. Also, older applicants were perceived as more resistant to change. Getting them to follow directions, learn new processes and perform tasks would result in conflict. The interviewers, one representative said, have a specific idea of what image they want to project for their company, and often, gender, age, race, and socioeconomic status play a large part in the decision making process in spite of these factors being discriminatory.

Despite the fact that I was willing to perform even menial jobs, I was passed over time and again by companies interested in hiring younger employees, paying them less, and managing them more easily. I came across a photo meme that summed up the job industry up quite accurately:

We're looking for someone from twenty-two to twenty-six years old with thirty years' experience.

Using this information, I tweaked my résumé and sent it out once more. I removed any information about age and socio-economic status, which included removing my specific street address and other references to my position in society. I even declined to provide the requisite Equal Opportunity Employer (EOE) information tacked on to many online application sites. That way race and other perceived cultural differences were removed as well. Despite the fact that I presented as exactly who I am, a man in his forties, I wanted a level playing field where I could express *in person* my knowledge, willingness to adapt, and most of all, my youthful energy.

Did it work?

Yes. I was able to work around the biases I knew were firmly in place. Also, I learned more effective ways to present myself in person. I wore non-threatening colors and muted tones so my skills would stand out, not my clothing. I wore a tie if a particular company's culture indicated it appropriate and landed a position at a reputable Fortune 500 company.

No matter how much we'd like to believe that bias does not or cannot exist in current society, it does. Experience is overlooked in favor of youth. At the end of the day (which comes so much earlier as we grow older) it's up to us to recognize age bias when we encounter it and take measures to address it.

CHRISTIAN MARCUS LYONS, b. 1961, is an award-winning writer whose work has appeared in *The Bark, New York Magazine, The Edge, Babel,* and in the fiction anthologies *Darker Times* and *Pull the Trigger.*

Subjective Age: *Most days I feel like I am 20 years old . . . that is until I have to climb up off the floor after playing with the dogs.*

The Freaking Autumn of My Life

Julie Gray

I have been pretty worried about turning fifty for about three years now. When I turned forty-seven, the voice in my head was saying sure, sure, forty-seven WHICH IS ALMOST FIFTY I'M GOING TO DIE!

Of course, at that time, I was living in Los Angeles, or Land O' the Youth Obsessed. In LA, when you turn fifty, you are either put out to pasture in your Malibu Mansion of Quiet Regrets or, more often, taken out behind the Hollywood sign and shot.

When I heard people, friends maybe, bemoaning turning forty, I wanted to scream OH, PLEASE, but then I didn't because that's rude and immature.

A few years ago, maybe four or five, I don't know, my memory is going, I had lunch with Shane Black, the gifted screenwriter of movies like *Kiss Kiss Bang Bang,* and he said to me, about turning fifty, "I feel my mortality unfurling beneath me." I thought it so beautifully put, his poetic declaration of his new, near-death status. Touching, really, from where I stood, a good half decade away from the Gates of Death.

But now it's coming this summer, ironically, the freaking autumn of my life. Fifty. Which is probably, oh, say, the early September of the autumn of one's life. Or so. But then, we never really know, do we?

Yes, my mortality is unfurling beneath me. But so is yours so put that in your pipe and smoke it.

I choose, instead of living *The Death of Ivan Illych*, in which death draws me inevitably closer to its bony chest, to allow this unfurling to lift me to greater heights. Like some kind of reverse-gravity-boot type of thing. I don't know. I'm not a scientist.

Interestingly, the inevitability, the unstoppability of growing older has made no inroads on my deep dislike ("outright hostility, let's explore that," my therapist says) of pictures of kitties on Facebook with captions under them about cherishing life and whatever.

But an acceptance of stuff I can't help has led me to a greater wisdom, a patience, call it whatever you want—maybe resignation—which gives me license to scoff haughtily at things like high heels and huge, stupid, fashionable purses.

(Full disclosure: I never wore high heels or carried big, stupid, fashionable purses, so honestly the scoffing is come by pretty easily. But because fifty has a certain gravitas, I can say that to someone much younger *and they believe me because I'm older.*)

Do you see where I am going with this?!

Why let them down, I say? Unfurl that mortality and pass the opinion sauce!

Remember when you were younger and your parents and various "old people" would say stuff like "you aren't experienced enough" or "you'll find out one day"? Well, we have! We found out! We ARE experienced enough! And I intend to lord this over as many people as possible.

Recently, someone twenty-five years younger than me suggested that I hadn't gotten a particular opportunity because I was "like, too old maybe?" I gave her quite a scolding by way of freaking out internally and crying later. I made a mental note to come right back in HER face in twenty-five years but then I'll probably be dead or incapacitated by then so it won't really have the same impact.

But youth, as everybody but the young know, is way overrated. Besides, I've been to Burning Man, I've seen the Smiths live TWICE, I know what Twitter is and who Miley is and what doing really dubious things is like. I've been around the block. And I don't want to go back.

Some say that it takes losing those you love to really cherish your life. Or seeing third world suffering. I can't say either of those experiences has shifted my point of view toward cute-kitty-gratitude about life. In fact, I have a theory that those who favor Facebook status updates featuring kitties, ponies and beaches with captions like "Dance the dance of life! Today! Because life is so special and stuff!" are honestly deluded. Newsflash: Life is like a carton of eggs. Some have poop on them. Dance on that.

Despite my best efforts to stay firmly rooted in my Scottish, inherited death-be-not-soon gloom, something shifted within me recently. Perhaps it's the inevitable date of June ninth; it keeps getting closer no matter what I do (HINT: please send gifts), but in any event, my attitude, my coping mechanism, some might say, is to feel a great wave of not gratitude, exactly, and not fear, either, but of motivation to do the things that I've not done yet.

I've done a lot of things, mind you, I did my bucket list a long time ago, stuff like going to Cairo or seeing the Smiths—TWICE—no, I'm talking about the ordinary things that I never used to make time to do. Things like swimming more, trying out a dance class and reading the books I never got around to. To chill out more, call people back when I damn well feel like it and take more walks before I'm in a Mobility Scooter.

I want to do more of these things now not because I have the fear of impending old age and death but because now seems like a good time; I'm twenty-five years older than OMG-he-didn't-call-me-back and twenty-five years younger than I-wonder-if-this-is-my-last-birthday. So I'm right where I want to be. Right in appreciation and enthusiasm but, at long last, secure enough and smart enough to enjoy it.

And that's a pretty nice place to be.

JULIE GRAY, b. 1964, is a writer and media literacy advocate living in the Middle East, which has truly honed her sense of humor and tolerance for heat and chaos. Julie writes for the *Huffington Post, Script,* and the *Times of Israel,* and is the founder of the Tel Aviv Writer's Salon and the Middle East Media Literacy Initiative (MEMLI).

Subjective Age: *While my actual age is fifty-something, my subjective age is, oh, about thirty-five.*

Repose

John Griswold

It was finals week at Hinterland, and students were permitting their parents to drive three hours south to pick them up for a summer at home. Outside one residence hall a dad in expensive shorts barked orders at his son's friends humping stereo components to the car. Mother, in her nylon tracksuit, did the cha-cha of uselessness, trying to be helpful but also getting yelled at by her husband as if she were a child. Several younger parents in the drive seemed eager to relive their own college glory; they shouted to each other and giggled and went into football stances and paced up the block, evidently looking for the Skulls kegger. An older mom and dad trudged from dorm to curb, hardly looking up; their demeanor said, It's OK, run over my feet again with your wheeled Vuitton luggage, I'm of no great consequence anyhow. All the students were embarrassed and begged to get on the road. It's an awkward time.

Disengaging suddenly and finally from my students each semester fills me with nervous energy. I walked to, and from, and then back to, campus—more than four miles—for no good reason other than to focus my eyes on something more distant than a page of student writing.

. . . .

Do you have repose? Take the Patillo test. It's named for an army friend who used to try to annoy us by always asking, "Ain't you itchin'?"

"No," we replied, even when covered in ticks and leeches and dying the death of a thousand cuts from sawgrass.

"Bet you are," Patillo said. "Bet you're itchin' right now. Huh? You itchin'? Up there on your scalp? Top of your left ear?"

"Hell we are," we replied.

"Oh, yes you are, you can't help it," Patillo said. "It's just a little tickle, but it's growing, isn't it? Now it's on your right shoulder blade, and it itches like hell. Jesus, it's on your lip. Scratch it. Scratch at it. You know you want to. You got to. It's in the hair on your shin, it's like you got fleas and they're bitin' you. They brought the mosquitoes with 'em. And the earwax is in on it; it's tickling the little hairs in your ear canal; my God, it's the most sensitive place on your body. Scratch it! Rub it! Git it!"

Last I heard of Patillo, he was training helicopter pilots. Imagine yourself wrestling the collective, the cyclic, and both pedals on a big turbo-charged aircraft known in aviation circles—due to its capriciousness—as the Death-Jet Ranger. It's been painted bright orange so it'll be easier to find from the air when it crashes. Sweat runs into your eyes, where you can't reach it under your helmet visor, even if you could take your hands from the controls. Your instructor, Warrant Officer Patillo, tells you you're doing fine.

Then: "Hey, are you itchin'?"

If you can say confidently that you wouldn't be affected, you may have repose.

. . . .

At some point every semester, a student asks, "Why is literature always about bad stuff?" It's a good question, since that perception keeps so many—especially those in the middle class who want only happyhappy—from art. Part of the answer is that drama is conflict.

So we've heated up the earth, and the last of the polar bears may be gone within twenty-five years. So what? In the cosmic view, it's no big deal, but I have a hard time with it. And you know who's next, after the polar bears: your third-grade teacher, Miss Benzene, that great hulk in polymer pearls who for years dressed her snarling Chihuahua in little red pants, a fur-lined jacket, and a Santa hat, and brought him to school the last day before winter break. She slapped Danny Tule, the littlest kid in class, right out of his desk for bragging about being a tap dancer while she was trying to explain the pageantry of the birth of the Christ child.

Miss Benzene, god love her, finally retired to Boca last year. She's ninety-eight. Too mean to die and too stubborn to move back to the Midwest, she too will be washed out of being in another fifty years or so.

"Get the hell out of my Florida room!" she'll yell at the Atlantic as it rises against her, but the waves, as salty as tears, will lap over her and the fourteenth incarnation of her hateful rat dog anyway.

I'll have to find and text Danny Tule from the nursing home I'll be in by then, to tell him there's justice after all. The cosmic narrator, who has ultimate repose, will yawn and chug a quart of neutrinos right from the carton.

. . . .

I've always felt repose was possible, else what's a minor in philosophy for? But loss is an obstacle. When events throw you off balance or give you pause, how can you be "below freshet and frost"? I'll never get over the fact that I won't play pool with Sam Clemens, or that I didn't catch Mozart live in London on his European tour of 1764. I wholeheartedly regret that my writing didn't make me rich and somewhat famous until now, so I never got to do coke off a toilet seat with Mick and Bianca at Studio 54, or use my influence to be an extra in the film *Magical Mystery Tour*.

I grew up thinking of the Beatles as the older brothers I never had, though John and Paul were already fathers when I was born. Now my sons love them too. Starbuck knew all the words to "Yellow Submarine" when he turned three, and his favorite curse was "Aw, Bonka!" (It referred to the Apple Bonkers, the Blue Meanies' skinny henchmen.)

One day not so long after my mother's funeral, Starbuck asked, "Daddy? Are the Beatles alive?"

I instantly saw his new understanding of things. "The Beatles don't play as a group anymore," I said, dodging.

"But where do they live?"

"Oh, Paul lives in England, I guess. Ringo is more of an LA guy. Vegas, maybe."

Then he had me. "What about John? And George? Where do they live?"

I hesitated. He was our first child, after all; how does one answer, except honestly? "They died," I said.

"John and George died?" he asked.

"Yes," I said.

That was all he seemed to need to know for several weeks, but I knew there were harder questions ahead. Grandma Helen had died, we told him, because she was very old and very sick. It was true enough, and he needed reassurance that my wife and I wouldn't die for a long time and neither would he. So that became the rule for him: you got very old, and very sick, and *then*, maybe, you could die. But to Starbuck, John Lennon was the handsome young man in *A Hard Day's Night* who bats his eyes at the British banker and says, "Give us a kiss." It wouldn't help any to tell him that Lennon was younger than I was when he died.

It came on the way home from his school. We were laughing at John's high-pitched shouting ("Yassuh! Take one, the United Jumbo Band!") at the start of a bootleg version of "Ob-La-Di, Ob-La-Da." I replayed it several times so we could mimic it well.

Unexpectedly, Starbuck asked, "Did John die?"

"Yes," I said and let the music play.

"Did he get old and die? Was he sick?"

I tried to make my voice matter-of-fact—a sort of cruelty, I felt, which meant that I was so callous that I could abide the horrific, and that he could be asked to do so too—and said, "No, a man hurt him."

"How?"

"The man shot him with a gun. He hurt John so badly that he couldn't stay alive."

"Oh," Starbuck said.

Of course, I didn't tell him the accounts I'd read of John alone in the backseat of the New York City Police car that sped him from the Dakota in an attempt to save his life. A policeman named Moran turned and asked, "Are you John Lennon?" unintentionally sounding like an interrogator, a hopeful fan, or St. Peter. John, in the voice as familiar as a father's to millions of us, croaked, "Yeah." He had lost 80 percent of his blood volume and died of hypovolemic shock by the time they reached Roosevelt Hospital. I thought of how Paul McCartney said that one of the last times he saw him, John hugged him and said quietly, "Touching is good."

"Will we ever see John again?" Starbuck asked. He was near tears.

I paused, because I wasn't sure of my voice. It seems impossible we can lose people along the way as if they were only eyeglasses or extra sets of keys. I told Starbuck that through John's music and films we can be with him and the Beatles anytime we want, and that books and paintings and films and music and theater are like wonderful friends because they contain the best that human beings have ever thought and felt.

I rubbed the back of my neck and looked over the top of my glasses at Starbuck in the rearview mirror. It was a sure tell of unease, but he was only four. Besides, I thought I meant it, that stuff about the miracle of art. Yes, I do.

JOHN GRISWOLD, b. 1963, has published three books, including *Pirates You Don't Know, and Other Adventures in the Examined Life*. He is the editor for a creative nonfiction book series and teaches in an MFA program in creative writing. He believes his sons are the best thing that ever happened in his life.

Subjective Age: *I wrote "On Repose" when I was forty-two years old and I felt twenty-seven, which I had felt for many years. Now, after several years in a stressful workplace and constant societal pressure to own up to being old, I often feel my chronological age. But as soon as I get in the rental car and head on down the road to the next thing to be examined, I shed the years and feel, oh, let's say thirty-three.*

On Interruptions

Sarah Ruhl

I remember reading Alice Walker's essay in my twenties about how a woman writer could manage to have one child, but more was difficult. At the time, I pledged to have no more than one, or at the very most two. (I now have three.) I also remember, before having children, reading Tillie Olsen, who described with such clarity: thinking and ironing and thinking and ironing and writing while ironing and having many children—she herself had four. I myself do not iron. My clothes and the clothes of my children are rumpled. The child's need, so pressing, so consuming, for the mother to *be there*, to be present, and the pressing need of the writer to be half-there, to be there but thinking of other things, caught me—

Sorry. In the act of writing that sentence, my son, William, who is now two, came running into my office crying and asking for a fake knife to cut his fake fruit. So there is also, in observing children much of the day and making theater much of the night, this preoccupation with the real and the illusory, and the pleasures and pains of both.

In any case, please forgive the shortness of these essays; do imagine the silences that came between—the bodily fluids, the tears, the various shades of—

In the middle of that sentence my son came in and sat at my elbow and said tenderly, "Mom, can I poop here?" I think of Virginia Woolf's "A Room of One's Own" and how it needs a practical addendum about locks and bolts and soundproofing.

But I digress. I could lie to you and say that I intended to write something totalizing, something grand. But I confess that I had a more humble ambition—to preserve for myself, in rare private moments, some liberty of thought. Perhaps that is equally 7.

My son just typed 7 on my computer.

There was a time, when I first found out I was pregnant with twins, that I saw only a state of conflict. When I looked at theater and parenthood, I saw only war, competing loyalties, and I thought my writing life was over. There were times when it felt as though my children were annihilating me (truly you have not lived until you have changed one baby's diaper while another baby quietly vomits on your shin), and finally I came to the thought, All right, then, annihilate me; that other self was a fiction anyhow. And then I could breathe. I could investigate the pauses.

I found that life intruding on writing was, in fact, life. And that, tempting as it may be for a writer who is also a parent, one must not think of life as an intrusion. At the end of the day, writing has very little to do with writing, and much to do with life. And life, by definition, is not an intrusion.

SARAH RUHL, b. 1974, is a playwright whose works include *For Peter Pan on her 70th Birthday*; *The Oldest Boy*; *In the Next Room, or the vibrator play*; *The Clean House*; *Orlando*; *Dear Elizabeth*; and *Stage Kiss*. She is a two-time Pulitzer finalist and a Tony nominee, and has received a PEN award for mid-career playwrights and a MacArthur Foundation grant. "On Interruptions" opens her book, *100 Essays I Don't Have Time to Write*.

Lessness

Lance Olsen

A little less of us every day.

Seven words, nine syllables, twenty-three letters.

That's all that is the case, precisely what we really know about ourselves, sans irony, sans wit, sans posturing, sans philosophy, sans desperate belief; how it is impossible to reason with our own bodies.

There is hope, Franz Kafka once wrote, but not for us.

Blessed is he who expects nothing, Alexander Pope once wrote, for he shall never be disappointed.

An email, from a friend, her lung cancer having recently metastasized to the brain; "They have me on this experimental chemo pill, long-term, which is supposed to reduce the risk of recurrence greatly. The problem is it made my face break out in this horrendous acne-like rash. So I've cut back to half a dose and begun taking antibiotics as well as using all sorts of creams. My dermatologist's assistant spent nearly an hour with me showing me how to use makeup to cover the rash. I've never used makeup in my life, and really hadn't planned on starting now, but it does seem to make a difference."

Grenz-Situationen, was Karl Jaspers' term.

We seem to believe it possible to ward off death by following rules of good grooming, Don DeLillo once wrote.

How we keep writing anyway.

Grenz-Situationen: Limit Situations.

How we keep writing anyway until we don't keep writing anyway.

The bioengineered replicant Roy Batty to his creator, Tyrell, in *Blade Runner*, a moment before Roy crushes Tyrell's skull, drives his thumbs into Tyrell's eyes: *I want more life, fucker.*

How I saw the writer Ronald Sukenick for the last time one humid rainy April afternoon in his Battery Park City apartment two months before he died of inclusion body myositis, a muscle-wasting disease that eventually makes it impossible for one to swallow, then to breathe.

Jaspers' philosophy being an extended effort to explore and describe the margins of human experience, an effort to confront what he thought of, beautifully, as the Unconditioned.

Death is so terrifying, Susan Cheever once wrote, because it is so ordinary.

Ron couldn't use his fingers anymore, so he bought a voice-recognition program and wrote by means of that.

Ridley Scott re-editing the scene so that in the final cut Batty says: *I want more life, father*—thereby draining the life out of the line, making it into mere Frankensteinian, mere Oedipal, cliché.

How my wife and I strolled along the banks of the Bagmati River in Kathmandu among myriad cloth-wrapped bodies burning on funeral pyres.

How Ron and I both knew this was it, how there would be no future meetings. How we both understood there were no social conventions to cover such an event. How the unsettling result was that each of our simple declarative sentences seemed anything but.

When we speak of "seriousness" in art, Thomas Pynchon once wrote, ultimately we are talking about an attitude toward death.

How, shortly before his in 1631, John Donne obtained an urn, his own burial shroud, and the services of an artist. He wrapped himself in said shroud, posed atop said urn, and had said artist render a charcoal sketch of him, which the poet kept by his bedside throughout his final illness.

The distance between the real and the ideal.

Two large framed photographs hang on the walls of my writing studio, both by Joel-Peter Witkin. They are the only ones by an established artist my wife and I have ever felt a need to purchase. Each is a still life, a *nature morte*, constructed from corpse parts the photographer found and posed in morgues in Mexico and France.

Families of the dead in prim circles around the pyres along the river.

Holy men spattering butter on the fires to help them burn faster.

How, to pass time on the Paris Metro once between stops, I asked my sister, with whom I was riding during a visit, how old she wanted to live to be, and, instead of answering, she began to cry.

Jaspers referred to the ultimate boundaries of being as *Das Umgreif-ende*—The Encompassing: the indefinite horizon in which all subjective and objective experience is possible, but which can itself never be apprehended rationally.

How, after fifty, your face becomes an accomplishment.

Eighty-three, less than a year before he died, Kurt Vonnegut: "I've written books. Lots of them. Please, I've done everything I'm supposed to do. Can I go home now?"

One only becoming authentically human, in other words, according to Jaspers, at the instant one allows oneself awareness of the Encompassing by confronting such unimaginables as universal contingency and the loss of the human, the loss of the body—the latter otherwise known as death.

Everything else refusal, fear, repression.

How the last words Roy Batty speaks, huddled on a dark rainy L.A. rooftop in 2019, are some of the saddest, the most powerful, in the entire film: "I've seen things you people wouldn't believe. Attack ships on fire off the shoulder of Orion. I've watched C-beams glitter in the dark near the Tannhauser Gate. All those moments will be lost in time, like tears in the rain. Time to die."

How it is the case, precisely, that life can be defined as a slow dying.

A terminal illness.

Birth, Beckett once wrote, was the death of him.

The goal of all life, Freud once wrote, is death.

How it is the case, precisely, that death is a protracted amnesia visited upon those who live beyond the lost one's passing.

Ernest Becker: The irony of man's condition is that the deepest need is to be free of the anxiety of death and annihilation; but it is life itself which awakens it, and so we must shrink from being fully alive.

Remembering, Milan Kundera once wrote, is a form of forgetting.

My dying friend: A lot of the brain motor difficulties that I was expecting after the first surgery seem to be appearing now. My left hand feels more or less like a stroke patient's, unable to do very much except spill a glass of water on a computer keyboard or leave A. walking two blocks behind me because I had no sensation that I let go of his hand. For about two weeks there I was having some real palsy tremors, what they're calling *mini-seizures*.

On a large enough time line, Chuck Palahniuk once wrote, the survival rate for everyone will drop to zero.

That's it. That's all.

How, as I was working on my novel about Friedrich Nietesche's last mad night on earth, I couldn't shake off the abrupt uncanny realization that inside always becomes outside in the end. The simple, brutal notion: how that which separates us from the world—our sphincterial control, our skin, our existential deep-sea suit—gradually goes away.

We are always becoming something other than we are, something other than we want to be.

Traveling.

Every once in a while, Ron stopped talking, shifted in his electric wheelchair, looked out his picture window at the Hudson, then drifted back to what we were saying, and we would pick up where we had left off. I drank bourbon, Ron tea through a straw. He was having trouble swallowing. He was becoming tired very quickly. You could see it.

Every parting gives a foretaste of death, Schopenhauer once wrote.

How I could hear steam building in the skulls of the corpses as I moved along the banks of the Bagmati.

How Hemingway turned himself into a character in one of his books and shot himself in the head. How Hunter Thompson turned himself into a character in one of his books and shot himself in the head. How Yukio Mishima turned himself into a character in one of his books and committed *seppuku*. Publicly. In 1970.

Outside, people not cheering him on, but heckling him, jeering, as he disemboweled himself.

Gradually, or not so gradually. It depends.

I lost all my hair two weeks ago, my dying friend wrote. One of the things they talked about was the need to keep the head covered at all times and I ended up buying a large assortment of what they call chemo turbans, some of them reasonably stylish, to wear around the house. I mean, it's a perfectly good wig, and I'm sure was once a very nice beaver or groundhog or whatever it was, but I hate it. The hair of my nightmares.

The head. Not *my* head.

As if she had already begun to become something other than her own body.

My sister-in-law was in town, my dying friend wrote, and her comment was it looks okay, it just looks nothing like me. I'll use it for teaching, since it still masks hair loss, and there's no need to impose my limitations on the students. Then I decided to say screw the chemo turbans and looked at some hats. I ended up buying three outrageously exquisite retro-style felt fedoras which cover the whole head and are marvelously comfortable. You won't believe these. I've never been so stylish in my life.

Roy Batty, a replicant, virtually identical to humans in every way except for the fact that the memories he believes are his own are really someone else's, except for the fact that he has a four-year lifespan, is more human than the other so-called humans around him.

A ball will bounce, Richard Wilbur once wrote, but less and less.

How the sadhus, Hindu holy men who live by begging, cook bread by burying it among shards of smoking human bones.

I want to enjoy my death, Beckett once wrote.

Presumably with some irony.

In that race which daily hastens us toward death, Camus once wrote, the body maintains its irreparable lead.

But how Tennessee Williams accidentally swallowed the cap of his nasal spray and suffocated alone in his hotel room.

How Sherwood Anderson choked on a toothpick at a party in Panama.

How Maupassant tried killing himself by slicing his own throat, failed, was declared insane, spent the last eighteen months of his life in an asylum, dying from syphilis he contracted in his youth, as did Manet, as did Gauguin, as did Schubert, as did Nietzsche, as did Scott Joplin.

How, after a little more than an hour, I realized I should take my leave of Ron. How I don't believe I ever experienced more difficulty closing a door behind me.

How that door both shut and remained wide open.

How the only real closures come in mimetic fiction and memoir, redemption and faux wisdom hardened into commodity. Like an order of Arby's Cheesecake Poppers.

How a group of children stood knee-deep in the river, oblivious, in the black oily water that used to be strangers, throwing a red rubber ball through gusts of coppery haze.

Charles Sanders Pierce: If man were immortal he could be perfectly sure of seeing the day when everything in which he had trusted should betray his trust, and, in short, of coming eventually to hopeless misery. He would break down, at last, as every good fortune, as every dynasty, as every civilization does. In place of this we have death.

The graveyards are full of indispensable men, Charles de Gaulle once wrote.

Death is not an event in life, Wittgenstein once wrote: we do not live to experience death.

Yes, I want to say, and no.

My mother waiting primly in her living room in suburban Dallas, also dying, also of cancer, this time breast metastasized to the spine, the liver, the brain, inventorying the clutter that took her nearly seventy-four years to quilt around herself, noting out of the blue, almost casually, to no one in particular: *All these things will forget their stories the moment I'm gone.*

A little less, and then a little less.

The first Witkin photograph on my wall: a plump old woman, the top of her head missing, her skin blotched, her body supported by wires, sitting at a chair next to a table in a sparse room. On the table is a book. Her finger holds her place, although the arm to which the finger is attached isn't itself attached to her torso. *Interrupted Reading,* the photograph is entitled.

Anna Karenina throws herself under a train.

His books are questions of survival of personality, Carole Maso once wrote of the narrator's former lover in *Ava.*

Yes, and no.

My cousin entered the hospital for routine hip-replacement surgery to fix his fullback years in college. The operation went off without a hitch—until an infection flowered within him, one of those virulent bacterial strains that chew through a patient's every prospect. One week my cousin was perfectly fine, minus the limp and a certain throbby stiffness. The next he was on a ventilator. The next his wife was emailing what amounted to acquaintances like me in an attempt to drum up something that looked like an acceptable audience for the memorial service I had absolutely no intention of attending.

Emma Bovary eats arsenic, Eva Braun cyanide, Alan Turing cyanide, Abbie Hoffman phenobarbital.

There is no boat in Hades, no ferryman Charon,
No caretaker Aiakos, no dog Cerberus.
All we who are dead below
Have become bones and ashes, but nothing else.

Someone once carved on a Roman tombstone. Two thousand years ago.

The second Witkin photograph: a woman's untorsoed head, eyes closed, atilt on some dark surface (let's call it a table), next to which a stuffed monkey is posed.

Patrik Ouředník recounts how, during the first months Buchenwald was open for business, those in charge gave the inmates postcards that said: *Accommodation is wonderful, we are working here, we receive decent treatment and are well looked after.* The inmates were made to sign them and address them to relatives, some of whom apparently believed what they read. One Greek prisoner mailed his postcard to his father in Pyrgos. Three months later, his father arrived for a visit.

At the railroad platform, the son leaping on him and strangling him to death before the Germans could get their hands on the man.

My wife's grandmother refused to be buried, insisting on being entombed in a mausoleum instead because, she said, she didn't want to get dirty.

The distance between the real and the ideal.

Whatever opinion we may be pleased to hold on the subject of death, Proust once wrote, we may be sure that it is meaningless and valueless.

How it would be a perfect misreading of his work to suggest that Witkin's intent is to shock, disgust, exploit his subjects, his viewer's vision.

My uncle had a heart attack on a beach while feeding pigeons. A good Scandinavian, he was too embarrassed to draw attention to himself, reported his wife, who had been sitting beside him at the time, and so he expired, *sotto voce*, on the spot.

Diane Arbus swallows barbiturates and slashes her wrists, as does Mark Rothko.

The living being is only a species of the dead, Nietzsche once wrote, and a very rare species.

Death is the mother of—

No, that's not it.

Another dying friend. Another email. Another cancer. Another metastasis to the brain. Sorry not to have updated you sooner, but the fog is settling in so even this will have to be short. Not much news. I wish I could write something light and cheerful, at least something light and pomo-ish, but, fact is, cancer does suck. Or, rather, it's the treatment that sucks: makes me want to do nothing but sleep all day (and night). Not much pain—occasional headaches, joint aches. What's most scary is the felt deterioration of my mental abilities (such as they were)—each day, I get dumber and dumber, and know it. Memory loss, inability to follow conversations, inability to find words. B. finds it inevitably frustrating, seeing me standing in the middle of a room, clearly without a clue what I'm doing there; and never sure if I understand or will remember two minutes later something she asked me to do. Frustrating for me, too—feeling like a retard who needs to have notes pinned to his shirt, reminding him what he's supposed to be doing.

Every plot being an education, ultimately, about how everything ends.

Jerzy Kosiński swallows barbiturates and puts a bag over his head, as does Michael Dorris.

While I thought that I was learning how to live, Leonardo da Vinci once wrote, I have been learning how to die.

Witkin's work performing an act of reminding.

This is how to say it.

Every narrative being, ultimately, a study in death.

Freud overdoses on morphine.

How, as one gets older, deaths begin arriving closer and closer, like mortar shells zeroing in on their target.

Death being the one idea you can't deconstruct, David Lodge once wrote.

How I was reading to my mother from Eliot's *Four Quartets* when she died. My wife was holding her hand. We were at her bedside, talking to her, trying to comfort her, even though she was already unconscious, even though she had been for more than a day. After a while, I began reading to her, to us, a little from her favorite book, the *Bhagavad Gita*, a little from late Eliot. She suddenly flinched and stopped breathing.

She was herself and then she wasn't.

One thousand and one things change the meaning of any book on any given reading.

Witkin's goal slant-rhyming with Viktor Shklovsky's: the technique of art being to make objects *unfamiliar*, to make forms difficult, to increase the difficulty and length of perception.

Alice Bradley Sheldon, aka James Tiptree, Jr., mercy-kills her terminally ill husband and then shoots herself.

Near death and incoherent, Nietzsche lay in his narrow bed in a small room on the top floor of the archives his sister Lisbeth had had built in Weimar. The people Lisbeth had brought in with the hope of establishing a lucrative cult around her brother were talking about literature. Nietzsche roused, opened his eyes briefly, said *I too have written some good books*, then faded back into silence.

Gregor Samsa starves himself, as does the Hunger Artist, as does Kurt Godel.

And I have come to relinquish that most modern of stances: uncertainty, Carole Maso once wrote. I am certain now of what will happen.

How my mother changed tenses before my eyes.

They said the side effects of these last two chemo sessions would be the hardest, my dying friend wrote. The latest development is that I'll suddenly pass out for a few minutes. Yesterday I was teaching and woke up as they were loading me into an ambulance. They checked my vitals, did a quick EKG, I signed a waiver stating that I didn't want to be taken to the hospital, and I went back to teach without incident.

Witkin's goal slant-rhyming with Gaston Bachelard's: art, then, is an increase of life, a sort of competition of surprises that stimulates our consciousness and keeps it from becoming somnolent.

Edwin Armstrong, inventor of FM radio, jumps out a window, as does Gilles Deleuze, as does F. O. Matthiessen.

In heaven all the interesting people are missing, Nietzsche once wrote.

Witkin asking his viewers to sympathize with the fragility of the human flesh, the human heart, the act of lessening that we call ourselves.

Birth was the—

The head. Not *my* head.

Everything else refusal.

Grenz-Situationen.

Everything else fear and repression.

Yes, I want to say, and—

It happened on a Sunday when my mother was escorting my twin brother and me down the steps of the tenement where we lived, Joel-Peter Witkin once told an interviewer, recounting a pivotal moment from his childhood. We were going to church. While walking down the hallway to the entrance of the building, we heard an incredible crash mixed with screaming and cries for help. The accident involved three cars, all with families in them. Somehow, in the confusion, I was no longer holding my mother's hand. At the place where I stood at the curb, I could see something rolling from one of the overturned cars. It stopped at the curb where I stood. It was the head of a little girl. I bent down to touch the face, to speak to it, but before I could touch it someone carried me away.

How the angelic four-voice vocal texture of Guillaume Dufay's masses make the day on which you hear them feel thoroughly lived. How your consciousness arranges the entire piece of theater called living into a series of remarkable paintings called recollection.

A *polyptych.*

How each morning, as you rise from your bed, the belief hums through your head that you are going to die, going to die, going to die, yes, surely, no doubt about it, but not today—an observation that will remain correct every morning of your life, except one, because—

Because—

To hope, E. M. Cioran once wrote, is to contradict the future.

LANCE OLSEN, b. 1956, is the author of more than twenty books of and about innovative writing, including *Theories of Forgetting*, a novel based on Robert Smithson's earthwork the Spiral Jetty, and *[[there.]]*, a trash-diary meditation on the confluence of travel, curiosity, and aesthetic/existential experimentation. Olsen has been a recipient of both a Guggenheim and an NEA Fellowship, as well as the Berlin Prize, a DAAD Artist-in-Berlin Residency, and a Fulbright Scholar grant. He teaches experimental narrative theory and practice at the University of Utah.

Subjective Age: *Body: somewhere, depending on the day, between twenty-seven and 279. Mind: thirty-two. Social: twenty-two. Imagination: five. Wisdom: it comes and it goes; like a bad cold, only better.*

5Os

Katie Couric Is No Friend of Mine

Paul Casey

Time was when turning fifty for a man meant buying a red convertible or taking up with a blonde secretary. Or both. Now, thanks to Katie Couric, that bitch, turning fifty means having a colonoscopy.

In the waiting room, the first thing I noticed was the bathroom. Not down the hall, *but right there in the waiting room.* Just like the friendly hints in the written instructions on colon cleansing, I suspected irony: After drinking the liquid laxative diluted in 12 ounces of fluid, and drinking an additional four eight-ounce glasses of clear fluid, *you will want to stay near a toilet.*

Little wonder that I am also instructed to have some moist towelettes on hand and Desitin for chapping. I remember a boss once saying, "You know what chaps my ass, Casey?" Now I know. Given my gurgling bowels, I decided to be heartened by the nearby facilities.

The elderly gentleman nearest me wore a Ricky Ricardo two-tone shirt, khakis, brand new white sneakers. His close-cropped silver hair and tanned narrow face made him look like a military man, his eyes staring into the distance. When the nurse called his name, he got to his feet in one motion, turned to leave, stopped, pivoted back, leaned down to kiss his woman on the forehead, then marched to meet the medicos.

I've spent my adult life avoiding doctors. Last time I visited a doctor was ten years ago when I turned forty and my wife threatened divorce if I didn't submit to a physical. I submitted. A mere decade later and she's nagging me to get another one, and I know exactly where this will lead. A bad bit of business, that's where. Thanks, Katie.

Fucking doctors.

My mother was a willing victim of Western medicine, which excels at treating symptoms but rarely seeks causes. Consequently, on the counter flanking the kitchen sink, my father's quart of Seagram's VO was surrounded by my mother's pill bottles: steroids, painkillers, mood elevators, tincture of opium. My mother had a lot of illness in her life, so she took a lot of medication. Naturally, I developed an aversion to legal drugs, even the over-the-counter stuff. Doctors weren't my favorites either.

Growing up, I thought everybody's mother went into the hospital one or two times per year for one or two weeks. I have early memories of standing outside the Stanford Medical Center and my father pointing up to the window of my mother's room. Me and my brothers and sisters stood there so she could look down on us. It didn't strike me as unusual until I was a teenager and noticed other parents rarely, if ever, went into the hospital.

The doctors couldn't cure her. Her stomach hurt, she couldn't eat, lost weight; then she was hospitalized where they were happy to try out another cure. Drug treatments, surgery, diets, there was always something new to try. Stanford was a teaching hospital, after all. My mother happily agreed to every treatment, though. Eventually, she was diagnosed with Crohn's disease. She lived with that for twenty years until leukemia got her in the end.

In my late twenties my wife noticed a small extra flap of skin in my armpit.

"It's nothing. Get the scissors."

"You're going to the doctor."

I didn't have a doctor, so I ended up in the urgent care clinic with a young, male physician's assistant, and he decided I needed a finger wave because of a harmless growth *in my armpit*. Later, curled on the couch at home, I attempted to explain my sense of violation. My wife said, "I've birthed your three children, so don't complain to me about doctors poking you."

Philosophic hindsight now allows the possibility that the finger-wave procedure was strictly diagnostic. If not, then fair play to him. I was a handsome buck then. Still, the incident did little to change my opinion of the medical profession.

Many years later my wife grew restive about a marble-sized bulge on my neck. "That has to go. It's freaking me out."

The first doctor reported that it was a fat deposit; insurance would not cover cosmetic surgery.

"Did you tell him about the cancer on *both* sides of your family?" my wife asked.

Actually, I *had* told him and was shocked when, after cursory fingering of my neck bulge, he hustled me out of his office. Thrilled, of course. But a little alarmed, too.

"We're getting a second opinion."

A young surgeon did finally see me and said insurance wasn't a problem. And somehow I got the idea that the surgery was on a par with a trip to the dentist. "Local anesthetic; he'll flick that thing out with a melon baller," I explained when my wife offered to accompany me. "I'll be fine."

I firmly believed this, too, until the morning of the surgery when the nurse called to make sure I didn't eat anything. "Since 10:00 p.m. last night, right?"

I cradled the phone to my chest with my chin to free my hands to spread the mustard on the salami sandwich the call interrupted. I replied, "No, nothing." Then ate my sandwich. I didn't see how a salami sandwich could affect anything one way or another.

My next clue that this was more than getting a tooth filled was the puzzled, concerned look on the admitting nurse's face when I answered, "Well, no, I came alone."

She craned her neck to look past me. "There's nobody with you, really?"

I felt lonely when she said it like *that.*

Then the orderly took my book away.

"No," I explained, tightly gripping the novel I happened to be reading at the time, "this is how I relax. It will help me."

He was a young, pasty-faced fellow; he easily yanked the book out of my hands. "Not sterile."

The more awful memory, an icy jet of fear freezes my bowels when I think of it, was the gurney ride: strapped in, flat on my back, fluorescent light fixtures passing overhead, wind playing down the length of my body, rolled and steered by a stranger's hands. For me, a vision of the future—*this is how you will end, right?*

I was given Versed. I remember the anesthesiologist telling me what a great surgeon was operating on me. Then I was in the recovery room and they started in on somebody accompanying me. "Mr. Casey, you can't drive yourself home. It's illegal."

"My ride is waiting for me outside," I said.

"Outside?"

A candy striper rolled me out to the exit. It was raining past the awning, the parking lot streaked with the overhead lights. "Mr. Casey, I don't see a car out there."

She stopped the wheelchair in between the sliding double doors. "Sure," I said, standing, "it's right down there."

"Mr. Casey, please."

My house was less than a mile away; I easily drove home.

Before you get to have a colonoscopy you receive a physical. Avoiding doctors meant I didn't have a doctor, so my wife worked the phones, which is how I ended up with an attractive young female doctor instructing me to bend over the examination table.

At work the next day, Andy Seubert asked me how it all went. I replied, "A beautiful young woman shoved her finger up my ass and told me I was too fat. All in all, not bad."

My name was called. I remembered to kiss my wife—mental tip of the cap to Mr. Ricky Ricardo shirt—and squared up. I was shown to a curtained-off area that contained a chair and bed and was handed a gown. Once I was gowned and on the bed, an IV was started and I was left alone. That's when I noticed activity in the room across from me. When I figured out the gloved, masked woman's task, I remembered my advice to my teenage daughter one evening while we sat on the couch watching *Friends*. Sarah, who had the cat on her lap, suddenly thrust the animal off of her lap and screamed. I spotted the problem right away, a turd clinging to the fur on the cat's ass. When my daughter returned from putting the cat out, I told her if that happened to me I would kill myself.

That's how I felt when I observed the woman place the black, serpentine cameras into a dishwasher. They could never get the water hot enough, could they? Each soiled camera was delivered in a large, rectangular plastic container, maybe even Tupperware. Did they scrub those fuckers out?

Eventually, they rolled me a few feet from the prep area into the procedure room where I received an ugly surprise when the doctor instructed me to turn on my left side.

"My *left* side?" I asked. Because then I faced the high resolution screen, a 52-inch terrifyingly clear panel that already contained a white spiderweb with thousands of strands that turned out to be a piece of gauze the camera rested on.

The nurse answered for the doctor, "Yes, your left side. Is there a problem?"

Oh, you glib…you think you're going to force me to face my inner self when the camera is inserted in me? Fuck that machine. Fine, I turned on my left and *closed my eyes.*

They dripped the Versed into me and I opened my eyes to visual wonders, like gliding in an airplane over sand dunes sunset pink.

I am fucking beautiful!

The camera hesitated, hovered over a white flat area, lowered to what appeared to be a slight protuberance. A small claw came into view and gnawed on the polyp and a thin stream of blood bisected the white area and for that brief moment I understood religious ecstasy. It was all so lovely and it was in me. I am lovely inside.

After thirty minutes of recovery, I dressed in my street clothes; the nurse ushered me into a consulting room and then went to the waiting area to call my wife in. Once all three of us were seated, the nurse explained that everything looked good, that they did take one small sample but it was nothing to worry about, worse case is that instead of waiting ten years for the next examination, it might be changed to five or three. "But I don't really expect that," she summarized, and was proven correct when the tersely worded lab results arrived a week later.

In a hurry to flee I walked ahead of my wife, exiting the room and then down the corridor, eyes on the door out of there. Door knob in hand, I looked back and saw my wife standing in front of the consulting room next to ours, head cocked as if trying to hear through the closed door. I couldn't wait. I skipped out.

She caught me on the sidewalk, said, "They're still in there." Foggy from the Versed, I wanted to go home.

"The older man, the one in the black and tan shirt, the one they called before you. When they called his wife I knew it was your turn—but they're still in the little room."

I turned to the parking lot. "Ricky Ricardo?"

She continued, "Early detection, though, leads to extremely high survival rates. What do you think of Katie now?"

I kept silent and followed my wife out to the parking lot. Dull, gray clouds filled the sky. I hoped Mr. Ricky Ricardo shirt lived a long marching life, but Katie Couric was no friend of mine.

PAUL CASEY, b. 1956, lives and works in the Portland, Oregon, area. In addition to working full-time jobs in marketing and sales in the thirty years since moving to the Pacific Northwest, Paul has also taught various writing courses as an adjunct instructor at local colleges and universities, serving longest at Washington State University in Vancouver.

Subjective Age: *Although I am about to turn sixty, I will always feel twenty-seven, because that's when fatherhood started.*

Women over Fifty–
The Invisible Generation

Hilary Mantel

On Sunday last I had a shock, waking up to find that my novel *Wolf Hall* was the 2-1 favorite to win the Man Booker Prize. It was almost as much of a shock to be described in the press (repeatedly) as "the fifty-seven-year-old novelist from Glossop." I've never been coy about my age, so I don't know why the truth should take me aback when set down in print. It made me laugh; I just couldn't think how I got to be fifty-seven. Do men ask themselves this question—how did I get to be thirty, to be fifty, to be ready for my bus pass? Or is it, as I suspect, just women who can't fit the puzzle together, who feel that a reference to their age is not neutral but a sort of accusation?

We've heard so much recently about the disappearance of older women from our TV screens, and about the difficulties, for older woman, of negotiating public life. Every media picture of the rare and glowing Joanna Lumley feels like a challenge; why can't you all be like that, why does she look like a princess and you look like a potato? Many women of a certain age, when a peer of ours is flashed up on screen, run an instant comparison: is it worse to have her jowls than my wrinkles?

Celebrities trade on their image; perhaps it's mean to snigger at their Botox, but their faces are their fortune and they set out their stalls to attract envy. Not so women politicians. We know we're being unforgivably shallow when we judge them on their looks, but we do it all the same. I have been known to say, regarding Ann Widdecombe, that you get the face you deserve. And my mother, who is the same age as Margaret Thatcher, could never see her in her heyday without remarking, "I wish that woman would go home and look after her neck."

When I was a child—in Glossop and district—no one supposed that women over fifty were invisible. On the contrary, they blacked out the sky. They stood shoulder-to-shoulder like penalty walls, solid inside corsets that encased them from neck to thigh, so there was no getting past them: if you'd rushed them and butted them with your head, you'd have careened off, sobbing. They stood in bus queues muttering dark threats against the driver. They stood in line in the butcher's shop, bloodied sawdust clogging their bootees, and amid the loops of sausages and the tripes they talked about My Operation—they boasted of their surgical crises, as Coriolanus boasted about the wounds he got for his mother country. Almost every one of these women was called Nellie, and the others were called Cissie. Why these names are synonymous with effeminate weakness I cannot imagine. They wore vast tweed coats or impermeable raincoats in glass-green, and their legs were wrapped round and round with elastic bandages, so they took up plenty of space in the world; to increase their area they stuck their elbows out. They had baskets and brown paper parcels. They said, "That child wants feeding/slapping/its bonnet on," and younger women jumped to it. They'd been nowhere but they'd seen everything. They never laughed with you, they laughed at you. They did not use face powder but scouring powder. They could add up grocery prices at calculator speed, and they never took their eyes off the needle of the grocer's scale. Show them the aging heroines of today, and they'd have snorted—they were frequent snorters. Helen Mirren, Joanna Lumley they'd have called picked wishbones. They'd have sneered "bleached blonde" at Madonna, while grimly rating those sinewy arms; she looks as if she could scrub a step or mangle a bucket of wet sheets.

At fifty-plus, these women ran the world and they knew it. When I was a child I assumed that I would grow into one of them, and have a stubby umbrella which I'd use to point at the follies of the world. I never imagined I'd still be parting with money at makeup counters, or that I'd be racing off for a blow-dry when threatened with a photographer. I assumed I'd wear my hair in round perm, the color of steel and as tough. Think of the time I'd save; vanity is such a consumer of the hours. With the spirit of my foremothers inside me, I would write even bigger novels, fortified by pies, and any impertinent reviewers would get a clip around the ear. They were tough as the soles of their shoes, these grannies, and they often lived to great ages; but when one of them died, her funeral stretched right down the main road, and a week later her daughter had stepped in to replace her, packed like an iron bolster inside her ancestral coat.

They were not, these women, peculiar to my birthplace; their geographical spread was the whole British Isles. Except for their accents, they were interchangeable in their pride. They were unyielding, undaunted and savagely unimpressed by anything the world could do to them. We could revive their dauntless spirit, instead of dwindling, apologizing and shrinking from the camera lens; though one problem, I fear, is that you can't get the corsets these days.

HILARY MANTEL, b. 1952, is the two-time winner of the Man Booker Prize for her best-selling novels, *Wolf Hall*, and its sequel, *Bring Up the Bodies*. The Royal Shakespeare Company recently adapted both titles for the stage and a BBC/Masterpiece six-part adaption of the novels was broadcast in 2015. Mantel is the author of fourteen books, and is currently working on the final book in her Thomas Cromwell Trilogy.

Our Terrible, Beautiful Existence

David Shields

Several years ago I wrote a book that looks without blinking at our blood-and-bones existence, at the fact that each of us is just an animal walking the earth for a brief time, a bare body housed in a mortal cage. Some people might find this perspective demoralizing, but I don't, truly. Honesty is the best policy; the only way out is deeper in: a candid confrontation with existence is dizzying, liberating. This was my ninth book and the one that has changed me the most, by far. I still see life entirely through its Darwinian prism. I keep trying to shake off the aftereffects of writing *The Thing About Life Is That One Day You'll Be Dead*, and I find I can't. All good books wind up, I think, with the writer getting his teeth bashed in.

My ninety-seven-year-old father is the book's principal catalyst, subject, star, anti-star, death star, antipode, blocking figure, hero, anti-hero, life force, Energizer Bunny, counterpoint to my death-haunt. I think of the book as a meditation on the brute fact of mortality—"our birth is nothing but our death begun," as one of the chapter titles has it—but all anyone wants to talk about is my impossibly vital dad (at eighty-six, he had a "mild" heart attack on the tennis court and didn't leave the court until he'd won the set). What began as a gathering of thoughts about the body became, through my father, much more than I'd bargained for: a tug-of-war between him and me, between existence and non-. It's the story of how, via him, I got my groove back. He learns that he's really going to die. I learn that I'm really going to live. That's the book: my body, my father's body, data tracking the human physical condition from crib to oblivion, aphorisms about sex and death—all held together by the radiance and brevity of our sojourn on earth.

Centenarians tend to be assertive, suspicious, and practical. Natalie's former day-care teacher, now a manager for the outpatient clinic of a cancer-care center, says, "It's the assholes who always get better." My father isn't an asshole, but he is mightily self-involved (more self-involved than anyone else?—maybe he simply masks it less well), which seems to have had no ill effects whatsoever on his health or longevity.

What will my father's last words be? What will mine be?

All human beings have bodies. All bodies are mortal. Yours, too, is one of these bodies.

What the book winds up getting to is this: the individual doesn't matter. You, Dad, in the large scheme of things, don't matter. I, Dad, don't matter. We're vectors on the grids of cellular life. We carry ten to twelve genes with mutations that are potentially lethal. These mutations are passed on to our children—you to me, me to Natalie. Aging followed by death is the price we pay for the immortality of our genes. You find this information soul-killing; I find it thrilling, liberating. Life, in my view, is simple, tragic, and frighteningly beautiful.

DAVID SHIELDS, b. 1956, is the bestselling author of twenty books, including *Reality Hunger*; *The Thing About Life Is That One Day You'll Be Dead*; *Black Planet*, which was a finalist for the National Book Critics Circle Award; and *Other People: Takes and Mistakes*. The recipient of Guggenheim and NEA fellowships, Shields' work has been translated into twenty languages.

Subjective Age: *Twenty-seven*.

Ten Ways to Look at Boob Jobs

R. A. Rycraft

The breasts I knew at midnight beat like the sea in me now.
—Anne Sexton

ONE: The basic Boob Job is not necessarily a matter of choice. Take my own, for instance. I never wanted one. But menopause hit with its extra twenty pounds (and counting) and I have a free Boob Job. I'd say nature has out-jugged itself when it comes to my bust—not to mention the rest of me. Turned my 34Cs into 38Ds. I stand in front of the mirror and check out my bare breasts. I tell myself, They don't look so bad. Your fifty-five-year-old puppies look pretty good, especially when you factor in the four kids they've survived. Pendulous, maybe, but not bovine.

I turn this way and that, cup them in my hands, push them together, evaluate the cleavage and am shocked to realize that no push-up bra is going to help. Clearly, gravity and two pounds of connective tissue, ligaments, milk-glands, fibroid cysts, and fat are sufficient to push them over the edge. The weight of them sagging into bra-cups, Judi Dench-like, rather than spilling out of them, Helen Mirren-like. That blue corset I wore as a "treat" for my honey before his research trip to the Yukon nine years ago? History. The black leather one I wore for our eighth anniversary? Hasta la byebye, baby. Any sexy-little-thing that's a "Medium"? Gone.

So far, I hear no complaints from my honey even though he once proclaimed perfect my 34Cs—"a nice, perky handful." He is silent about my matronly rack. The way it fills out blouses, sweaters, and lingerie; the way it weighs down a bodice and reveals too much cleavage or pulls at frontal buttons. Not one word. Mum's also the word for the not-so-pretty, seamless underwire, full-coverage, full-figure bras. He is a wise man.

TWO: The Jobs of Boobs include the following: attract a mate; boost aesthetic effect; convey the life and death powers of female deities; embellish the chest; enhance a sense of self; fill a man with delight; flirt, tempt, and seduce; interact with partners as sex, fetish, and erotic objects; nurse a child; provide subjects for art (the simply nude, the suckling mother, the suckling lover, the ravaged woman, the Venus on a half shell); reward men in Muslim Paradise: voluptuous/full-breasted virgins with large, round breasts, which are not inclined to hang (oh, yeah…the virgins will also be non-menstruating, non-urinating, non-defecating, child-free, and possess "appetizing vaginas"); shape clothing; substitute for paint brushes; suggest femininity; supply names for mountains and restaurants; and work as business assets, sexual signals, milk-squirting deadly weapons, and vehicles for drug trafficking.

THREE: Before her Boob Jobs, D. told me she suffered from low self-esteem because of how she looked during adolescence, pointing to the "ugly" middle school pictures taken before she had braces—her first augmentation. If you could see the dramatic before and after difference, you might appreciate how the ordinary experience of successful orthodontia predisposed her to the assorted aesthetic interventions that pepper her life. The thyroid medication she took not because she had thyroid disease but because it helped her lose weight. The morph into fashion freak, starting when she was a teenager, escalating as she approached middle age. Approached now. The diets. The Zone. The South Beach. The Nutrisystem. The Jack LaLanne Juicer juices. The bioidentical anti-aging hormones. The expensive face and body creams. Clinique. Repairwear Laser Focus Wrinkle and UV Damage Corrector. Repairwear Laser Focus All Smooth Makeup. Repairwear Intensive Eye Cream. Which didn't work. Which suggested a face lift. Which suggested a Boob Job. Which wasn't enough. Which suggested another Boob Job. Which seemed to satisfy D's lover. Which seemed to satisfy D. too. Which seemed to cure her low self-esteem—for now.

FOUR: Heaven help me. My granddaughter has boobs. One day she was my sweet, little flat-chested grandchild. The next she's my sweet, grown-up and curvy grandchild. The staples of her wardrobe? Tight camis under tight t-shirts. The layers enhance rather than conceal. The necklines plunge. And she has beautiful, eye-catching cleavage. Oh. My. God.

FIVE: Famous Boob Jobs: Artemis is particularly well-endowed with about seventeen teats—or is it two teats and fifteen bull testicles? If you want your phallic arrow to fly straight and true, you cut off your right breast like Amazon warrior queen, Hippolyta. Martyr Saint Agatha of Sicily's breasts? Crushed and hacked off. Picasso dislocated his subjects' shard-like globes in *Les Demoiselles d'Avignon*. Germaine Greer burned her bra and liberated tits everywhere. Those bad, blonde girls in Austin Powers? Their knockers sprout cannons. Lady Gaga's bazongas can shoot fireworks as well. Joan of Arc and Gwyneth Paltrow bound their bumps to look like men. Barbie had a reduction. Elizabeth Edwards had a double mastectomy. Olivia Newton-John reconstructed hers. Christina Applegate lopped hers off in a pre-emptive breast cancer strike. Chastity Bono decided hers were optional, added a penis, and changed her/his name to Chaz. Porn star Sexy Cora died during her sixth enlargement surgery (34F to a 34G), doctors telling her husband as she lay there dying, "the brain damage was too big."

SIX: My lesbian friend baked her lover a cake. We're not talking about your regular, run-of-the-mill flat cake with chocolate icing and sprinkles. No. As it happens, while scrounging around in the cupboard, she discovered heart-shaped pans once used for a Valentine's Day party. And there, inside the hearts, were the sports ball pans she'd used to try to make a baseball cake for her son's first birthday—eight years ago. Seeing the half balls upside-down in the hearts like that gave her the idea. A bikini cake. They'll make nice ta-tas, she thought. The two hearts, with a few nips and cuts, made the perfect hourglass shape. And then, with a glob of icing on the flat side of each half-circle and two straws as anchors, my friend did her Boob Job magic. She iced the cake smooth with flesh coloring. Nude, the buxom, no-nippled torso was unnerving, but my friend wasn't yet done. There was the skimpy, blue, string-bikini bottom yet to be applied. After that, she painted a hot pink butterfly tattoo on one hip. The final debate was whether to cover the areola area with a couple of ribbon tassels or flower pasties. She finally opted for a matching bikini top, leaving the strings untied with one erect nipple exposed. The laces spelling JUST across the upper chest and FOR FUN across the bare belly. In a magnetic frame on the fridge is the snapshot my friend took capturing her lover's reaction to the cake. She is, of course, grinning like a Cheshire cat.

SEVEN: Tomorrow your daughter gets a Boob Job. Your baby. Just twenty-four. And she is getting a boob job because, she tells you, she is done having and nursing kids. Nursing your two adorable granddaughters obliterated her breasts. Not that she had much to begin with. And while you don't like the idea, you get it. She did not inherit your breasts. No. She inherited the small, fried-egg-shaped breasts of your sister, the same breasts found on an aunt, several cousins, and one or two of your nieces; breasts that do not fill a bodice or shape a sweater without a thickly padded Wonder Bra. Your aunt and sister reconciled themselves to their cleavage-less chests.

As far as you know, only one of the cousins could afford an enhancement, the same one who has four or five kids. The same one married to an oral surgeon and living in a high-priced Southern California community near the beach. But then, technically, your daughter shouldn't be able to afford a boob job. She is a stay-at-home mom. Her husband is the family's sole provider. Theirs is a tight budget. Yet, somehow, she has the money, having squirreled away earnings from odd jobs, like selling airbrush tattoos at Mud Runs and 4th of July carnivals, and saving her half of income tax refunds. You're not surprised, really. Your daughter is patient and relentless when she wants something. And she wants new boobs.

EIGHT: J. said, I want those movies out of my house. You watch them when I'm not home. You jerk off to them on the couch when I'm in bed.

Her husband said, If you watched the movies with me, maybe it wouldn't be an issue. I'd get excited; you'd get excited. Voyeurism feeds desire. Don't you know that?

J. said, It's not just that they're vulgar; it's that I'll never be porn-worthy. What real woman can compete with a perfect-bodied, submissive nympho? What happened to the eroticism of simple lovemaking?

He said, You might try bikini wax. A Boob Job. I could get you one for Christmas.

J. said, Fake boobs and boobiferous are not synonymous.

He said, Sure they are. And we'd both get the breasts we've always wanted.

NINE: Many Boob Jobs has E.

A. A mastectomy. The impact of the empty space hits hard. Surprisingly unanticipated. Unexpected. E. has always worn layers, so there's no need to hide what's missing with a wardrobe change. It's just that she doesn't feel like wearing colors anymore. E. is more into black with white…mostly black.

B. A reconstruction. E. hates the prosthesis, but she wants to fill out her clothes; she wants a natural look with or without cleavage. But then the reconstruction…it doesn't work out as hoped…more hard chest mound than soft breast. Not that it matters. The fact is she can't imagine ever letting a man fondle anything on her chest again, can't imagine taking off her top for a man again, not since her husband said, I didn't think it would look like that.

C. Redux. A few years later, the cancer invades E's remaining breast. Another empty space. Less unanticipated? Less unexpected? E. can't say for sure. Back in her hospital room, E.'s husband says, There was a problem; he says, The doctor closed you up. At which point he leaves for home. Fourteen excruciating hours later, the doctor tells E. the problem is her skin—not metastasis. She's not going to die. Not today, anyway.

D. Another reconstruction. E. is disappointed. The new chest mound is higher, larger, and harder than the old one. Her arm is swollen to three times its normal size. But it is her skin that causes her the greatest concern. It is thin and giving at the seams.

E. Enhancements. E. has made several important decisions. It's time to leave her husband, so she rents a little house and moves in alone. It's time to risk a new relationship, so she allows herself to get involved with a friend. It's time to make love again, so she does—with her blouse held firmly in place. It's not as if she's trying to fool anyone. The man knows what's under the blouse. And she's beginning to believe he won't turn away in disgust should it slip loose. But for now, he doesn't push to see what's hidden, and she doesn't offer to expose much, preferring, instead, the most extraordinary of pleasures: cuddling with him on the couch.

TEN: My eighty-something-year-old neighbor claims that sooner or later in every woman's life, boobs, the jobs of boobs, and Boob Jobs become irrelevant. Take hers, for example. She was a curvaceous 1940s bathing suit model. Movie star material—Ingrid Bergman comes to mind. But then she fell in love, got married, and had a few daughters. A typical woman of her era, she gave up her career and embraced the role of stay-at-home mom—a good thing since the pregnancies took their toll on her model's body—particularly her breasts. Hers was a happy, till-death-do-us-part marriage, and that took its toll, too. The lithe look of her model days was lost forever, evolving into a form she prefers and finds more comfortable—a home body.

Then her husband died. She's not inclined to replace him. A few years after his death, she required a double mastectomy. She's not inclined to replace her breasts, either. She says, I'm done. There will be no more men. She says, "Why conform to a self-image we cannot sustain or make work for us?"

R.A. RYCRAFT, b. 1956, is nonfiction editor at *Serving House: a Journal of Literary Arts*, and has published stories, poems, essays and reviews in numerous journals and anthologies. Rycraft is the English department chair at Mt. San Jacinto College in Menifee, California and co-editor of *Winter Tales II: Women on the Art of Aging* and *Steve Kowit: This Unspeakably Marvelous Life*.

Subjective Age: *My subjective age is thirty-three. That's when I began to get a grip and started welcoming wisdom born of experience; that's the Me I still hope to see every time I look in the mirror.*

Baby Boom

Andrew McCarthy

My wife is pregnant. Few phrases speak to such an utter, irrevocable change in the trajectory of one's life. That my wife is with child is, of course, good news. It's fantastic news. And yet it is news that does not sit easily with me.

I already have two children, one by my first wife and another with my current—and currently pregnant—wife. My oldest lives with us half the time and with his mother, a few blocks away, the other half. I adore my children, naturally. My son is eleven; my daughter recently turned seven. Like most parents, I believe my children to be more dynamic, more charming, funnier, smarter, more perceptive and sensitive, more athletic, and more beautiful than other people's children. My wife has accused me of not liking other people's children. I like them fine, I tell her, but I love my children. At this moment they still adore us. It's a lovely time of life.

The thing is, I turned fifty this year. I was fairly old getting into the child business to begin with, but now...

My own parents were in their twenties and early thirties when they had children. These days people are waiting longer, so long that refrigeration is often involved. We're postponing the responsibilities of parenthood for careers or personal pleasures, waiting until we're ready. But are we ever ready? Much like the presidency, doesn't the job of fatherhood make the man?

When I do the math, and I have, repeatedly, I will be nearing seventy—s-e-v-e-n-t-y—when my youngest child goes off to college. That is, assuming I live that long and that I can still afford college. From everything I hear, seventy is no longer seventy. At least, that's what the seventy-year-olds say. If the view from fifty is any indication, I'm sure they're right. It's just that I was looking forward to a little more time to be left with an empty nest.

These newly added years of child rearing on the horizon will swallow up nearly an entire decade. And as one gets older (like, say, fifty) one realizes that time is the most valuable of commodities. It's the discovery that choices must be made, that everything is no longer going to be possible; it is a view into the void and perhaps the true sign of aging. And now, with the notion that my sixties will be spent with a teenager at home, I am left gasping as I watch pipe dreams of extended travel, time with my wife, and visions of blessed solitude go up in smoke.

I used to be grateful I waited so long to start a family, glad I was more emotionally mature when my kids came along. But I never imagined myself one of those fathers mistaken for Grandpa at morning drop-off. All my supposed accumulated wisdom goes out the window every time my son tortures his sister. I don't see this situation improving, as I now need longer naps than my children.

Since the day my first child was born, seasoned parents told me to enjoy it. "The time flies," they all said. And that has been my experience as well. It seems just yesterday that I sat with my son on my lap at his preschool orientation, but earlier this week I waved goodbye to him outside our apartment as he pedaled his bike into Central Park to go off to school, out into the world alone, without looking back.

The greatest, deepest joys in my life have, without doubt, been associated with my children. So why this apprehension about another? Is it just fear, the same corrosive agent that lurks beneath so many of my less noble characteristics? But fear of what? That everything won't be okay with the delivery? Or maybe it's worry that my relationship with my wife will get sliced even further, with yet another piece of her going to someone else who cries out for attention. Or how the new baby will affect the ever evolving dynamic within the family. We already have a house filled with four divas and no chorus—can we really take on another star? There are a lot of unknowns at this point.

I take solace in the knowledge that there's still time. As I write this, we have another five months before the baby is due. My mother likes to say that the nine months give you a chance to get used to the idea— though I know I'm grasping at straws when I start quoting my mother's pliable wisdom.

In any event, we are preparing. My wife has plunged into serious and classic nesting mode. She has become urgently obsessed with finding a bigger, better home. Now, I, on the other hand, have recently been employing an equally time-honored response: denial. Just last week I was on a plane. Sitting across the aisle was a crying child in the arms of an exhausted, panicked-looking father. The man helplessly bounced the unhappy infant on his lap, but the kid just shrieked louder with each jostle. I thought, "I'm so glad I'm past that phase," all the while knowing that in less than a year I will be that exhausted, bug-eyed man. Again.

Another thing I thought was behind me was the playground. I always hated the playground. A few months ago I was struck suddenly with relief and a strange form of pride when it occurred to me that the hours spent chasing my kids under the jungle gym and pushing them on truck tires hanging from heavy chains were mostly over. The idea of zooming down the slide with my new infant on my lap fills me with exhaustion. Been there, done that.

And yet, if experience tells me anything, it's that all this hemming and hawing, all my resistance, is just "by the way," a time-filler of sorts. History promises—and I trust the future will bear this out—that the moment my new child is born, all my misplaced anxieties and selfish doubts will be swept away. Love will rush in and save the day, the way it always does when new life is welcomed. My heart will sing. I will be my best self once again.

At least, until the 2 a.m. feeding.

ANDREW MCCARTHY, b. 1962, is an actor, director, and an award-winning travel writer. He has appeared in dozens of movies, including *Pretty in Pink*, and has directed episodes of *Orange Is the New Black*, and *Grace and Frankie*. He is the author of the travel memoir *The Longest Way Home*, and his debut novel, *Just Fly Away*, will be published in 2017.

Subjective Age: *At 5:30 wake-up, I'm at least fifty-five. By lunch, I'm forty. By ten at night, it's over.*

A Temporary Insanity

Gail Wells

The possibility had been gnawing at her since the first grandchild came. The new parents, daughter and husband, brought the baby home to a tiny house in a town three hundred miles away from her. Visits were short and sometimes tense. The baby didn't sleep much. Nobody slept much. The dishes sat dirty in the sink, and there were piles of laundry on the sofa. The television was on more than she liked.

It was hard to be there and hard to leave. When they pulled away from the curb, she turned her head away and breathed hard through her nose. I just love her so much, she said to her husband. He was quiet for a moment. I remember us in those days, he replied.

The daughter's husband started nursing school and kept his old job at the equipment yard. He is a hard worker, and the daughter is, too. The day care person is wonderful but sometimes she is closed, and sometimes she is sick. Sometimes the baby is sick. I don't want you to put yourself out, the daughter assures her on the phone, the cheer not quite concealing the desperation.

She drives up to help whenever she can.

Sometimes she and the daughter let the little boy sleep in the car seat while they cruise the town looking at houses for sale. The town is a charming old college town in the Palouse country of eastern Washington, with avenues of mansions built by rich wheat farmers. They gaze at stately Queen Annes in the college neighborhood, deep front porches held up by lathed posts twined with wisteria growing from gnarled trunks. They look at sturdy ranch houses on half-acres of vegetables and dahlias, and low-slung glass-walled trophy homes facing the golf course. She can see the longing in her daughter's eyes. She remembers. Thirty-one years ago she brought this baby girl home to a dad and a big brother in a two-bedroom apartment with one bathroom and a coin-op washer across the parking lot.

She remembers wanting her mother then. Now the daughter says, Look, that one would hold all of us. You and dad could have the west wing.

You're kidding, she says. Maybe, says the daughter with a smile. But it gives her a thrill to think about it.

The possibility begins to grow, a temporary insanity. Isn't this how people did in the old days? Three generations under one roof, four adults raising the child, relief for the young working folks and care for the old ones as they get older?

She speaks her yearning to a friend. A sweet fantasy from our agrarian past, the friend says. Think about it. Do you really want to be the go-to babysitter? Do you want to live in each other's laps?

She thinks about it. I'd have to set some boundaries, she says.

Boundaries! says the friend. They didn't have boundaries in the old days. Boundaries are a modern construct.

The toddler learns to recognize his grandma and grandpa, though at first he is wary. He is an intense, emotional child, a thrower of monumental tantrums. The parents try ignoring, distracting, redirecting, reasoning. They impose time out, during which the toddler continues his tantrum in the corner. They bargain. They threaten. They yell, though they try not to. They are tired all the time. She knows this and she tries not to judge. She thinks, I could be a real help here just by setting an example of consistent discipline. She does not say this, although at one difficult dinner she ventures that negotiating with a three-year-old as if he were a grown-up…She doesn't get the thought out before the daughter blows up. What do you want me to do, beat him? She backs down in the face of the shouting. A moment later the daughter, tearful, holds both arms out and they embrace. Nothing more is said.

Sometimes she has to get out of the house. She pedals her son-in-law's bicycle through the neighborhoods, examines modest affordable houses that just need a little paint, a bit of fixing on the porch railing, someone to take the garden in hand. She peers at the flyers through the plate glass of the real-estate office. She can't stop her mind from doing the math: selling her house will yield $___ after the rest of the mortgage is paid, and if we put down, let's say, $___ on, oh, that little Craftsman (such a charming house and not too badly run down), then ... The numbers pulse like alternating current through her brain, and she feels her breath coming shorter and quicker.

She remembers the feeling she used to get as a kid at the swimming hole, grabbing the thick knotted rope and taking a running jump, swaying out over the water, slowing into the apex of the arc, resting in that eternal weightless moment, and then the drop. She remembers the bigger kids shouting from the bank, Let go! Let go!

It is hard to leave. Always hard. There are tears, awkwardly dashed away. But at Cascade Locks she starts to smell the river-loam, St. Helen's-ash, Douglas-fir perfume of the Willamette Valley, and she inhales it gratefully for the last eighty miles home. She steps through her own front door, drops her bag, and heads out the back door to her garden. Here are her tall oaks with their green branches bending tenderly over the creek. Here are her vegetable beds feathered with carrot tops, onion sprouts like green exclamation points. What am I thinking? she asks herself. How could I leave this place?

She closes her eyes and sees the toddler's grimy grinning face and her daughter's belly just rounding with the second pregnancy. She feels an almost physical tug from the northeast, and her heart quivers like a compass needle.

The baby is born, another lovely strong boy. The toddler learns to talk and becomes quite reasonable. The son-in-law finishes his nursing degree and gets a job at a hospital in a desert town only two hundred fifty miles away from her. Which is great, but oh! the town.

Oh, dear.

The town marches grimly over sagebrush flats, acres and acres of near-identical houses on grids of cutely named streets, each with its lavishly irrigated front and back lawns (in the middle of a desert!), and the neighborhoods cut up every few miles by rectilinear four-lane commercial strips, and the whole thing straining against a tangled net of freeways.

She tries to like it. She walks to the store from her daughter's house and buys groceries and carries them back in her canvas food co-op bag. She does this all the time at home. Lots of people in her town walk their groceries home in canvas food co-op bags. Some people carry their groceries home on bicycles with smug bumper stickers that say One Less Car. (In a university town, she thinks, people should at least get the grammar right.)

Here she catches curious looks from passersby. Twice she has to jump back onto the curb to let a heedless driver turn in front of her. She realizes that nobody walks in her daughter's town, and that only children and poor people ride bicycles.

She realizes she disapproves of this town and of everyone in it. Nearly everyone. She is ashamed of her disapproval.

But the daughter and her family finally have a big house, and they are thrilled. They don't mind if it looks like all the others. There are enough bedrooms for themselves and the boys, and for her and her husband when they visit. She is not unhappy to trade the old lumpy futon for a real bed. There is a rumpus room with a pool table.

While the men putter with the cars or shoot pool over beers, she and the daughter browse Walmart and Costco, pushing the wire cart with the infant in his car seat and examining sofa pillows and side tables. Sometimes they leave the boys with dad and grandpa and go out for sushi, just the two of them. She loves this; she loves this.

She loves this, and the insanity comes back, and the prospect of cutting all her ties and changing her whole life makes perfect sense. What is it about a quandary that splits reality in two? She looks up quandary and finds that its etymology—fittingly—is uncertain. It may be derived from a Middle English root meaning evil, plight, peril, adversity, difficulty, or it might come from the Latin root *quando*, meaning *when*.

Neither of these satisfactorily explains the pickle she feels herself in, of being so strongly pulled in two directions that she doesn't know who she is. When she is home she is one person, the sensible cautious woman she's known her whole life, the person who has adjusted to a comfortable middle age with some resignation but mostly with gratitude; things could be worse. At her daughter's she is someone else entirely, a bolder, freer, more adventurous woman who looks to the future and sees an infinity of bright possibilities.

She doesn't know this woman very well, but she'd like to know her better.

She takes the son-in-law's bicycle out again, keeping a weather eye for clueless drivers. The houses are cheap. She finds one for sale across from the elementary school, decent-sized, three bedrooms, bigger than their own house. The price is astonishingly low. If we sold our house tomorrow, she calculates, we could buy this house outright. And it's bigger! Three bedrooms! Is it a sign from heaven?

She constructs an elaborate fantasy of the older boy walking from kindergarten to grandma's house. She welcomes him with milk and wholesome crackers, she lures him away from his video games with a jolly round of double solitaire. Or they play catch in the backyard, or ride bicycles if it's not too hot or too cold or too dusty or too windy, if they can find a place away from traffic.

She vows not to tell her daughter about the house, but she can't stop herself. Her daughter sighs and says, Mom, it would be so wonderful to have you and Dad here, but I know you have your own life. She tries to read her daughter's face, her sigh. Is this permission to go ahead? Or a warning not to? Maybe her daughter needs boundaries of her own.

On the long, coffee-fueled drive home the insanity swells to a tsunami in her head, and she is swept away on a foamy crest of reckless planning, endlessly elaborating on the permutations:

They could sell the house (they'd have to put in a new bathroom vanity and of course repaint inside and out and a bunch of other stuff but that's no big deal). They could buy a new house in their daughter's town. Yes it would be a cookie-cutter house but they could make it their own inside. She would rip out the damned lawn and grow raspberries with drip irrigation.

Or they could rent their house out and rent something up there, an apartment or a condo. She conjures up renters for her own house: a visiting professor, polite and accented, with an accomplished wife and adorable children. Or they could sell their house now and rent up there and bank the money. As her husband drives, she scribbles numbers on the back of her magazine, does long division, figures out a purchase price and a down payment that would put them in the sweet spot of being mortgage-free. See? It would be a good financial move!

Those boys are going to be teenagers before we know it, she tells him. It's now or never. She imagines them walking up the daughter's driveway carrying an ice cream cake for the baby's first birthday. She imagines the older boy hitting a baseball off a tee, and a couple years later, when he plucks a soaring fly out of the air and trots back to the dugout, she and her husband stand up and yell, the grandparents, rapt and loyal and present.

The next morning she wakes up in her own bed and pings her emotional circuits and finds them still charged with electricity. She thinks about her church, her friends, her volunteer work. I gathered a community around myself when I moved here, she tells herself, and I can do it again. At this she feels but prefers not to register a momentary dimming, like what happens to the lights when a tree grazes a high-voltage line.

Two weeks go by. She sits on her back porch and drinks her coffee and contemplates her garden, the way old people like to do. It's May; the lilacs are blooming and the rosebuds are starting to swell. The creek bank is lush with new growth of Indian plum and oak leaves unfurling and billows of Himalayan blackberry. The neighbor's backyard is fifteen feet away across the creek, but she can't see it through the green blanket, which makes her feel enclosed and protected.

She pictures her daughter's backyard: a rectangular patch of irrigated grass, a reef of concrete patio bleached by the desert sun, a few tough rosebushes around the fence line.

If she had to pick a totem plant, it would not be a rose or a sage or a tumbleweed. It would be a foxglove or a peony, something wet, tender-walled, fragile. Difficult to transplant. This garden, the sitting, the quiet, all give her a peace she never had when she was her daughter's age. But of course she didn't need it then, didn't want it. She was young.

She probes herself for the insane electricity. It's gone.

Yet sometimes the peace feels like a coma. Sometimes the green blanket feels like a shroud. Sometimes she wants to thrust her arms through her safe life and rip her way out. What if I die in this house? The thought fills her with dread.

The evening before another trip north, she's out checking the sprinklers when a deer peers into the yard from the creek bank. She recognizes him. He's a regular, a yearling buck with two nubbins on his forehead. Go home, she says, without conviction. The deer pauses and stares at her. She picks up a piece of gravel and throws it awkwardly. It falls short, rustling the shrubbery. The deer retreats a couple of steps. Well, are you going or staying? she asks him. He gazes back at her with his long inscrutable face.

The older grandson boils out the door when they arrive, wearing a bicycle helmet and clutching his Power Ranger. He gives them extravagant hugs and showers them with chatter. The baby toddles behind, holding his mother's hand. I'll bet you hardly recognize them, says her daughter. Yes, she replies, they're different boys every time we come.

She says this every time they come.

The older boy wants to ride bikes with grandma. They wheel wide circles in the street, she shouting at him to watch for cars, he shouting at her to watch him go so fast! Afterward they pump up his bike tires. She presses the end of the pump's hose into the fleshy web between her thumb and forefinger and says, Now push on the pump. The hose emits a farting noise, which cracks him up, which cracks her up. They do it again and again. Her daughter sticks her head through the garage door: What are you two doing? They are laughing too hard to explain. She loves this. She loves this. How can she leave?

GAIL WELLS, b. 1952, is a journalist and an essayist and is the author of six books, including a memoir about raising her family in a converted old schoolhouse. She is finishing a biography of Norma Paulus, a prominent Oregon lawmaker. Gail lives with her husband in a house next to a creek and gardens in her backyard.

Subjective Age: *Our neighborhood has a resident herd of deer, who visit our backyard garden as if it's their special deli. Common as they are, they fill me with wonder, and I can't bring myself to be harsh with them. My age at these moments is about three-and-a-half.*

Passing Fifty

Mark Greene

I just finished a crazy bike ride down Ninth Avenue through midtown Manhattan.

Barreling down the long slope from W. 57th, southbound on Ninth Avenue, is to be part of a sun-glare avalanche of surging yellow cabs and pothole-banging delivery trucks jostling through bottlenecked mobs of aimless texting pedestrians. It's pure chaos. It's funny and crazy and dangerous and I love it. There are moments when I am tracking so many visual variables that the ride becomes a peripheral-vision fever dream. You shoot past cabs, people's startled faces visible for the briefest of moments in the passenger window. Who are they? What is their life like? Are they happy?

Ninth Avenue is a symphony of variables, all in motion. Some drivers notice you, some are oblivious. You have to know which are which. You see the whites of their eyes as they glance at you in the side view mirrors. Each person texting on each passing corner could be the one. Lady. Pink blouse. Man, black backpack. Kid, smoking. Women, two kids. Baby stroller, no, two baby strollers. Looking. Not looking. Any one of them could be the one that steps off, absentmindedly, just as you are shooting the gap.

. . . .

I'm fifty-three years old.

I'm going to miss riding crazy like this. Some time in the next few years, I'll wake up one day and that will be that. I will still ride my bike, but biking Ninth Ave. will recede into yesterday. For me, that part of my life will be finished. It's so tempting to boil aging down into some bleak list of things you can't do any more. It creeps up on you in your forties. Your eyes go. Then your joints. It's weird how quickly we adjust to and accept this daily paring away of our physical prowess.

I feel like I'm bidding a long farewell to my younger self. A friend who's gathering his coat and cap to leave. He is lingering at the door now. Reluctant to go. But he's got a train to catch. He'll go.

That youthful self is still vibrant within me. And I'm working to bring the essence of him forward in some form, spiritual or otherwise, into tomorrow, a gift to the old man I'll become in fifteen years or so. But who are our younger selves? And how do these energetic, vibrant hungry beings inform us as we age? Can our older selves find connection and continuity with the remnants of youth in us? I can tell you this much, those two selves, young and old, will either be adversaries or partners. I feel my job is to teach them to be friends, before it's too late.

Take drinking, for instance. I used to drink a lot. I don't any more. My body simply can't take it. I guess I'm lucky that way. It hurts too much the next day. So two glasses of wine and I'm done. But I know guys my age who still sit up all night drinking beer. Ten or twelve beers, one after another, till 2 a.m. And I'm left wondering, is the young in them punishing the old? Did the old do something wrong? Are the ways they lived when they were younger, the solutions that gave them joy, reluctant to step aside for something new?

Just as my youth goes, the old man I will be is coming. As much as I'd like to bar the door, he's out there, just raising his hand to knock. I know that knock is coming. I can feel it in my right shoulder. In my knees when I push myself too hard. I feel it when a drowsiness creeps over me during a long day. Old age wakes me in the dead of night, worrisome thing that it is.

I used to sleep like a baby. But now I wake sometimes. I lie there and take stock. Over and over. Like a grocer who can't believe his inventory. Did I order that? Where are my customers? I turn decades-old events and relationships over in my mind. Examining the emotions they give rise to. Regrets wheedle in. Money gone wrong. Some empty aimless relationship I wasted precious years on, or the woman I should have stayed with. People who have already died. People who got famous while I didn't.

What you are in the world can seem vague and uncertain as you age. The long night of the soul they call it. As you age all the pat ideas about success and failure creep up on you. You played your cards wrong somehow.

You can do this 2 a.m. exercise endlessly if you are not careful. You can obsess on a cycle of questions that have no end, because they are the past and the past cannot be undone. The past can be a carnival wheel of garish emotions and old tapes you spin again and again. Eventually, if you're smart, you say "don't do that any more," and you'll let it rest.

Because even as age exacts its price, it brings great gifts. If you shift your focus, you'll realize that something remarkable is happening.

. . . .

With age, over the last few years, I've found that my mind is synthesizing information in startling and deeply satisfying ways. It's as if all the cramming of experience into my head and heart has finally resulted in a reliable sense of self. It manifests as a higher awareness; very much spiritual in its nature. It manifests as a capacity for calming and ordering one's reactions to the world. It has made me smarter and sweeter and more self-assured. And the source is hard for me to pin down. But I believe it will come to any of us who are actively engaged in life. It's as if the divine says, "You've done enough struggling to understand. Here, have a glimpse of peace."

I do credit the birth of my son and the years of service I have given him as part of what got me here. My connection to him has made me a more patient, thoughtful and self-assured person. My wife is a huge part of it. Her path has made mine so much more meaningful. The people I have known in my life, the places I have seen, they all play a part. But it's more than any person's influence, or even the map of our choices.

I think, perhaps, we're designed to evolve in our fifties. There is clearly a refining of skills that takes place. If you spend a lifetime writing or designing or dancing, or building, the pursuit of your craft as a practice of order and structure falls away and intuition takes over. It's a synthesis of years of work, resulting in flow. What you have sought to master, thought about, processed for decades becomes transcendent. You hit your best years. You get the payoff.

This is what happens in living, too. If you can turn your attention from what is past, towards the miraculous things that are coming, you will see the patterns of divinity that younger eyes often cannot spot. The trappings, appetites, desires and demands of youth are driven by the need to experience life and validate ourselves. Once we are validated, it's time to set aside appetite and seek something higher. If you look for it, it is right there, waiting.

I can't say for sure where life will go. What is emerging may work out or it may not. But I can tell you this. Life seems like a huge adventure now. What once was a struggle to create sense of the world, now feels like a single long clear note of something peaceful and full of love. I only catch a glimpse of it, this note of peace, this sense that things fit together, are beautiful, can be loved … but it's there. I've seen it right there on Ninth Avenue, in the sun washed faces rushing by.

So if you're young, be young. Try not to do any damage if you can help it. But be young. It's your job to take it all in.

But if you're wondering about getting older, trust me, there's some amazing stuff coming. For real.

MARK GREENE, b. 1960, is Executive Editor for the *Good Men Project;* his articles have received over 250,000 Facebook shares and ten million page views. His work examines the life-affirming changes emerging from the modern masculinity movement. Greene writes and speaks on culture, society, family, gender and fatherhood for the *Good Men Project*, *The Shriver Report*, *The New York Times*, *Salon*, the BBC and *The Huffington Post*.

Subjective Age: *I was born in 1960. And, oddly enough that's how old I feel.*

Beyond Chagrin

David Bradley

When I was in the second grade I wet my pants.

It happened during a rehearsal of my elementary school's annual pageant, just before I spoke my lines—well, line. But, according to the director, a fourth-grade teacher who'd minored in drama, that line *was crucial.* For as she envisioned (and had rewritten) "Little Red Riding Hood," the BIG BAD WOLF (Yours Truly) who lurks upstage, growling (*Grrr!*) through Acts One and Two, overhears a Sunday School lesson, is transformed from predator to protector and in the final scene comes downstage to Our Heroine's rescue, growling: "Leave her alone!"

My casting came with … obligations. I was one of only four or five colored children in the school. All the other speaking parts been assigned to fifth and sixth-graders, all of them white. At seven, I'd absorbed the understanding that black Americans had been struggling to be seen as respectable—e.g., as Negroes, not as colored people—since before I was born, and I was expected to add and not detract. So I practiced my growling and studied my line, the better to be a credit to my race with, my dear.

The trouble was, I had a sixth-grade reading level, but only a second-grade bladder, and the script called for the WOLF to lurk on stage in every scene. I made it through rehearsals, thanks to frequent breaks, but midway through the first full-length run-through, I was *grring* not in anger, but agony. As I rushed downstage to the rescue, I felt a cathartic release of dramatic tension. I spoke my line clearly and with authority, then exited, stage left, dripping.

Lurking in the Boys Room, waiting for my mother to fetch fresh pants, I *grred* at myself furiously, teeth-bared in chagrin. BIG BAD WOLF? Big, bad disgrace—to myself, my parents, the entire Negro race. Next day, I told the teacher/director I could not go on.

She told me not to worry. I'd spoken my line despite the deluge, which proved I was a trooper. She'd added a stage direction for the WOLF to slink off and back on midway through the final act. As for the previous day's mortification, she told me, "Don't worry, it's not the most embarrassing thing you'll ever do."

Don't *worry*? How could I not? That was a terrifying prophecy which too often came true. In high school: a plethora of peccadilloes, like that chemistry experiment that produced not the predicted white precipitate but a green cloud of poisonous gas, and that jump-shot at the buzzer that swished through the opponents' net. In college, in the city: a myriad of misdemeanors arising from my rural Protestant upbringing. Yes, I did ask the *itamae* at Benihana, wasn't he going to *cook* that? Yes I did whisper to the nun, one Wednesday morning in February, "'Scuse me, Sister, but you've got a smudge on your forehead." No, I did not order a ham-and-cheese in a kosher deli; but yes, I did order a hot pastrami and a glass of milk.

And yes, I did call myself a Negro...to the derision of the Society of African and Afro-American Students and the pity of the Students for a Democratic Society. I did ask, Where *was* It Happening? and what *were* the Usual Places to buy tickets to It...and by the way, what was It?

Often, I found out by stepping in It. Worse, in attempting to save face, I tended to insert my It-covered foot into my mouth. (Well, where *I* come from we *fry* our fish.) Afterwards, I'd lie awake, recalling with incredulity (I can't believe I sucked the tail, too) not only the present gaffe, but boo-boos, flubs, fluffs, goofs and howlers past (Yes, I did ask him why he'd been living in a closet. And yes, I did ask her how long her friend would be visiting.). When at last I slept my dreams were often haunted the ghost of *faux pas* future.

In later life I learned—the hard way—to check my facts, my pronunciations and my fly. (Yes, I did give that reading with my zipper down; worse, I pulled it up during the Q&A.) I developed protective strategies: a deadpan affect that suggested my miscues were calculated comedy; a Socratic style that masked clueless questions as intellectual interrogation; an ironic tone that could be rapidly deployed whenever my *savoir* fell behind my *faire*.

But no strategy could protect me from my own awareness. *I* knew I did say, "Why can't your friend Bill meet us at the bar?" *I* knew I did believe that working girl was a grad student doing fieldwork in ethnography, and though the judge found it hilarious and dismissed the case, I was left paralyzed by the premonition that the worst still lay ahead. That grade-school teacher's prediction proved a curse that hounded me even unto middle age.

But shortly after turning fifty, as I stood in the wings, listening to an old friend introduce me to a distinguished academic audience with a much-embellished account of one of my Greatest Misses (for the record: I did *not* attempt to leap It in a single bound, although I *was* trying to climb the thing) and thinking, a bit sadly, that I could no longer lift my leg that high, it came to me: at my age, the most embarrassing thing I'll ever do is probably something I've already done. Suddenly I saw myself not as aging, but *transcending*, entering a state of grace beyond disgrace, beyond shamefacedness, beyond chagrin.

DAVID BRADLEY, b. 1950, is the author of the novels *South Street* and *The Chaneysville Incident* (which won the PEN/Faulkner Award). His short story "You Remember the Pinmill" won an O. Henry Prize, and his personal essay, "A Eulogy for Nigger," won the Notting Hill Prize. Born in western Pennsylvania, Bradley is a graduate of the University of Western Pennsylvania and the University of London. He now lives in Southern California.

Subjective Age: *When I get up in the morning I am 103. After coffee, I am a chronologically accurate sixty-five. When I start out on a walk or a bike ride I think I am thirty-two, but feel like I am seventy-five until I get warmed up; then I might feel like forty-five, but I take it easy because I'm no fool, no siree, I want to live to be 103. When I watch the news I am over thirty-five. When I am writing I am ... ageless.*

Like Landing a Man on the Moon

Ralph Robert Moore

I turned fifty today.

I'm half a century old.

This birthdate is frightening only if you're young. When I was in my teens, I could never, ever imagine myself being this old. Fifty was too close to death, too far from the excitement of being a teenager. Those I knew who were old, meaning above thirty, seemed almost a separate race, an undignified people who didn't read or hold meaningful conversations, who wandered around with pot bellies and balding heads in badly-cut clothes, like giant toddlers who had somehow, inexplicably, been given control of the world.

I first felt my own mortality when I turned twenty-five. I was sitting in my suit at my desk, one of dozens in a beautiful, high-vaulted marble chamber in the Bridgeport, Connecticut bank where I worked, and realized I didn't like my job, was never going to like my job, and was probably going to be stuck in that job until I turned sixty-five.

For the first time in my life, I felt real depression. It seemed like out of all the infinite possible ways I had imagined, while a teenager, I might make money, to be able to continue to have the good time I was having, but now be on my own, all of the possibilities exciting and emotionally rewarding, I had somehow managed to fall into the dullest, most demeaning job of all. Plus it paid so little there was almost nothing left over after rent and food.

So what did I do? Something that seemed, in my mind-set then, almost logistically impossible, like landing a man on the moon. I moved from Connecticut to California.

Where did I wind up? In an industrial park in Santa Barbara, doing piece work for a small company that manufactured credit card readers (the box with a slot on top your card gets swooped through at the cash register).

I was making even less money than before, and the rents were higher, but I had learned an important lesson, and it was exhilarating.

I had control over my own life.

If I didn't like something in my life, I could change it.

In the years that followed, that's exactly what I did, and what I've continued doing. I've never felt depressed since.

Even at turning fifty, which I see as a badge of honor.

No matter who you are, or what you've done with your life, or not done, there is some merit in the simple accomplishment of having made it this far. Not everyone does.

After fifty years, what's the most important thing I've learned?

Things work out.

No matter how hopeless a situation may appear to be, it does, eventually, change. And when it does, it's almost always for the better. If you graph your life, you'll get dips and spikes, but the overall trend is upwards.

Don't get discouraged by first drafts.

RALPH ROBERT MOORE, b. 1950, grew up in an age when children walked anywhere they wanted, knew they could be killed at any moment by a big bomb, and after midnight, there was nothing on TV but test patterns. He is growing old in an age of Mars land rovers, terrorist explosions, and the ability to reach anywhere in the world, at any time, with the click of a mouse.

Subjective Age: *I remain in my early forties, when Mary and I moved into our current home. Our weekends were spent digging under the hot Texas sun in our back yard, slowly transforming it into a beautiful small park, and then collapsing in chairs under the trees at the rear of our property each sunset to drink cold beers.*

Grandmother

Kyoko Mori

In Japan, where I grew up in the 1960s, longevity was considered the most auspicious gift bestowed upon mortals. Pine trees, cranes, and turtles, all believed to live for a hundred years or more, decorated the screens and tapestries in noblemen's homes from the feudal times. The designs in gold foil and silk made longevity seem grand in museum displays, but for ordinary people in our own time, the path to longevity was littered with boring admonitions: eat regular meals, dress appropriately for the weather, get up at dawn, take naps, and go to bed early except on New Year's Eve, when eating long white noodles at midnight would ensure many healthy years.

My maternal grandmother, Fuku, came from a family famous for their longevity. Her mother and aunts had lived to be over ninety-five. Her back bent, her white hair put up in a bun, Fuku was the shortest, smallest adult I knew. She and my grandfather, a retired country school teacher, lived in a drafty house among rice paddies. During the weeks my mother, brother, and I spent with them every summer, Fuku scolded me daily for my picky eating habits. "If you don't finish your food, you won't live a long life like everyone in our family," she fretted. When she frowned, her whole face creased into a spider's web of wrinkles. She always wore the same clothes—a gray blouse and a black skirt shaped like a tea cozy. I didn't want to be ninety-five, I decided, if it meant years and years of eating food I hated and looking old like my grandmother.

I snuck out of the house during nap time to wander around the rice paddies where my great-grandfather had been bitten by a poisonous snake. He would have died instantly if he hadn't borrowed a sickle from a farmer and cut his leg open to let out the poison. The moral of the story was that we shouldn't let a minor inconvenience, like losing a little blood, stop us from living a long life, but my great-grandfather didn't live happily ever after. He once owned every rice paddy in the village and supported his family with the rent he collected from his tenant farmers. After the Second World War, however, the landowners had to surrender their land to the government so the paddies could be distributed among their tenant farmers. My school history books presented the land reform as a great democratic event that modernized our country, but my great-grandfather had survived into old age only to lose his land and be reduced to poverty.

Perhaps my mother, Takako, was thinking of the people in our family who had endured a long but unhappy life, when she chose to kill herself at forty-one. She left a note saying we would be better off without her, but I knew—as my grandmother must have, too—that her misery was caused by my father. He had several girlfriends and seldom came home to us. The following year, when I was thirteen, he remarried and decided I could no longer see my mother's family. My grandparents lived a half-day's journey away. I managed to disobey my father to visit them only twice before I left the country at twenty to attend an American college. When I returned thirteen years later, my grandfather was dead but Fuku was managing alone in their old house. It was mid-summer, the season of my childhood stays.

A month before turning ninety-four, Fuku looked even smaller than I remembered. Although I was short and thin as well, she only came up to my shoulder, and my wrist looked enormous next to hers when I took her hand. She was dressed in her usual gray blouse and black skirt. All afternoon, she led me from room to room, opening and closing the drawers in the rickety cabinets stuffed with envelopes, boxes, and scraps of paper. She gave me the photographs of our family and the letters my mother and I had written to her—saved in bundles tied with cotton twine. "Everything will be ashes when I die," she kept saying.

She lamented she had no fancy kimonos to pass on to me as heirlooms. "All my kimonos turned into rice," she sighed, a refrain familiar to me since childhood. During the Second World War, Fuku sold her kimonos to buy food on the black market. Shortly after my grandparents moved back to the country, the war ended and the family lost their land. Whatever kimonos Fuku had left were sold then, along with some of their furniture.

One of the drawers contained a dozen new dish towels. "I want you to see this and remember," Fuku said. "When I die and people come to the house after the funeral, you have to make sure your uncle's wife is not going to be drying the dishes with a dirty towel. Promise to remind her where I keep the new ones." I said, "Don't worry. I'll tell her. But you're not going to die any time soon. You'll live to be a hundred."

During the years I wasn't allowed to see or hear from her, I realized that Fuku had nagged me because she loved me. Once my mother was gone, no one worried about me. I regretted snapping at my mother for hovering over me whenever I had even a minor cold. I regretted belittling my grandmother's concerns for my longevity. Coming back to her house as an adult, I knew Fuku wasn't saving those dish towels out of vanity. My grandmother longed to exert influence over us even after she was dead. She couldn't imagine not being connected to us; if she could, she'd worry about us for an eternity. The towels were plain gray like the blouses she wore. Her fierce love, combined with her frugality, scared me.

Two years later, when my uncle telephoned with the news of her death, I was in my kitchen in Wisconsin peeling tomatoes by dunking them in boiling water and running them under the faucet. The red globes, with cracked skin, reminded me of broken hearts. Both my mother and I had abandoned Fuku in her old age.

Over the years, I lost touch with what was left of my family in Japan. Divorced and childless, I now live alone in Washington, DC. I love my independence, but when I think of getting old, I worry about being all alone in the world. In a year and a month, I will turn sixty, the age my grandmother was when I was born. How will I live as an old woman? What will I do if, or when, my health begins to decline?

Watching my friends with parents who are in their eighties and nineties, I can see that even the closest family cannot save us from the pain and anxiety of illness or the heartbreak of moving into a retirement facility. No wonder my ancestors prayed to their gods to protect them. We can't bestow upon ourselves a long and healthy life by eating the right foods, getting enough sleep, saving money, surrounding ourselves with friends, or having children who love us. Our health and safety are beyond our control at any age. As we get older, we have even less resilience—and time—to recover from setbacks. Everyone must experience aging and death alone.

Even so, I wish I had a role model, someone to show me how to age with dignity in the face of this uncertainty. My mother chose to die when she was barely middle-aged. Fuku was the only person in my family I knew as an old woman. Why wasn't I more respectful toward her all those summers I stayed with her as a child? Why didn't I visit her sooner and more often from the States? After a thirteen-year absence, I spent only two days with Fuku because I didn't want her to have me as a house guest for longer—she would worry the whole time—and out in the country, there was no other place to stay. She has been dead for twenty-three years, but I'm still trying to make peace with her.

We had the afternoon to ourselves before my uncle, his wife, and one of my aunts would be over for dinner. Between cleaning out her drawers, I asked Fuku to show me her garden. She used to have flower beds and vegetable plots all around the house. I recalled sitting in her tomato patch with a damp cloth and a salt shaker, picking the sun-warmed tomatoes off the vine and eating them on the spot. A ripe tomato from the garden was one of the few things I ate without being nagged. On the phone, my uncle's wife had told me that Fuku still had a small patch of vegetables and flowers.

The patch was in the front yard, near the door, so she wouldn't have to walk far to get to it. There were several heads of lettuce, four potato plants, some herbs; purple asters and late summer chrysanthemums were already blooming. Fuku pointed to the bucket left nearby, with some hand tools in it. She asked me to get the trowel and dig up the potatoes.

I removed the soil from around the largest of the plants.

"Pull out the whole thing," she said.

I grabbed the stem and yanked. Several potatoes, smaller than children's fists, dangled at the bottom.

"Pull the others, too," she said.

"Are you sure?" I asked. "These potatoes are small. Wouldn't they be better in a couple of weeks?"

"I have no reason to save them," she said.

That evening, my aunt cooked the potatoes into a stew with bite-sized pieces of meat I picked out and did not eat. My uncle laughed and said, "Still a picky eater. How do you expect to live a long life eating like that?"

I had always been sickened by the taste and texture of animal flesh in my mouth. So I continued to spit out the meat pieces and put them on the edge of the plate. It wasn't the most polite or mature thing to do, but the best I could manage.

After dinner, my uncle opened the bag of summer oranges he had brought. "These oranges are full of Vitamin C," he told me as he peeled the thick pock-marked skin and put the individual sections on Fuku's plate. "When your grandmother was staying at our house with a bad cold, summer oranges cured her. Now she really loves them."

"Of course," my uncle's wife piped up, "she only tried them after your uncle recommended them to her. When I offered them, she said she only ate oranges in the winter because the ones we get in the summer are bitter."

Pretending not to hear, Fuku popped an orange section in her mouth. Earlier, she had told me that my uncle's wife made her coffee too weak and splashed her plants with too much water from the watering can. My grandmother hated having to accept her daughter-in-law's help; instead of thanking her, she talked behind her back and tried to appeal to my guilt and sympathy. Now she was ignoring a comment that showed her in a bad light.

My grandmother was behaving in a willful, stubborn, and manipulative manner, but I couldn't blame her. She was caught between her love and her worry: what if there was too much or not enough food for us, what if we were disappointed because she was too old to entertain us, what if we didn't leave her house with perfect memories of our visit? She wanted our time with her to be *just so*.

I didn't inherit my grandmother's frugality, and because food was always available to me, it doesn't interest or worry me. All the same I recognize Fuku in myself. Like her, I have a hard time letting go of ideas, small or large, that lodge inside my head. I become irritated with people who try to help me because, as soon as I get their attention, I long to be left alone. When conversations take turns unfavorable to me, I clam up or else make sarcastic comments. These, I know, are the traits commonly associated with the elderly: the inflexibility, the insecurity, the unwillingness to accept help without resentment.

I hope not to become the worst of how Fuku was, but I don't want to turn her into a counter-example, the Person I Don't Want to Be, either. I'd rather accept and resist her at once, remembering her with respect even as I note and avoid her shortcomings. Accepting and resisting simultaneously is all we can do with family members who annoy us. I will become my grandmother, but not entirely. It's not so different from swallowing the potatoes and spitting out the meat.

Fuku had two older sisters named Masu and Ko. If you said all three names together, masu ko-fuku, it meant "increasing fortune and happiness." Her sisters had also married into land-owning families and lost their land after the war. Fuku believed their parents had invited bad luck by giving the three of them such auspicious names. "It's presumptuous to wish for too much fortune and happiness," she said. Avoiding extravagances, even in the form of wishes and expectations, was my grandmother's strategy for survival. She dressed plainly, ate simple food, and tried not to call attention to herself, as though moderation could ward off further bad luck.

My mother hated the drab and shapeless clothes Fuku wore. "Your grandmother dresses too much like an old woman," she complained. "I gave her a pretty maroon skirt and a paisley scarf, but she stuck them in a drawer. She never buys anything for herself even when I send her money." Takako, who was very beautiful, wore dresses with a cinched-in waistline and darts at the bust, the feminine colors and styles of the mid-1960s. If she had lived past forty-one, she wouldn't have considered her mother a good role model for growing old.

I am now on my mother's side when it comes to keeping expectations high, especially for beauty. In my youth I believed that being concerned about appearances was a waste of time. Small and plain like my grandmother, I assumed there was nothing I could do about my lack of natural beauty. My husband and I didn't know how to shop for furniture and made do with mismatched tables and chairs that various friends passed on to us. It took me well into middle age to care how I dressed and how I decorated my home, to understand that choosing my clothes, furniture, and dishware can be a pleasure. I don't want to become an old woman dressed in gray and black in a drafty house with bare walls. I prefer my mother's pretty dresses and the tapestries she embroidered with butterflies and roses. My life has been an attempt to honor Takako by making the choices she couldn't: to leave my father, get an education, become a writer, marry and divorce on my own terms. I'll continue to surround myself with beauty and pursue the happiness that eluded her.

I turn to my grandmother, though, for her persistence. She worked hard for her life of modest pleasures: the summer oranges on her plate, the patch of vegetables and flowers outside her door. Her name, Fuku, without the names of her sisters, meant "happiness." In Japan, "happiness" is indistinguishable from "contentment" and "luck." It's the quiet contentment we are lucky to have at any age.

Fuku never wore the clothes Takako gave her, but she planted the seeds from the sweet peas that climbed the banisters to our balcony. All summer long, she was delighted by the profusion of pink, white, purple, and red flowers. Her flower beds contained an impressive variety of perennials and annuals. Almost any flowering plant I see at gardening centers in Washington, DC, whose climate is similar to Japan's, I know from my grandmother's garden. Fuku's flowers served no purpose except to look beautiful. And my mother, who couldn't plan for a life beyond forty-one, had foresight and persistence when it came to gardening. She made sure that her flower beds had something beautiful in them no matter what the season.

When I moved into my apartment in Washington, DC, I bought terracotta window boxes to grow petunias, my mother's favorite summer annual. The red and purple flowers cascaded down my window ledge and attracted swallowtail butterflies and ruby-throated hummingbirds. When frost killed the petunias in October, I replaced them with pansies, mixing the colors the way my mother did so the yellow flowers, little cat faces, popped out among the purple flowers plush as velvet ribbons. The pansies flowered till the heat in May wilted them and it was time for petunias again. I also planted sorrel—a hardy edible perennial—in a small orange pot in a grandmother's honor. Even in the dead of winter, I can open the window and pick a handful to toss into my salad. The slender arrow-shaped leaves have the sharp citrus taste of Fuku's summer oranges.

Kyoko Mori, b. 1957, is the author of three nonfiction books (*The Dream of Water*; *Polite Lies*; *Yarn*) and five novels (*Shizuko's Daughter*; *One Bird*; *Stone Field, True Arrow*; *Barn Cat*). She teaches creative writing at George Mason University and for the low-residency MFA Program at Lesley University. Mori lives in Washington, DC, with her two cats, Miles and Jackson.

Subjective Age: *On a good day, I think of myself as forty-eight, the age I was when I moved to DC, knowing I had found my real home; on a bad day, I am reduced to the girl I was at thirteen—determined to survive her mother's suicide but not knowing how. But mostly, I think of my essential self as a runner, moving forward in whatever (aged or ageless) body I'm in.*

Hark

Achy Obejas

The start of your day looks like any other. You tap the wristwatch that buzzed you awake and grab for your phone to read the morning headlines. There's a coup on a distant island that's sinking into the sea, shortages in a neighboring country leading to violent unrest (you know someone there and make a mental note to write to see how they are). While you're reading you get an email alert: it's from Stanford University—their hearing clinic—saying they appreciate your interest but they're still only doing animal testing and you can help with a donation. You let your legs drop over the side of the bed and listen hopefully for the groan of the floorboards. You pivot your waist and gaze at your wife and your four-year-old still tangled in blankets. Soon they'll be up, playing a game devised by your wife to see who can give you the most kisses. You glance at your phone and measure the time. In the kitchen, you make a cup of chai (now that you're avoiding caffeine) with coconut creamer and cashew milk (now that you're avoiding dairy) and take the first two of six Lysine capsules, one Vitamin C and a Zantac (your reflux is under control). Later, you'll fill a baggie with the twenty-four other pills and supplements you'll take throughout the rest of the day. It's so incredibly quiet you make a point of rattling the spoon in your cup, of shaking the Zantac bottle, of sniffing and clicking your teeth just to hear sound rattle through your skull. You know all about sound: how waves travel into the ear canal until they hit the eardrum, where they vibrate the skin like the head of a tambourine, then continue to the inner ear, that treacherous snail called the cochlea that runs the waves through thousands (though ever-decreasing) of hair cells where they're mutated into electric signals that run up the auditory nerve to the command center in the brain. You've seen pictures of hair cells: tender, almost transparent sprouts lined into soft 'V's, like something growing at the bottom of the sea or on a distant planet. And you've seen what yours probably look like: scattered, flat, milky white. You rap your knuckles against the dining room table, listen for the creak as you open your laptop and the scrape of the power cord on the floor as you plug in. You check your bank balance, think about the clinic in Germany that promises that for ten thousand (maybe twenty, maybe forty thousand) dollars they'll flood you with stem cells and ease your arthritis and maybe, just maybe—if you're lucky, because, of course, this is the part that's off the books, that's not guaranteed, that they can't really talk about—they'll reinvigorate those hair cells into beautiful V for victory lines that will hum and help you note the teeniest flick of your four-year-old's eyelids opening in the bedroom as he scrambles across the blankets to find you, you who were hoping for ten or fifteen or twenty more minutes. You, who always want more and more time. If it was just you, you would go for the stem-cell treatment, not in Germany but in Mexico, where a suspicious clinic on the border promises essentially the same thing for much less, though it's still a lot. You'd roll the dice. But it's not just you now. You can't just take the savings and run. This is why you're always tallying: You know you have maybe ten, fifteen years of productivity but it'll take Stanford fifteen, twenty years to find the formula to revive your hearing. You've calculated you'll be a well-seasoned senior citizen by the time your son graduates from high school. And you want to hear yourself clapping as he crosses the stage, as he pumps his fist in the air and shouts out whatever high school graduates will shout out then. You ask yourself, constantly, why you waited so long, why you squandered time, and when you squeeze the boy, he's always asking, Mami, why are you crying, which makes you feel weak, then panicky, as you wonder how long, how long, until you're just reading those words on his lips. This is not how you imagined your old age: in motherhood, deaf. You were always so slow, always late to the party, to the office, to the milestone. You were running a lazy, unequal race with time because, well, you were busy. You figured time would slow down too, to keep pace with you. It would have been the fair thing to do. Anyway, science was running a much more intense race: bio-carbon dating and silicon chips, antiretroviral drugs, the birth control pill, the polio vaccine, high-yield rice, the Internet, Kevlar, MRIs and GPS, genetic sequencing, Lasik eye surgery. There would be time to change your diet, and time to really start running, and time, later, when things were calmer, for a morning swim. Surely, when you finally caught up with whatever your destiny was going to be, those fucking scientists would have figured something out, wouldn't they? God, if only you'd known, if you'd had an early clue or symptom, you might have taken the time to learn lip reading, ASL, to develop a community other than all these hearing folks you love so much. You study your face in the dark and awkward reflection on your laptop computer screen. You stretch your neck, you rap the table again with your knuckles. You know that meaning is made up of movement, of music, and so you rap the table yet again, let your fingers pound the keyboard and listen, listen, listen…for anything.

ACHY OBEJAS, b. 1956, is the author of *The Tower of the Antilles & Other Stories*, *Days of Awe*, *Ruins*, and many other books. She has translated Junot Díaz, Adam Mansbach, and Wendy Guerra, among others. She is also the founder and co-director of the low-residency MFA in Translation program at Mills College. Married to Megan Bayles, she lives with their son, Ilan, in the waterfront town of Benicia, California.

Subjective Age: *I became a mother at fifty-five, which is now the only age that matters.*

Falling through Space

Ellen Gilchrist

I turned around the other day and realized that summer was beginning to end. Late August, early September. The leaves will change and I will return to my books. Time to learn something. Time to study stars or atoms or time itself. Not that time exists. It is a construct, like language or belief. I intend to stop believing in it.

It has been a wonderful summer in the small university town where I live. Children came to visit and stayed for weeks. They had parades and sang to me and slept without moving through the long, hot nights. I slept near them, dreamless, timeless, caught in the wonder of their lives.

The days run away like wild horses over the hills, a poet wrote. It is that keen ecstasy which ends as summer ends. Time to open my closet and look things over. Move the dark clothes a little closer to the front. The black wool suit, the tweed jacket, the cocktail dress. Serious clothes. Not these cotton rags I pull on in the morning and dust the piano with on my way to bed at night.

There is a roadrunner living on my roof. He moves from the old hickory tree at the back of the house to the hickory in the front yard. This is a well-established pathway, having served generations of squirrels. We knew he was in the neighborhood. Several people had sighted him. I myself had seen him once, running beside the fence line in the direction of a wooded lot behind the houses. There has been a plethora of development in our town. The wildlife is doing the best it can under the circumstances.

It was my lifelong devotion to the theatre which led to my discovering that the roadrunner was living on the roof. An eight-year-old named Aurora and an eight-year-old named William were in the bathroom putting on clown makeup for a clown show. "Will you put up the tent cover so the show can go on in case of rain?" they asked me. "Of course," I answered. "Anything for art."

I went outside and began to drag a set of steel tent poles along the concrete porch. The noise startled the roadrunner from his afternoon nap, and he came tearing down across the roof. He spread his six-foot wingspan and flew the length of the porch, amazing my Bavarian daughter-in-law, who clutched the baby to her breast, believing she had seen an American eagle.

....

Where will the roadrunner go when the leaves turn yellow and carpet the concrete porch? Perhaps he will still find a way to live in my yard. Perhaps he will go back down the hill and live in one of the houses the greedy contractors are building in the floodplain that used to be a woods and a pasture. People in my neighborhood have watched with great interest as the new drainage ditches have failed to carry away the water when it rains. Surely no one will buy a house built on the lowest place in ten square miles. Perhaps they will. Human nature is very strange and hard to understand. Perhaps I will turn into a social critic now that fall is near. I will go down there and put up a sign that says, DON'T BUY A HOUSE HERE UNLESS YOU WANT WATER IN YOUR BASEMENT.

What *will* I do now that fall is coming? The children have all gone home. I can't hide behind my grandmother plumage any longer. I have a book to write. And one that will be published in September. That should be enough for anyone. But this time of year is insatiable. It wants vastness and adventure. Some hard use. Learn the Chinese language. Build a cathedral. Do yoga. Study Zen. Stop desiring anything. Anger, Greed, Pride, Fear, Desire, the five daughters of Maya, King of Darkness.

Hurry up, fall is always saying. Time is growing short. We don't have forever. Except I don't believe that. We have whatever we decide we have. Weeks spent with children pass like hours. Months spent writing a book seem like a weekend. Hours wondering what to do next seem like eons. Minutes waiting for someone are a well-known eternity. The main thing is to keep moving. Keep the pace that children keep. They rise from sleep and move into a day like sunlight. They burn until they fall. We are tilting on our axis. We are tilting further from the sun. Cold days and long nights are waiting. Exciting. I will shake out my sweaters and get my high-heeled shoes, get airline tickets to northern cities, get a flu shot, get ready.

Enough of all this leaf, flower, bole. Enough of watching my neighbors water their lawns. Fall is the time for flowering. Gather in the sheaves, take the goods to market. I want to see Angel Corella dance at the American Ballet Theatre. I want to fly to London and see *Richard III*. I want to work all morning and exercise in the late afternoons and watch the senators fight on C-SPAN. In short, I am waking up, here at the end of summer, in the temperate climes, on the planet earth, in the only world there is.

I got out my Ansel Adams engagement calendar to see what I was doing this time last year. I had written on August 17, "You must change your life," Rainer Maria Rilke. Last fall I was passionate about that. I stopped taking estrogen. Nor for any medical or scientific reason but because I was tired of thinking about it. Since then I have learned that the estrogen I was taking is derived from mares who are deprived of water to make the urine stronger. It was bad karma to take that stuff and something in me knew it.

Also, I threw away my papers. I have no interest in some graduate student wasting her time going through the xeroxed copies of drafts of my books.

Next I suffered through the very last book signing I will ever do. I am writing books to be read, not to be collected as souvenirs.

I won't have to look far to find other interesting junk to divest myself of this year. I have plenty of fears, dumb habits and insidious little prejudices I could pitch into the fires of autumn. The eight-year-old named William has a campground in his backyard with a ring of stones for building fires. Sometimes his parents let him cook his dinner there. The next time I see his smoke I will write down some stupid things I keep doing and take the paper over and burn it on his fire. On that day I will officially declare that summer is over.

ELLEN GILCHRIST, b. 1935, received the National Book Award for her 1984 collection *Victory Over Japan*, and is the author of more than twenty books including novels, short stories, essays and poetry. *Acts of God* is her most recent collection of stories; her most recent essay collection is *Things Like The Truth: Out of My Later Years*. Gilchrist lives in Fayetteville, Arkansas and Ocean Springs, Mississippi, and teaches creative writing at the University of Arkansas.

Subjective Age: *I don't have one. I feel like I've always been exactly the same person.*

THE
60s

This Vast Life

Susan Moon

Every morning, I vow to be grateful for the precious gift of human birth. It's a big gift, and it includes a lot of stuff I never particularly wanted for my birthday. Some of the things in the package I wish I could exchange for a different size or color. But I want to find out what it means to be a human being—my curiosity remains intense even as I get older—so I say thanks for the whole thing. It's all of a piece.

In thirteenth-century Japan, Zen Master Dogen wrote, "The Way is basically perfect and all-pervading." I'm already in it. We are all in it; we are made of it.

When my granddaughter was just over two, I visited her and her parents in Texas. She doesn't have a lot of ideas yet about how things are supposed to be, or what's supposed to happen next. She's glad to be alive. I was babysitting for her one afternoon, and part of my job was to get her up from her nap. I was reading in the next room, and I knew when she woke up because I heard her chatting away to her bear. I lifted her and her bear out of her crib and we went downstairs. While I fixed her a snack of crackers and cheese, she danced around a purple ball that was lying in the middle of the living room, singing an old nursery rhyme that she had learned in her preschool: "Ring around the rosies, pocket full of posies, ashes, ashes, we all fall down." And then she sat down on the floor—*ker-plunk!*—laughing. She was fully present, fully joyful. Actually, the song she was singing is a very old chant about the plague, and the last line about the ashes refers to our mortality. But she wasn't worrying about that.

In his poetic essay "The Genjokoan," Master Dogen wrote, "A fish swims in the ocean, and no matter how far it swims, there is no end to the water. A bird flies in the sky, and no matter how far it flies, there is no end to the air."

When I get unhappy about something in my life, I think: "Wait, no, this isn't the right life, it isn't what I want, I need to find the edge of this life and leap over the fence into a different life." But that's not how it works. My life is vast. I can't find the edge of it, just like a fish in the ocean or a bird in the sky. There's no getting out of this life, this ocean, this sky, except by dying. If I try to change oceans, I'll never find my way or my place—there's no place else to be but here, in the big mystery of it.

It happened that only a few days after visiting my granddaughter I visited an old friend in his eighties who lives in an assisted living facility. He's a Catholic priest and monk who has dedicated his life to solitude and spiritual study. He's well read in multiple spiritual traditions, including Zen, and he is an important mentor to me. For many years he has been leading me in an ongoing conversation about prayer, mysticism, and spiritual inquiry, through correspondence as well as face-to-face visits.

He's not well physically, he's weak, on oxygen, and confined to a wheelchair, but his mind is fine.

He told me, "If I've died before, I don't remember it, but I recognize what's happening—that's where I'm going." Years ago he had a coffin built for himself by a carpenter he knows. It stands upright in his little apartment like a roommate, a reminder, keeping him company. He sits at his table and looks out the window at a pear tree, and watches its leaves turn, and fall, and bud again. He watches the seasons, the whole universe, in that pear tree. He reads, he prays, he receives an occasional visitor. Like my granddaughter, he is completely present in his life. Like Dogen's fish, he is swimming around in his ocean, and there is no end to the water, even in this tiny apartment.

Moments after I entered his room he was talking to me about Isaac of Ninevah, the eighth-century Syrian hermit, whose writings he had been reading when I came in.

Like my granddaughter, he, too, is singing his version of ring around the rosies, dancing until he falls down and turns to ashes.

In between that toddler and that old man is a span of over eighty years—and most of us, in those intervening decades, tangle ourselves up in knots over the things we don't have that we want, and the things we have that we don't want. We run around trying to fix things, in our personal lives and in the life of the planet. It's a good thing we do, because it's actually our responsibility to fix things; we need to fix the plumbing, for example. The toddler and the old monk aren't fixing the plumbing. They need us to take care of them, but we need them, too, to remind us that everything is already taken care of.

I like to think about how we are completely held by the atmosphere in a literal way. The air that surrounds each of our bodies, that flows in and out of our lungs, is not nothing. It's thick with molecules, and it fills up all the gaps and cracks between us and the other bodies and objects around us: the furniture, the walls of the room, the trees outside, the buildings. There's no empty space. The air is fluid, making room for us, so that each of us inhabits a nook that is exactly our size and shape. The air kindly moves with us when we move. It's like those soft rocks you can find on the beaches of northern California that have tiny mollusks living inside them in the holes they made for themselves. We're all connected, molecule to molecule. I'm held by everything that's not me.

The last meditation retreat I attended was beside the ocean, and while I was sitting I listened to the surf. The surf is the sound of the ocean breathing. It's never still. Sometimes the sea is so loud and crashing that I crave a little silence, and so I listen for the silence between the waves, but just as one wave recedes from the shore, flowing back down the sand into the ocean, getting quieter and quieter, just before it gets silent, the next wave always breaks. The ocean never stops breathing because it's alive. As I sit on my seat in the zendo, following my breathing, I follow the breathing of the ocean, too, and I begin to breathe in rhythm with the ocean.

The sound of the ocean is the sound of time passing, the sound of one moment giving way to the next. Each wave, each moment, is a gate that I pass through into the next moment.

And even if I'm not sitting by the ocean, one wave of my life is still followed immediately by the next, with no completely quiet place in between.

I love the vow: "Dharma gates are boundless; I vow to enter them." I keep giving myself away to the next moment, and the next moment receives me. I just have to step through.

SUSAN MOON, b. 1942, is a writer and lay teacher in the Soto Zen tradition, and leads Zen and writing retreats internationally. Her books include *This Is Getting Old: Zen Thoughts on Aging with Humor and Dignity*; *The Hidden Lamp: Stories from 25 Centuries of Awakened Women*, with Florence Caplow; and, most recently, *What Is Zen: Plain Talk for a Beginner's Mind*, with Norman Fischer. Moon rejoices in her three granddaughters. She lives in Berkeley, California.

Subjective Age: *It's sort of a truism that we think of ourselves as being younger than we are, and this has been the case for me all my life. But it's changing now that I frequently have to ask younger people for help in opening jars and such, and this reminds me of my age. So does leaving my purse on the floor of the gas station restroom, and having to drive back an extra half hour to get it. (At least I remembered it later!) Still, I notice a strong tendency to think of myself as the same age as whoever I'm taking to, as long as they are younger than I am. If they are my age or older, I think: "Poor old thing! Though I suppose she's doing pretty well for her age."*

Activiaism

Kate Clinton

Recently when I went to an eye doctor for floaters, a common vision problem for older people, an assistant asked me if I had ever thought of cosmetic surgery for my droopy lids.

In a Kiehl's store I bought some hand cream and the cashier, in his white faux-doctor jacket, tossed too many packets of "youth regenerating skin cream with Rare 'Resurrection Flower'" into my bag.

At a cocktail party reception before a fund-raising dinner I was emcee-ing, a gorgeous woman came up to me, told me she was an aesthetician and that she could get rid of "those things" on my face.

I like getting senior discounted movie tickets, but I like to ask for them.

After a matinee of Robert Redford's film, *The Company You Keep*, about older radical revolutionaries, I was in a bathroom stall, listening to the usually astute film critiques of the Upper West Side set. "That Redford, he's been in the sun too much." "And Julie Christie? Was that a wattle?"

For sure there is such a thing as gravity. And it's true that I spent a number of summers in my youth slathering on baby oil and floating around in aluminum canoes on upstate lakes. I did not know floaters are so common, or someone told me but I forgot.

My mom used to say, "My face I don't mind it, because I'm behind it." I think I look like Jamie Lee Curtis. I apply a dab of Activia every morning and evening to my face and neck.

KATE CLINTON, b. 1947, is a humorist on many platforms, except heels. She posts regularly on her website, kateclinton.com.

Subjective Age: *I am 68. But with the wind chill, it feels like 59.*

April's Cryalog

M Cx3
T NC
W Cx3
Th Cx3
Fri Cx1
Sat Cx2
Sun Cx2
Mon Cx3
Thes Cx3
Wed Cx2
Thurs NC
Fri Cx1
Sat Cx1
Sun NC
Mon Cx1
Tues Cx2
Wed Cx2
Thurs Cx1
Fri Cx1 very bad
Sat Cx4 very bad
Sun Cx1
M Cx1
T Cx1
W Cx1 a little
Th NC
Fri Cx1 ↑ 16th?
Sat Cx1 my birthday I think
Sun NC
M NC
T CCCCC
W C pm
Th C am
Fri C
Sat C

Sun NC
Mon CCC
Thes CCC
Wed CCCC
Fri CCCC
Sat CCC
Sun CC
M CC
T CC
W CC
Th CC
Fri CC
Sat CCCC
Sun CCCC
Mon CCC
T CCC
W CCC
Th . CCC
Fri CCC
Sat CCC
Sun CCC
M CCC
T CCC
W CCC

April has 58 days.
after which it
can't go on.

and so on.

Pause

Mary Ruefle

I recently came across an old cryalog that I kept during the month of April in 1998. 'C' stands for the fact that I cried, the number of C's represents the number of times I cried, and 'NC' indicates that I did not cry on that day.

The saddest thing is, I now find the cryalog very funny, and laugh when I look at it.

But when I kept it, I wanted to die. Literally, to kill myself—with an iron, a steaming hot turned-on iron.

This was not depression, this was menopause.

Reading this, or any other thing ever written about menopause, will not help you in any way, for how you respond to menopause is not up to you, it is up to your body, and though you believe now that you can control your body (such is your strength after all that yoga) you cannot.

Of course, you may be lucky: I know a woman who experienced menopause in no way whatsoever except that one day she realized it had been a couple of years since her last period, which was indeed her last.

You hear a lot about hot flashes, but hot flashes are the least of it, totally inconsequential in every way: you get as hot as a steam iron at odd moments—so what? The media would have you believe that hot flashes are the single most significant symptom toward which you should direct your attention and *their* products, but when I think of menopause I don't think of hot flashes; I am not here to talk about hot flashes.

Except to tell you that they do not cease even after you have completely gone through menopause; they become a part of your life the way periods were, they are periodic and, after a while, you stop talking about them.

No, I am here to tell you that one woman, a woman who is the most undepressed, optimistic, upbeat person I know, awoke one morning and walked straight into her kitchen and grabbed a butcher's knife (she is a world-class cook) with the intent of driving it through her heart. That was menopause.

If you take the time to peruse the annals of any nineteenth century asylum, as I have, you will discover that the 'cause of admittance' for all women over forty is listed as 'change of life.'

In other words, you go crazy. When you go crazy, you don't have the slightest inclination to read anything Foucault ever wrote about culture and madness.

It may be that you recall your thirteenth year on earth. Menopause is adolescence all over again, only you are an adult and have to go out into the world every day in ways you did not have to when you were in school, where you were surrounded by other adolescents, safe, or relatively so, in the asylum of junior high.

You are a thirteen-year-old with the experience and daily life of a forty-five-year-old.

You have on some days the desire to fuck a tree, or a dog, whichever is closest.

You have the desire to leave your husband or lover or partner, whatever.

No matter how stable or loving the arrangement, you want out.

You may decide to take up an insane and hopeless cause. You may decide to walk to Canada, or that it is high time you begin to collect old blue china, three thousand pieces of which will leave you bankrupt. Suddenly the solution to all problems lies in selling your grandmother's gold watch or drinking your body weight in cider vinegar. A kind of wild forest blood runs in your veins.

This, and other behaviors, will horrify you. You will seek medical help because you are intelligent, and none of the help will help.

You will feel as if your life is over and you will be absolutely right about that, it is over.

No matter how attractive or unattractive you are, you have been used to having others look you over when you stood at the bus stop or at the chemist's to buy tampons. They have looked you over to assess how attractive or unattractive you are, so no matter what the case, you were looked at. Those days are over; now others look straight through you, you are completely invisible to them, you have become a ghost.

You no longer exist.

Because you no longer exist, you will do anything for attention. You may shave your head or dye your hair or wear striped stockings or scream at complete strangers. You've seen them, haven't you, the middle-aged women screaming at the attendant in the convenience store?

You are a depressed adolescent who sweats through their clothing and says terrible things to everyone, especially the people they love.

You begin to lie. You have the urge to shoplift and if you drive an automobile you have the urge to ram your car into the car in front of you.

Nothing can prepare you for this.

The one thing no one will tell you is that these feelings and this behavior will last ten years. That is, a decade of your life. Ask your doctor if this is true and she will deny it.

Then comes a day when you see a 'woman' who is buying tampons and you think of her as a *girl*. And she is; anyone who has periods is a girl. You know this is true and it is very funny to you.

You are a woman, the ten years have passed, you love your children, you love your lover, but there are no longer any persons on earth who can stop you from being yourself, you have put your parents in the earth, you have buried the past. Of course in the meantime you have destroyed your life and it has to be completely remade and there is a great deal of grief and regret and nostalgia and all of that, but even so you are free, free to sit on the bank and throw stones and feel thankful for the few years or one or two decades left to you in which you can be yourself, even if a great many other women ended their lives, even if the reason they ended their lives is reported as having been for reasons having nothing to do with menopause, which is thankfully behind you as you would never want to be a girl again for any reason at all, you have discovered that being invisible is the biggest secret on earth, the most wondrous gift anyone could ever have given you.

If you are young and you are reading this, perhaps you will understand the gleam in the eye of any woman who is sixty, seventy, eighty, or ninety: they cannot take you seriously (sorry) for you are just a girl to them, despite your babies and shoes and lovemaking and all of that. You are just a girl playing at life.

You are just a girl on the edge of a great forest. You should be frightened but instead you are eating a lovely meal, or you are cooking one, or you are running to the florist or you are opening a box of flowers that has just arrived at your door, and none of these things are done in the great spirit that they will later be done in.

You haven't even begun. You must pause first, the way one must always pause before a great endeavor, if only to take a good breath.

Happy old age is coming on bare feet, bringing with it grace and gentle words, and ways which grim youth have never known.

MARY RUEFLE, b. 1952, is the author of many books of poetry and prose. Her latest book is *My Private Property*, which includes this essay. She lives in Vermont.

Subjective Age: *My subjective age is 100, as I feel I have lived in the world of 10,000 things for a very long time.*

These Vanishing Hills

Steven Faulkner

Our white car with its green canoe roped on top is singing out of the short-grass prairies of Montana into the dry hills of Wyoming and then east toward Spearfish and Deadwood. Far off to the south and west, a strange sky leans over strange land.

Beside me, my eighteen-year-old son Alex rests his head against the window, half-asleep, his long legs folded beneath the dash. After four weeks hiking and canoeing, his face is tanned and shows traces of a young beard. He'd rather spend time with his friends than four weeks with his father, but he's joined me—one last trip before he leaves for college.

Earlier this afternoon, we passed the Crow Indian Agency. We followed the Little Bighorn River along the dry hills where George Armstrong Custer and his 210 men, on a hot day in June 1876, scrambled up through sagebrush and prairie grass to escape their deaths. Surrounded, cut off, cut down by as many as 2,000 Sioux, Cheyenne, and Arapaho, they were backing along the highest ridge they could find. They must have seen that there was no way out, no way out at all.

Custer has become an icon of those surprised by death.

As we drive, that mottled barrier far to the southwest rears up, pushing high into mist and storm. It leans toward us. Even the nearer shadowed hills seem to be blowing our way, mixed into a thickening sky moving low and fast from that distant shadowland. *Must be mountains*, I tell myself. *They don't look like mountains.*

Alex is now awake and staring out the window.

The road rises into higher hills. A single deer grazes in a passing meadow. Now, dark forests crowd us left and right. Then suddenly, a heavy wind beats us sideways, and the canoe atop our car screeches and bounces against the ropes. A low, black, running ceiling of cloud rushes over us, and then a slashing, lashing rain. Hard. Harsh. Blinding. I hit the brake, slowing us, slowing us.

And then, as if in a dream, an old man is pedaling a bicycle in front of us, miles from any town, bent over and pedaling, his gray rain gear flapping hard in the dark wind and rain, but not stopping, pedaling alone, his balding head like a thin crockery bowl turned against the battering rain, but not stopping, pedaling patiently, neck and shoulders braced grimly against it all, and our white car easing past his maybe seventy-year-old figure bent and flapping behind us now like a storm-driven pelican. Our windshield washers are jumping back and forth, and I'm thinking we should stop and pick him up, but he is clearly not asking for help. Perhaps this old man has chosen his way, and like it or not, chosen this storm, as Alex and I chose four weeks of cold mountains and rushing rivers in the Bitterroot Mountains. And now he is behind us, gone, and the windshield wipers leap to the flood. With dark clouds chasing the rain gusts in rapid succession across the highway, other cars resolve into shapes, some pulled over on the shoulders, others easing along, the rain battering us all, and Alex beside me peering into madness.

His mother had called hours earlier, worried we were in trouble. She awoke from a dream in which she saw an airplane go down in a lake. Alex took the call. I saw him lean back, smile, and rub the soft stubble on his cheek as he told her we'd keep an eye out for low-flying airplanes.

But I know that her dreams are not to be taken lightly. One night Alex's older brother was driving his convertible through a thunderstorm at seventy miles an hour, not wearing his seatbelt. He hydroplaned—slammed the little car into a concrete wall, flipped it, and shattered every window. His mother was lying in bed in his grandmother's trailer house 200 miles from him. She woke up sweating, gripped with a terrible worry, her mind fixed on Justin. Outside the trailer house, violent winds were thrashing the hickory trees and rain was drumming down on the tarred tin roof. She knew Justin, specifically Justin, was in terrible trouble. She prayed for his life. He survived, though for two weeks, she was extracting pieces of glass from his body as they worked their way to the surface.

Days before the Battle of the Little Bighorn, Sitting Bull told a dream. He saw U.S. cavalry soldiers falling from the sky, shorn of their ears, dropping like locusts into their camp. Sitting Bull told his nephew it was a sign that the Sioux would soon have a great victory, though many would die.

. . . .

We all know, with or without dreams, that death rides with us. And of course we accept its presence because we have no alternative. Perhaps we even take pride in our ability to face the inevitable. But I find myself unable to accept that this boy beside me, so full of adventure and camaraderie, of jokes and sympathy, can vanish. He loves me. He loves his mother. He loves his brothers and sisters. Can such love be extinguished? His courage and all his many friendships snuffed out with nothing but the fading, blowing smoke of a memory spiraling up, till even that lingering scent is washed away in storm?

Fatuous fool, you say. Clinging to a hope when you know none exists.

Perhaps, but there is no indigenous tribe that I'm aware of that does not believe in an afterlife. The tribesmen of Southern Sudan where I grew up spoke of spirits that lived in a baobab tree, of little black dwarfs that came up out of the ground and spoke to them. The Cheyenne believed that when the breath leaves, the spirit travels up the long fork of the Milky Way to *Seana*, the camp of the dead. Some argue that these many beliefs are coping mechanisms. Recalling the past and contemplating the future, we would prefer that our lives not end, so we propose an afterlife. Yet even scientists long for life beyond the temporal. They stand beneath massive telescopes peering into the cosmos and search for planets like our own, yearn for communion with other life, intelligent life, somewhere out there. But we know that the distances are prohibitive. Speculating about hypothetical wormholes or practical space travel to near stars seems delusional. Having rejected gods and devils, writers and movie-makers and scientists invent a romantic and frightening cosmos filled with aliens. If there is life in the "crushing black vacuum of the universe" beyond our tiny system of circling rocks, we will find it only in our imaginations. The distances are far too great. We are physically alone. Time and distance provide room for the afterlife fantasies of scientists, but we will never encounter a passing star rover, nor hear on the wind a hymn from Orion.

A million years from now, what remainders on earth? What reminders? Perhaps a fossilized bone in a gravel pit, worn shards of glass blown bare on a creek bank, dust of brick and concrete sweeping by in a nameless wind: scant record left of all humanity and its brief sojourn on this spinning, swirling globe of amethyst and emerald, of blowing clouds and rushing rivers, of dry hills and humid jungles, of quiet ponds and booming oceans.

In time, they tell us, there will be nothing here but hot, dried rocks staring blind and dumb across lifeless deserts. I look at my son: this leaping, bounding, surging current of a boy will bounce down through pebbles, swirl and crash around boulders, push his way through sedges and reeds, laughing and leaping over logjams and ledges. He will join others like himself, running and shouting beneath starlight and sunrise. But one day his body will age like mine, and sink like a seep into cracked clay and sand and dust. We know this. But if this be all, it is an atrocity.

. . . .

Alex and I spend the night in Spearfish, then drive the canyon route through the Black Hills, turning and curving just above the sunlit stream that jumps and turns, catches the light, and ducks into shadows beneath cliffs of gray stone thatched with pine trees. The Precambrian granite cliffs and outcroppings are two to three billion years old. Volcanic activity caused by the shifting of three supercontinents and as many as nine microcontinents forced huge magma intrusions of granite and pegmatite, and over the eons titanic pressures squeezed and crushed later sediments into stone, then buckled and folded and twisted the rock, thrusting it all upward over 7,000 feet into this strange mottled island of rock and pine standing alone within a surrounding sea of treeless hills. For millions and millions of years, the place was just another aggregate of eroding stone, blowing winds, and harsh sunlight. Now, upon this particular desert of ancient rocks and sediments, life thrives: the pines, junipers, willows, mule deer and pronghorns, coyotes and cougars and bears. Also the grasses and cattails, pink anemones, clustered broomrape, black snakeroot, curled dock. With dung beetles and tiger beetles scrabbling over pebbles, and ebony jewelwings alighting on green knobbly twigs, and dirty-orange skippers and black-laced monarchs and cabbage-white butterflies sucking sweet nectars before flitting away erratically, and green bottleflies and bluebottles swerving to a cluster of fresh deer scat, a black-and-gold spider hanging elegantly from a torn, spiral web laced to standing thistles, a fat tick sucking the diaphanous ear of a rabbit, a black squirrel high up a ponderosa pine blinking, scratching its hip, a Bullock's oriole with orange head hanging upside down from its woven, feather-lined globe of grass, hair, and twine, and yes, even a flying squirrel leaping now, gliding now, from a high oak, slap into a lower trunk of pine, and chipmunks and mice skittering through dead leaves and dried grass and a western meadowlark pouring out a lilting liquid call, and two dark vultures hunched on a high rock observing while a redtailed hawk drifts along an eroded escarpment maybe two billion years old, and three brown horses that took 50 million years to evolve crop the meadow grasses, when suddenly a falcon flashes straight down through the limbs of an oak in direct pursuit of a screaming jay—a thousand forms of life all acting and reacting and interacting through and around and above and below these Black Hills.

The Lakota Sioux warred with the Cheyenne who lived here, wresting it away by 1776, driving the Cheyenne west and south. Having acquired the place, the Lakota felt its magic. They prayed to the spirits of wind and rock and beast. They found here in this outpost of life a sacred way of living. They say that at the creation of the universe a song was sung that only in these hills finds its completion.

· · · ·

Road work up ahead slowing a long line of cars. I don't mind. I would love to spend a summer here, a winter, a lifetime, several lifetimes. After the granite monuments of presidents at Mount Rushmore and the rocky stare of Crazy Horse at the Crazy Horse Monument, we leave the Black Hills heading south.

I look up and see a storm far off to our right, seeming to run with us, pouring out of the Black Hills, while beyond the running clouds the prairie hills roll away into white afternoon sunlight. We are heading south and away into the treeless hills, but the clouds brooding over these dark, magical hills these last two days will not let us escape. A gray, patchy string of clouds off to our right seems to be keeping pace with us, running like an outrider of the building storm flowing out of the dark hills.

Alex is driving now: at seventy miles per hour. I know the storm cannot keep up with us, and I say so. When I look up again, the storm has drawn closer, and long strands of ragged cloud seem to be reaching out toward the prairie grasses with a great darkness building behind.

"I can't believe that storm is keeping up with us," I say. "Look at it, Alex. That cloud looks like a dragon."

Alex glances over for a moment, then returns his attention to the highway.

The storm is still running with us, miles to our right, but not falling behind. "Look, Alex. It looks like a bony hand reaching out."

As we watch, the hand slowly fists and humps into the shape of a great bear snarling, intent on running us down. The wind is picking up and the canoe above us jumps and squeaks.

A half hour later, unexpectedly, the highway swerves westward toward the storm and for the first time I think we might not outrun it. The canoe begins jumping and bucking in a strong wind, and we stop to tighten the ropes.

Two men on motorcycles fly by us, leaning sideways into the growing gale. We jump back into the car and move out.

A hundred yards ahead, we see a quick gust drive dust and torn grass across the two-lane highway. Then something heavy bangs off the cab of our car, and another, and another. I tell Alex to stop.

"No, Dad! We've got to get away!"

"No. The hail will smash our windshield. Pull over."

He does. Huge balls of ice clang onto the roof, bounce off the windows, shatter the side mirror. Ice balls bound crazily over the blacktop all down the highway. At first there is only a scattering of golf-ball-sized clumps banging all around. Later, the weather service will report almost two-inch-diameter hail. A single tree near the fence line shudders for a few seconds, shakes, then suddenly bends over before a weighty rush of wind and tearing hail. The noise is outrageous, like being attacked by crowds of roaring rioters armed with hammers and iron bars beating us down as they rush past. The wind is flying horizontally, whipping a white blizzard of rock-ice against us, bashing our windows, beating canoe and cab and hood and glass. Alex grabs a pillow from the back seat and covers his head. I follow his example, expecting the shattering of windows any second.

The wind rises, a continuous shout of driven hail. We pull the pillows around our ears. We can see nothing at all outside. Our white car sits there rocking anxiously as the great gusts shake us. I will read later of whole trailer houses lifted and thrown one on top of another just a few miles south. The roar, if possible, grows louder.

For a long ten minutes we endure this tension, waiting for glass to shatter or the car to overturn or scoot across the blacktop, and then, suddenly, the hail ceases. We look up from our pillows. It's still raining hard. Then the storm turns and takes another look. The wind that had broadsided our right side now swings behind us and hits again. Then a new sound rises, a low, heavy moaning.

Alex yells, "It's a tornado, Dad!"

I turn quickly to the back window. I can see nothing but wind-driven rain. We are blind. Blind and helpless. The moaning increases to a nasal howl. No refuge, no escape.

"Dad! What do we do?"

I look at my son and shake my head. "Nothing we *can* do."

We wrap the pillows around our heads and wait for disaster, that strange moan coming and going, coming and going, like an old man's labored breathing, and I think of that old man precariously pedaling his bicycle. I think of the two men leaning into the wind on their motorcycles. I think of the centuries when Indian encampments on these open plains were ripped apart by hail and wind or stampeded by storm-maddened buffalo, or run down by thundering horsemen slaughtering men and boys and women and girls with their whips and their spears and their guns and their scorn and their fears. I think of Custer caught by the sudden roar of war, and his eighteen-year-old nephew, the flag carrier, killed.

I can accept the death of a ebony jewelwing because there are many more. But as every parent knows, my son is unrepeatable. Unique. A singularity. In astronomy, a *singularity* refers to the death of a burning star. Its heat and light gone, the mass of the star collapses and crushes into a point of zero volume and infinite density, an impossible place in which space and time become infinitely distorted, an image as incomprehensible as the final loss of my son, or the final ruin of the lovely Black Hills, or the extinction of all life on this planet.

After a time, the anguished howling gives way to moaning that gives way to a rumbling growl, then to a long, low sigh, as if the storm has grown weary and wandered away.

The outside world comes back to us. The lone tree beside the fence stands up like an old man with a wrenched back, its limp limbs and torn leaves dripping quietly in the last passing showers. Hail lies like white gravel in the ditches and across the pastures.

We open our doors and step out into clean, fresh air. We check the ropes and adjust the canoe, run our fingers over the dents that pit the windward sides of the car damage. But the hills are cool and wet, and you can see a hundred miles.

I put my hand on Alex's shoulder. "Quite a storm."

He smiles and shakes his head. "I thought it was a tornado."

"Maybe it was," I say. "Maybe it was."

We climb back into the car and within minutes stop in little Chadron, Nebraska: north-facing windows shattered, glass and pieces of roofing scattered, gutters ripped away, wet little mounds of hail beneath remaining downspouts, vinyl siding chewed up as if by a great machine, bits and pieces spit out into streets and yards.

We turn right and drive westward. Along the creek, trees have suffered little damage. In a nearby field, a 50-million-year-old horse lifts its head and looks at us.

Then Alex, who is still driving, points south: "Dad. Dad, look."

We pull over and step out.

Just beyond the hills the black clouds are in full retreat. The hills stand green and golden in the evening sun, with a few black pines scattered across the slopes. Beyond the hills, against that thick, rolling cloud bank is what you expect to see, somehow always unexpected: rising out of this quiet prairie of high hills and thin grass, vivid against the retreating bank of storm clouds, a rainbow: a windfall word.

We slide back into our battered car, make a U-turn, then, hungry for life, turn south to follow the storm.

STEVEN FAULKNER, b. 1950, grew up in Sudan and Ethiopia in Africa, and later in Kansas. After dropping out of college, he worked a variety of jobs: driving dump trucks, planting grave vaults, and delivering newspapers and doughnuts. He also spent fourteen years as a carpenter. He returned to school and now teaches creative writing in southern Virginia. His first book was *Waterwalk: A Passage of Ghosts*. His latest book is *Bitterroot: Echoes of Beauty and Loss*. Both are nonfiction accounts of father-son journeys along historic trails.

Subjective Age: *The more I think about my subjective age, the more it seems I am all my ages: I am still the boy in the African night listening to a lion fighting off hyenas; still the homesick boy in an Ethiopian boarding school; I still see the Kansas tornado skipping over our house and smashing into the church next door—and all the decades of marriage and children stay with me.*

Swimming at Adamsville Rec

Andrea Canaan

My daughter dropped me off at Adamsville Recreation Center Monday through Friday during my two-month visit to Atlanta where I swam laps for an hour and a half in their heated pool.

"Why hello Ma'am. How ya doin' today?" said a desk clerk in a warm-honey urban southern drawl. Even though I haven't lived in the south for twenty-five years, I used my New Orleans native cadence, rounded sounds, dropped word endings, and respectful friendly tone to reply: "Why hello to you Darlin'. I'm doin' just fine, thank you. And you?"

I paid two dollars for the swim and made my way to the women's locker room with its especially clean and well-designed disability dressing and shower stall. When I was ready, I headed toward the pool deck dressed in a black Speedo swim suit, size 24, black flip-flops, and a rubber-tipped black cane.

I pushed the women's locker room door open and began to make a hard right turn toward the Olympic size pool. I was looking forward to the twenty-five laps that keeps my recently replaced knee in good shape, and my un-replaced knee with minimal swelling, pain. Even more, I looked forward to basking in one of my places of meditation and prayer.

Coming out of the locker room, I nearly collided with a young boy walking with his swim teammates to the men's locker room. We were both surprised. He stepped back and moved out of my way, holding the door for me. He was a young black boy, ten, maybe eleven years old, with a wiry muscled and toned swimmer's body, water beaded on his skin that was the color of new pecans. He had a close haircut and dark caramel eyes. Other young men passed us by. Each of them said, "Evenin' Ma'am," "Hello Ma'am," "How ya doin' Ma'am," as they had been taught. The young boy who nearly collided into me, the one with the caramel colored eyes, had stopped to hold the door for me automatically. He showed his home training, his respect for an adult woman, especially for an elder.

As he held the door, he paused, turned his head to the side, moved his head back a bit on his neck, and tucked his chin in a little. In a second's silent exchange, he looked me up and down slowly, like I was a dark milk chocolate ice cream swirl, and said, "Well hellooo…there!"

His voice was a boy's and his look was pure delighted appreciation for an older woman's good looks and plus-size body.

I responded with a friendly, but elder-to-child, "Thank you, son" (for stopping and holding the door).

I passed to his right and walked toward the pool.

I didn't look back. I knew he was still looking, noticing the rhythm of flip-flopping steps, cane tapping on the tiled pool deck, wide coffee-with-a-generous-pour-of-milk-colored body, swaying hips, ample behind, thighs to legs to ankles and back up again, to silver-gray dreadlocks banded into a thick pony tail that falls to waist.

As I walked past eight lanes of swimmers, whose stroking hands and kicking legs made the sounds of a waterfall, I kept my smile small, but allowed beams of pleasure to enter with me as I stepped into the warm pool.

When I completed my laps, I returned to the locker room to shower and dress. When I walked out of the pool entrance with my swim bag over my left shoulder and my cane in my right hand, I noticed a list of the standings for each member of the swim team taped to the wall I walked along. I stopped and read each name. Next to this listing was a poster. It had a white background with bright red, blue, and green fish on it like a first grader would color. The words down the middle of the poster read:

In
This
Place
We
Are
All
Different
Fish

Maybe
But
In
This
World
We
All
Swim
As
One

As I nodded silent greeting to swim coaches blowing their whistles and shouting directions and encouragement, I felt my delight bloom as I remembered the look on the face of a boy and his easy delight in me. His eyes told me he treasured my size, and I was thankful to the boys and girls and men and women who made up the constellation of his living. His family and community must have taught him to praise power and grace whenever he found himself in their presence, no matter the age, shape, color or size.

ANDREA CANAAN, b. 1950, is a full-time student and a full-time writer, as well as a mother of three and a grandmother of three. She received a MFA in nonfiction from the University of San Francisco and is currently pursuing an MFA in fiction at Goddard College. Andrea resides with her partner of fifteen years in San Francisco, and is currently completing a memoir, *The Salt Box House on Bayou Black*.

It Was, as It Always Has Been, a Choice

Harold Knight

A serious question: What on earth would make a grown man take a month out from a busy career as a widely respected poet (at that time he'd published six books of poetry and a novel), teacher, and legal scholar (when he was much younger a law clerk to Justice David Souter) and run off to South Africa to save orphaned chacma baboons? I can't imagine.

Last night at the birthday dinner for a dear friend, one of the other guests and I suddenly found ourselves in a conversation that seemed as if we had stumbled into the middle of it and didn't quite know what we were talking about. It was much too serious for a party, and the subject was much too important simply to toss it off as party small talk.

All of us at the party were of an age—in our sixties. I was the oldest, but only by a year. The host and I had a slight disagreement when I said I am in my seventieth year. "But you're only sixty-nine!" she said. Think about it. Until a person's first birthday, they are in their first year, right? So once I've passed my sixty-ninth birthday, I am in my seventieth year.

The guest and I were chatting about why we don't go to church or synagogue (she is Jewish) these days. I think we were both trying to say the same thing. I was trying to explain that going to church, comforting as the Episcopal liturgy is, seems somehow so ephemeral, so otherworldly (Duh!), so removed from the immediacy of my day-to-day life that it feels like both a waste of time in the moment and somehow a deception. Especially since I don't think I believe in God.

For goodness' sake, Maya Angelou went and died—she had been a constant in my life since I read *I Know Why the Caged Bird Sings*. Maya Angelou was only eighty-six years old, only in her eighty-seventh year, seventeen years older than I. Seventeen years! My father was in his ninety-eighth year when he died, twenty-eight years older than I am now. Twenty-eight years!

You there, dear reader, you think you've got all the time in the world. Well, you don't, and the guest at the birthday dinner and I were trying to talk about that, but we didn't quite know how to fit it into party talk.

I'm going to be a shameless name-dropper. Michael Blumenthal told me a few month ago that if there is a "Michael Blumenthal fan club," I must be the only member. Yes, he told me that in an email after I told him I wanted to be a member of his fan club. He's a youngster—only sixty-five—but he has done all of these strange and wonderful things.

Tucked away in the back of my mind is the useless idea that I want to have lived the way Blumenthal has lived. Just read about the (almost bizarre) variations of "career" he has had. Lawyer, poet, professor, and savior of baby chacma baboons. This is not—as much as it may seem—a paean to Michael Blumenthal. He and I are so much different I suspect we could hardly be friends if we met face to face (that's probably not true—we're both too old to worry about each other's foibles).

It's okay for someone like me who wishes he had published eight books of poetry (or had some lasting "creative" legacy) to look at someone like Michael Blumenthal and think, "Now there's the guy who's done the sorts of things I wish I'd done." As long as thinking that does not either make of him some sort of hero that he would be embarrassed to know about or make of myself some sort of failure living with regrets too numerous to contemplate.

Nope. Michael Blumenthal and I are at exactly the same place. We have done what we have done—he perhaps with more energy and brains and discipline than I have—and we are both, according to Maya Angelou's example, about eighteen years from the end. It's okay to find his accomplishments fascinating. And it's okay for me to find my own life fascinating.

I've played the organ for more hours than most of my readers have been alive (even some who are dangerously close to being old farts). I've traveled the world—small portions of it—not for pleasure but for understanding. I've been married and divorced and had long-term relationships with men.

Do you want to know what's really important? A young man, thirty-something, whom I've known since he was about ten came to me recently, not knowing what to expect, but needing an "adult" to talk to about his growing acceptance of himself as a transgendered person. He came to me.

He didn't know that one of the most significant friendships of my life is with a transgendered man. He simply thought he could trust me. That's not as immediately exciting as going to Africa to save the baboons, but it's pretty damned miraculous.

So the conversation the party guest and I were trying to have is the same one everyone has. What's going on here? What is my life all about? Am I ready for it to end, or are there yet baby baboons I want to save? Or young friends I want *truly* to befriend when they need it?

Okay. So here's a sample Michael Blumenthal poem. And it fits at this point.

> *Self-Help*
> It was, as it always has been, a choice
> between *Twelve Steps to a Compassionate Life*
> and *The Story of O*, so I picked up *The Story of O*
>
> knowing it would be more interesting
> and, in the long run, better for me. I'd lived
> the compassionate life for years—it had proved
>
> far better for those around me than for myself.
> Now, I figured, it was time for *The Story of O*,
> *Tropic of Cancer, Philosophy in the Boudoir*, all
>
> the books that had inspired me in my youth,
> before altruism gave pleasure a bad name.
> We all go back to our origins, somehow, I think,
>
> ordering a cappuccino and flirting with the waitress,
> probably young enough to be my daughter. Isn't it,
> after all, pleasure we truly want, and decency
>
> the back road we use to get there? Why not, rather,
> speak our desires straight out, perhaps obliquely,
> as in a poem, but nonetheless without shame, so that

pleasure will ultimately reach those who deserve it,
and the books that once gave us so much bad feeling
toward our happier selves can go on doing their work

in the deeply literate darkness underground.

—Michael Blumenthal

See why I like his almost-old-man stuff so much?

HAROLD KNIGHT, b. 1945, discovered at age forty-nine what he wanted to do if he ever grew up: He resigned a tenured college music professorship in Boston and moved to Texas to study creative writing. At fifty-four he began teaching university first-year writing. At sixty-nine he retired and finally found his real passion, tutoring university athletes in writing. He still makes music, playing the pipe organ in his living room, and writes daily, keeping two blogs.

Subjective Age: *I feel about forty. I've been having a midlife crisis for thirty years.*

The Psychological Tasks of Old Age

Victoria Howard

In 1988 I wrote an article called "The Psychological Tasks of Old Age." I was forty-two years old. I had my reasons for thinking that I knew something about the topic. I had spent hundreds of hours with elders and their families. I was comfortable with old people and enjoyed being with them. As with many elder care professionals, my grandmother had been a loving presence in my childhood.

It was not my plan to specialize in the psychology of aging when I first came to Naropa in the summer of 1974. My intention was to study Buddhism with Chögyam Trungpa Rinpoche. In order to support my family and my studies, I needed a flexible work schedule. Caring for old folks in their homes seemed like just the thing.

I spent hundreds of hours on the meditation cushion and hundreds of hours in the company of elders. I began to notice the similarity. Being with age seemed to be a contemplative practice both for me as a caregiver and for the old people themselves. The gentle pace and simplicity of routine was spacious, almost monastic. The quality of attention to inner and outer detail was striking. I remember a friend of mine in the Buddhist community recounting his mother's comment when he described to her the practice of meditation. "You are getting the benefit of age without all the difficulties."

Now that I am an old woman, I can reflect on the conclusions that I drew during those first days of observing elders. At the age of sixty-eight, I am no longer simply watching in a detached way. I have the benefit of being the subject of my own study.

In that early article, I presented four psychological tasks "common to all elders." The first was Slowing. I described this deceleration as a "mark of mortality." That was my first mistake. In retrospect, I see this comment as unconscious ageism. It is true that, in the natural course of life, aging ends in death, but that does not define its nature. Biology and economics form the basis of our Western materialistic view. From this perspective, aging is a degenerative condition. James Hillman, in *The Force of Character*, speaks to this point:

> The convention of ageism, this "real truth," makes us feel caught—and conflicted. Either we collapse into increasing pessimistic misery, already at fifty obsessed with the decay of mind and body, or we optimistically deny the "real truth" with a heroic program of spiritual growth and physical fitness. The optimistic view and the pessimistic views share a premise: Old age is affliction.

The real affliction is thinking of aging in this way. Old people internalize this view. We look at our faces in the mirror with increasing despair. We give up on creativity, adventure and love because we are old. We narrow our lives and limit our possibilities because of this thinking.

It is true that we slow down in old age. We deal with aches and pains, bouts of illness and a feeling of vulnerability that we did not know in our bulletproof youth. We can focus on our complaints or we can appreciate the richness of slowing, the quality of awareness that it brings, the sense of connection to our bodies and the earth. Old age grounds us and from that grounded point of view, we can begin to attend to our inner and outer world in a way that we could not when we were speeding over the surface of things.

This brings us to the second psychological task: Life Review. In my doctoral research, I examined the way that elders do this. Reflection on the past is common in all stages of life. I remember to listening my eleven-year-old son and his sixth-grade buddies reminiscing about the "good old days" at their elementary school. They had just graduated and sharing their memories was their way of leaving a place that they loved and moving on.

Elders just have a much larger reservoir of experience to draw from. Weaving those memories together, finding the patterns and digesting the learning, is a huge job. This is where elder-as-artist begins to dawn. The power of creative imagination wells up in old age for just this purpose.

There is much more to say about Life Review now that I am in the middle of it myself and also about the mysterious upsurge of creative and erotic imagination that powers the process. For now, I will say that reminiscence and what comes of it is the means by which elders attain realization. Awakening is a natural human process that dawns in old age. Many cultural forces are aligned against it in our society. Ageism, the explicit and implicit devaluing of old age, does not support heroic elders undertaking this task. The Western world does not see that elders doing life review are creating the essential seeds of human culture. We old people are the makers of myth. If you are young, sit down with an elder and ask them to tell you a story. If you are old, gather the young ones around you and start talking.

The third psychological task is Transmission. The outer aspect of Transmission is elder-as-teacher. It can be the telling of stories or the very specific instruction that elders give about how to do things or how to conduct oneself. This is how human history is passed from one generation to another. In this age of libraries and computers, the actual person-to-person communication of elders can be dismissed as no longer relevant, but that is a mistake. It misses a key element of Transmission: the vibratory and energetic quality of the exchange. This is the inner aspect of Transmission. The Tibetans describe this quality of transmission between teacher and student as "Adhisthana." The word means "rain of blessings" or "grace." Elders give blessings. That is their archetypal duty. Without those blessings, given and received, the culture is weakened and impoverished. Blessings are our inner sustenance and they can only be passed from human hand to human.

The fourth task is Letting Go. I used to think of this as slipping away from life, relinquishing connection. Now I think of it as cutting loose.

VICTORIA HOWARD, b. 1946, trained as a psychotherapist. She is a student of Chögyam Trungpa Rinpoche and retired core faculty at Naropa University, where she helped develop both the Gerontology and the Master of Divinity programs. Co-founder of Dana Home Care and Windhorse Elder Care, Howard is mother of three, grandmother of three, and great-grandmother of one.

On Throwing Out My Journals

Jane Bernstein

After my mother died, and I went through the wrenching process of disposing of her possessions, I found myself thinking that I should throw away the journals I had stored in my basement. I'd considered doing this before but could not bring myself to put them in the trash. My mother's death made me think about it again. Someone would have to sort through everything I'd left behind after I died, I realized. Someone would have the wrenching job of choosing which items to keep, which to throw away, which to donate to a thrift shop.

On two occasions I did this for my mother: after she moved to assisted living, and again four years later when she died. Both times I had to empty her apartment quickly and felt overwhelmed by the effect her possessions had on me and by the sheer quantity of stuff, though my mother saw herself, as we all did, as someone who kept only what was necessary, who was averse to clutter to an extreme degree. The least sentimental person on earth, I used to describe her, remembering the way she was always marching me to the closet in my old bedroom and demanding I haul out whatever I had not used or worn that year. "It's a sin to save!" my agnostic mother would thunder. "Poor people could use these—" purses, shoes, skirts, clothes I no longer wore but for reasons I could not explain to her or to myself could not bear to give away.

Now I was ripping pants off hangers, shoving shoes into giant black bags, folding suits and dresses and winter coats, everything covered in cat hair and reeking from mothballs, the scent of her final years, when she had given up wearing perfume. As I bagged her clothing, I tried to push past my sadness by remembering that I had seen her do this same thing after my sister's death, and thirty-four years later, after my father's, coolly, with no emotion, or so it had seemed.

But what of her yarn and knitting needles, her slippers and hair brush, the framed prints, chipped ceramic ducks and cats, the photo albums filled with snapshots of trips she had taken with my father, one or the other of them posed in front of monuments in Prague, London, Jerusalem, or any of the dozen or so other cities they'd visited? What could I do with these things that were of no value to strangers, which I lacked the heart to simply throw out? All the storage space in my own house was already crammed with furniture from her last move, cartons filled with favorite toys, baby sweaters and art projects from my daughters' childhood and adolescence, with record albums, memorabilia and journals of my own?

What does one do with all the stuff that's left behind?

One summer, my daughter Charlotte bought an 8mm projector and home movies at a flea market in Cape Cod that had belonged to a dentist and his wife from Massachusetts. It made me ache to see these movies that had been so carefully shot, developed, and cataloged—their birthday parties and vacations—spread out on the parking lot of a drive-in theater, sold to strangers for a couple of bucks. I couldn't imagine anyone doing such a thing.

Ten years later, I understood it perfectly.

. . . .

Why save my journals when even I never read them? Before my mother died, when I'd considered getting rid of them, it seemed as if to do so was to throw out my past, discarding the girl, the single woman, the young wife, the mother of babies. When I considered putting the carton full of journals on the curb beside the trash cans, it seemed like a confession that I was done with my history, though all my life I have held onto the conviction that the past is the foundation and first layers of the present self, that remembering is everything. It isn't merely that I agree that, "Those who cannot remember the past are condemned to repeat it," as George Santayana wrote. I also believe that the only thing each of us truly possesses is our own history, that it is the stuff of life. So throwing out the journals felt like discarding pieces of myself. Leaving the carton in storage seemed easy enough when death was still remote, more a metaphor or a threat than something that would actually happen to me. Now my sister and parents are gone, along with all of their siblings. I'm at a point in my life where I can go away for a brief vacation and return to find that a friend, a contemporary, has dropped dead while I was out of town. These events have made me feel the reality of death. They remind me that if I don't take action while I'm still around, someone will be faced with the job of throwing away a massive amount of stuff that once had meaning to me, including my journals, and that these bound books full of my thoughts and observations will be incinerated, pawed over by strangers, or read by someone who'd known me when I was alive—someone with the patience to read my awful left-hander's scrawl.

. . . .

And what of these journals? I last breezed through some pages when I was preparing to move to a new house. Wearied by the prospect of hauling all my stuff from one basement to another, it had crossed my mind to get rid of the manuscripts and journals that I'd kept in storage for so many years.

I opened a carton and in one of the volumes found an entry about a series of strange encounters with a much older man—someone close to my father's age. I was stunned to read it and thought, that actually happened? I hadn't forgotten meeting the man thirty-seven years ago at the Cape, not far from the flea market where Charlotte bought the home movies. Instead, the events had been reworked by time, discomfort and memory, transforming something that had actually transpired into what I'd come to believe was a product of my imagination (reminding me how thin the membrane between verifiable event and what we imagine to be true). At the time I wondered what good it would do for anyone to read about this event or any of the escapades I felt compelled to record in my journals. And yet to tear out the pages with details I did not wish to share seemed bizarre, out of character. And so I was left wondering: What would I lose if I throw out everything?

Five years later, I still don't know the answer. What—if anything—am I saying about my life if I dispose of those boxes? Is my continued ambivalence about keeping them a sign that my mother's death has made me feel closer to my own?

. . . .

Some of my mother's possessions I am very pleased to have. Her flatware, the foyer table from our house, with hinged sides that turn the round top into a triangle—these things are now part of my everyday life. Her silver and champagne glasses, which I use for holidays, remind me what a gifted host she was. The watercolor of chicks, newly hatched from an egg, that was painted by a neighbor's father and hung with other pictures on the brick fireplace of the house where I spent my childhood, is now in my dining room. I don't care if it's awkward or sentimental; I like it a lot.

What I cherish most is the album with the photos from my parents' early life. When I found it in my mother's apartment, I stopped throwing clothes into bags and sat to look through the pages. There are three pictures from my parents' simple wedding ceremony, conducted in wartime. How lovely my mother is in her broad-brimmed hat. My father, with his dark wavy hair and cleft in his chin, is as handsome as a matinee idol. The kiss that was captured, the two of them wrapped in each other's arms, is a record of their passion, something I never thought about when I was growing up. And why would I, when they were my parents, whose style, common in that generation, I suppose, was to maintain a distance. They did not acknowledge their inner lives, and never spoke of love or loss.

In the album there are photos of my sister as an infant in a crib, and as a toddler, clutching a fence that surrounds the tennis courts in Lincoln Terrace Park in Brooklyn. No shadow darkens these early photos of my parents and sister; there is no hint of her awful demise at twenty. The snapshots of my parents picnicking, sweeping a cabin, sledding in a city park are sensuous. You can feel their youth and vitality. No one poses in these pictures, the way my parents do in the travel photos, where they stand as erect as the buildings behind them. My mother maintained that travel was the best part of her life, but the early photos—the one of my father flat on his back on the grass with my sister, a baby, on his chest, her fingers in his mouth—these tell a story that my parents never shared.

I wish I knew more than just the brief outline of my parents' lives and not merely as their child, forever their child, in the years after my sister's death, when I spent so much time in an awful dance of breaking away and drawing close, of trying to make up for their loss and knowing it was impossible, of hating myself for what I could not give them and resenting them for what they could not give me. I want the other stories that made up who they were, the stories I didn't know, the glimpses I could not have taken, a vantage point not my own.

· · · ·

In the few home movies we had—perhaps fifteen minutes in all—I am the little girl in the background, jumping and flapping my arms, dying to be noticed. I am that little girl still, wanting to be known in a rather frantic way.

My journals are not a record of my life. (Nor are my memoirs, since the scenes in each book are arranged to illuminate a particular story from life, rather than being about life in general.) If only I were a diarist and kept a record of where I went or what I felt about events of the time, I might have a different feeling about saving my writing. But, no. There's nothing about Vietnam in my journals, though my undergraduate days were shaped by protest, not a word about 9/11, though my roots are in New York, as I was, two days after the towers fell, when the city still reeked from soot and flesh. All I have of that event are a series of email messages, which will vanish in the ether, even before I do. My journals are not like those of M. F. K. Fisher, who wrote volumes about food and life, with such grace that even the record of what she drank on a single afternoon—"a poor white wine and a glass of good champagne and a very small brandy, over some three artfully prolonged hours"—is delightful to read. I am no Samuel Pepys, who lived through the plague and the Great Fire of London and recorded historic events and domestic ones with so much rich detail that a whole period of time comes alive for readers centuries later. Nor can I read my crabbed entries and find, as Joan Didion did when she came upon the scenes in her own notebooks, "what it was to be me." No grandchild or stranger at a flea market could read my journals and say: here is the story of a girl who lived in New York in the 1960s, a member of Students for a Democratic Society, a second-wave feminist, a struggling writer, a mother, a lover, a traveler. My journals, sporadically kept, are mostly records of despair. Some anecdotes appear throughout, some descriptions of various adventures, a few entries about my long labor and the birth of my first daughter, but they are without balance or context. Like my mother, I have lived through heartache, but I don't want to be remembered as someone whose life was about misery, when I have lived fully and loved with extravagance and laughed until I ached all over. My journals, taken alone, look like scribblings of a somber, unsmiling woman, a brief record of a lifetime of gloom.

I don't find myself thinking, "If only I'd lived differently!" as much as wishing my journals were worth someone's effort to read. Part of this is vanity; part springs from a lifetime of spending too many sunny afternoons reworking sentences and passages, aiming for perfection, while knowing it is impossible to attain. When I try to figure out what to do with that carton, I think, Wait! I'm not done yet! It's a sentiment that stops me cold. Not done living, for certain. As for the journals, I'm stuck with regret. If only my entries were a bright and witty record of my passage through a world long gone…if only I had revised…

. . . .

Part of what makes the process of sorting through the possessions of the dead so daunting is the sheer quantity of stuff that's left behind, the way after a while, everything starts to feel worthless. I yearned for more photographs of my parents' early married life, but the fact that there were so few snapshots heightened my emotions.

I'd like to imagine I will throw away all my detritus, including my journals, and leave behind a single object from each decade of my life, just enough to pique someone's imagination. A pressed rose, a silver lapel pin from a science fair; a peasant dress with pink and purple cross-stitching across the sleeves; a wrapped candy with a cellophane wrapper that says, "Mothers are Worth a Mint at Chemical Bank," a trophy from a road race. A divorce decree, a campaign sticker, a love letter—only one.

JANE BERNSTEIN, b. 1949, is the author of five books, among them the memoirs *Bereft: A Sister's Story*, and *Rachel in the World*. She is also an essayist, a lapsed screenwriter, and a member of the Creative Writing Program at Carnegie Mellon University. Visit www.janebernstein.net to read some of her shorter work.

Subjective Age: *When no mirrors are around, I am ageless.*

Where Have All the Old Ladies Gone?

Molly Giles

They used to be everywhere. One sat on every front porch, park bench, and bus stop of the town I grew up in. One watched from the front window of every house; one talked to another over every backyard fence. They stood behind the counters of the dime stores, drug stores, corner markets, florists, bookstores, and soda fountains. They taught every class in the grammar school. The library belonged to them. So did the churches. They ran the beauty shops. They operated the telephones. You could not take a music lesson without going to one of them. You could not make a bank deposit. You could not buy a stamp.

That was sixty years ago, when I was a child. I thought old ladies ruled the world.

Each one was different. Each one was alike. They all wore the same clothes: black shoes that laced, heavy dust-colored hose, hand-knit cardigans, silky dresses with hems that drooped. Rubber girdles. Veiled hats with feathers. Fur boas. They all carried pocketbooks and when they pulled the keys out of their pocketbooks they opened their doors onto the same sort of room: dim, clean, with an African violet near the radiator, a sepia photograph of someone dead on the desk, a pimpled milk-glass figurine of Cinderella's hollow slipper on the bric-a-brac shelf. They kept bowls of sweets—ribbon candy, lemon drops, green and white striped peppermints—on their coffee tables. None of them ate the candy.

Their names began with Miss or Mrs. They often called one another Miss or Mrs. Their first names linked, formed a gentle alphabet: Addie, Bessie, Clara, Dora, Edith, Fanny, Gertrude, Hazel, Ivy, Jewel, Kitty, Leila, Mabel, Nola, Opal, Phoebe, Queenie, Ruby, Stella, Theodora, Ursula, Violet, Wilma, Xenia, Yolanda, Zelda. They used these names at the tables where they played against each other in contract bridge, canasta, and mah-jong. They used these names in the basement restaurants of the department stores where they gathered to eat chicken pot pie and scoops of Neapolitan ice cream from stainless steel goblets. Their dentures clicked and some of the bolder ones, the ones with full sets of false teeth, bit into the ice cream showily and chewed, unmindful of the cold. Their voices, talking to each other, were harsh and hilarious.

They talked about train trips and movie stars and radio shows and yardage sales and the few relatives—rarely husbands—they were proud of. They talked about their illnesses. They were often ill, their bodies bent, bow-legged, breakable, subject to mysterious catarrhs, goiters, dropsies. Their skin was pale and delicate as plum petals, marbled with blotches, mustaches, warts, chin hairs, liver spots. Moles the size of pencil erasers hung off their lids and upper lids.

They didn't care. Their eyes were bright, magnified behind thick glasses or beaming out unaided from beneath brows that had either been plucked and penciled to improbable arches or left in a tangle. Their cheeks were softly wrinkled and rouged. Their hair was either white or gray or came in colors from a paint box: apricot, lilac, pitch black, blue. Sometimes their hair was skewered with sharp thin wires and caged inside a filmy net that looked like something insects might hatch from; sometimes it was tucked under a turban, a babushka, a snood. At night their hair floated down free and glowed like a ghost girl's.

They got up early. They went to bed late. They moved around the house where the rest of us were sleeping in long flannel nightgowns that smelled like Vicks VapoRub. They sighed and sipped hot water with lemon juice. Even at night their hands smelled like soup, their breath like sour tea. Their bellies smelled like baby talcum, their bosoms like funeral flowers—the rose, gardenia, violet, and lilac scents they sprinkled on stained handkerchiefs and tucked inside their brassiere straps all day. Their armpits were rank with faint sweat, their feet smelled like everyone else's, and an interesting rot came from their flanks when they crossed and uncrossed their beautiful blue-veined legs.

By dawn they were already in the kitchen. They cooked all day. Boiled green beans with gray slabs of bacon. Deep-fat fried chicken with blood at the bone. Sugary pie crusts. Watery custards. Milk toast. Aspics. Hard little lard cookies. Livers and tongues.

They were not good cooks.

No one could say this, except other old ladies. Other old ladies could say anything they pleased, about themselves, about each other, about the President of the United States, and about you. Old ladies saw you, when you were a child. They saw you in ways your peers and parents did not. They were not fooled by your dimples and curls. They looked right inside to something called your "character." They saw that your character was unformed and basically vile but salvageable and they believed that with a strict application of effort and will you could still become worthwhile, someday. They saw you had potential.

Because they believed in you—because they offered that great and terrible courtesy—you tried to measure up. You washed your neck and scrubbed your elbows. You stood up straight, kept your napkin in your lap, chewed with your mouth closed and did not pick your nose in public. You cleaned your side of your room, kicked your sister covertly, did your homework, double-checked your sums, said your prayers, and included them in it. You made way for them on the sidewalk. You offered them your seat on the bus. You helped them cross the street. Even though they acted as if they were helping you.

Some of them were witches. Some of them were saints. But most of them were simply the best friends you had.

I would have been lost without the old ladies of my childhood. Miss Buck taught me to read from the comics before I was four. Her maiden sister, The Other Miss Buck, taught me to tell time on a grandfather clock. Mrs. Istin made me paper dolls from the Montgomery Ward catalogue and taught me to knit with kitchen twine and two pencils. Mrs. Cotter took me rowing on the small city lake. Great Aunt Ethel took me to the Ice Follies. Great Aunt Rose took me to the ballet. Mrs. Brown, who wore a body cast, taught me to can-can. Mrs. Shippy taught me how to spell Mississippi. One of my grandmothers let me drink watered rose wine with dinner. The other grandmother sat by my bed when I was sick and made up stories about every square in my counterpane. In the white square we rode polar bears through the

Arctic, in the green we camped under redwoods, in the blue we sailed the cold Pacific.

This grandmother was the love of my life. Shy, restless, she never stood still long enough for a formal portrait, but I keep a snapshot of her on my office wall. She is dressed for Easter in a slippery ill-fitting brown and white dress and she is wearing a brown hat that squats like a brood hen on top of her bad gray perm. Her shoulders sag, as does her bust. Her stomach shelves out. Her glasses are crooked. She is wearing crystal earrings and a crystal necklace; this set, which I own now, she told me came from the chandelier of a French chateau. Elves gathered it, she said, and gave it to her so she could give it to me. Her feet, deformed by bunions, are encased in orthopedic boots. Her bare arms are heavy and slack; her watch cuts into the flesh of her wrist; her rings can't come off. Her face is downcast but her eyes flash up at the camera, bright, proud, and mischievous. And the smile that exposes her badly spaced, coffee-stained teeth is so genuine that my heart bows before it even now.

Her own heart was already burdened by then, her pulse slowed by long years of widowhood, her arteries clogged from gravies and cream pies, her blood pressure soaring from the daily demands of a menial job, her sciatica screaming, her arthritis a smoldering coal on each joint.

She was my age.

Only I'm not old. I wear jeans and lacy camisoles and cowboy boots. Sunblock, moisturizers, facials, and Retin-A have helped preserve my skin. Contact lenses have camouflaged the need for glasses. My teeth have been straightened, my hair has been curled, and both have been bleached. I go to a gym, lift weights, do yoga, Pilates, and hike. I get massages when I need to, see a psychotherapist when I need to. I have a job I enjoy, many friends. I travel a lot. I fall in love often. I beat the steering wheel and sing to Al Green when I drive. I weigh less than I did at eighteen.

Friends my age aren't old either. We all look good. Some have had plastic surgery to help them look good, but most haven't needed it. Charlotte, seventy-three, just came back from trekking through Myanmar. Jo, in her eighties, spent the last six months living on a barge in the Netherlands, researching a river. Barbara, sixty-eight, insists I take the wheel of her new Jaguar, and counsels as I edge down a steep stretch of coast highway,

"Don't use the brake, honey, don't use the brake." Kate, seventy-six, teaches yoga. Gina, ageless, accepting a national award for her latest book, stands at the microphone and stammers, in a young girl's voice, "I'm not ready." Susan, sixty, recovering from a bout of colon cancer, jumped on a Norwegian freighter, sailed around the world, and ended up marrying the ship's chief engineer. Eve, sixty-eight, just won her umpteenth decathlon. Esther, eighty, is building a back deck on her house by herself. Betty, fifty-eight, came back from Egypt with a twenty-seven-year-old tour guide.

"We're a different generation," I boast to my grown daughter who has come over with my grandson for dinner. I am whipping around the kitchen in my skinny jeans and ballet slippers, pulling out organic vegetables for a stir-fry.

"You are," she agrees. (She's a wonderful daughter.) She glances at the beginning pages of this article, which I have left lying on the counter, picks it up and reads out loud. "Where have all the old ladies gone?" she wonders.

"I know," my grandson beams. His eyes are dancing.

"You do?" We humor him. "Where?"

"Here! One lives right here! In YOUR house, Gramolly!"

What a lesson! Who needs it! I have seen the enemy and she is me. Only she's not an enemy and I couldn't have seen her without my contacts plus the huge magnifying glass I keep by the phone book. I throw the enoki and sustainable tofu back in the refrigerator; phone the pizza place for a Combination, Large; snatch my grandson up to shake the giggles out of him; and then follow him, still giggling, to my writing room where he settles before my computer. There, while we wait for the pizza to be delivered, he shows me how to Text and Twitter and I pretend to understand, delighted by the lights in his quick, intent, intelligent eyes. I watch his little hands continue to connect me to an iPhone and an iPad and an iPod and who knows what. Good heavens, I think. Where have all the children gone?

MOLLY GILES, b. 1942, has written four award-winning collections of short stories and a novel. She taught creative writing at San Francisco State University and the University of Arkansas for many years and presently leads workshops and mentors through Book Passage in Corte Madera. She recently completed a new collection of short stories about older women, entitled *CACKLING*.

Subjective Age: *Since I first wrote this essay, I am considerably less cocky about aging and somewhat less spry. I can still get down on the floor to tussle with the grandchildren, but I appreciate a hand getting up. I am seventy-four and it's a perfect age; I think I'll stay seventy-four for a while.*

Learning to Live Forward

Allan Gurganus

Mom and Dad made sure my three brothers and I had shoes roughly the right size. They bought us encyclopedias; they churched us verily unto atheism itself, Amen. I benefit from several other mistakes our folks made. They're dead now. I can finally be more candid. All of us are walking around with our parents' hopes for us branded on our foreheads. My Dad expected me to run General Motors. Or least to run their ad wing. And look how that enterprise tanked, even without me! Thank God for therapy and forgetfulness.

In fiction and daily existence, I value having learned to live forward, most always forward. In and out of print, I am cautiously pessimistic. But I still get these bouts of Hope. They come on like migraines. Entering middle age, we carry the growing quorum: all our loved ones who died first. There's an Auden line I love,

The nightingales are sobbing in
The orchards of our mothers,
And hearts that we broke long ago
Have long been breaking others;

Such tallying can feel oddly clarifying. Every decade I've lived has made me simpler, kinder, if five pounds heavier. My twenties looked good from the outside but lived as an inward hornet's nest. The decades since have each grown quieter, more replete.

I am teaching Chekhov. If I love his art, his life yields just that much to study. Whitman and Chekhov remain my spirit father-mothers. Both offered strangers medical help, often to these men's own detriment. My goal, partly based on such mentors' lived examples, is to leave every-body I meet feeling more powerfully themselves. This, insanely enough, includes grocery clerks, garbage men, my car mechanic. It's an extension of what we must do for our characters on the page: To allow them a vivid chance at feeling, at momentary dignity, at some lively Saturday nights. I know the man who cleans my Workshop office. I know all about his cockatiel's game of taking this fellow's cellphone from his pocket during naps. The bird loves to poke phone buttons, trying to make sounds, all while chewing off the cell's plastic numerals. We are sometimes so busy inventing clever issues and synthetic characters, we miss the person who all but shares our office. Chekhov insists that, on and off the page, no one must ever be humiliated.

ALLAN GURGANUS, b. 1947, writes fiction. His works include *Oldest Living Confederate Widow Tells All*, *Plays Well with Others* and, most recently, *Local Souls.* He has taught writing at Sarah Lawrence, Stanford, Duke and the Iowa Writers' Workshop.

Subjective Age: *My numerical age is, somehow, already sixty-eight. But that can swing from feeling as low as age eight then clear up to eighty. After gardening hard, I need an Advil, but I can still remember the joy of writing in perfect cursive circa 1953: 'Dwight Eisenhower is our nation's President.'*

Endings

Judy Blume

In her later years my mother, who enjoyed knitting for her loved ones, confessed to making bargains with God. He would not take her in the middle of a sweater. She was cagey about it though, always having new wool on hand to begin again the very next day. When I started to write I also made bargains with God. He, or she—because by then I had read Erica Jong—would allow me to finish my book before, well, whatever. And when I came to the end and sent it off in its plain brown envelope, I was filled with hope that this might be the one to make me a published writer. But just in case, the next morning I was back at it. I was in my twenties then and in a hurry; in my family life was short.

I grew up sitting *shivah,* shaped by death. Alternately fascinated, terrified, consumed by the ultimate ending, I developed my very own personal relationship with God that had little to do with organized religion. I believed deeply, as only a child can, that I was responsible for my beloved father's well-being, and that only I could prevent his untimely death. The year I was nine my father was turning forty-three, the same age his brothers had been when they had died. I secretly called it the "Bad Year" and invented a series of ritualistic prayers I would recite at least ten times a day, more if necessary, anything to protect my father, to keep him healthy and safe from harm. And it worked for a while. My father survived the "Bad Year" and lived for twelve more, then died suddenly on a sunny summer afternoon. I was twenty-one and had long given up the magical thinking that led me to believe I could save him, or anyone else. He was the last of seven siblings, none of whom lived to be sixty. Endings have always been hard for me.

Though I rejoice at writing that final line in a book, much as my mother did with the final row of each of her hand-knit sweaters, and I weep with relief at finding myself at the end at last, after months or sometimes years of struggle, I know that before long a melancholic funk will hit me and I'll go through a period of mourning. Parting with my characters is like saying that final goodbye to an old friend. Oh sure, they're still there for me if I want to pick up a book and thumb through the pages, but they're no longer part of my everyday life. Each time I have to learn to let go all over again, to send them out into the world without my protection. Lately, I've been allowing myself longer and longer periods of time between books. Now that I've passed my sixtieth birthday I'm in less of a hurry. I probably shouldn't admit this because my mother, if she were here tonight, would urge me to get back to work, and quickly. Then she would raise her finger and whisper a reminder, "You never know who might be listening."

JUDY BLUME, b. 1938, is a prolific American writer of popular children's and young adult fiction who writes for adult readers as well. She is known for exploring sensitive topics in a realistic manner. Her books have faced decades of banning attempts while selling 82 million copies. Blume has been named a Library of Congress Living Legend and received the ALA's Margaret A. Edwards Award and the National Book Foundation's medal for distinguished contribution to American letters.

Ripening

David "Lucky" Goff

Life apparently thrives by occasionally knocking over the apple cart. Just when I think I have something figured out, I am plunged, once again, in over my head. Sometimes I think Life has a wicked sense of humor and is a bit sadistic. I usually occupy this sentiment when I am feeling sorry for myself. I'm not in that place now. So lately, in the midst of my unforeseen happiness, where I am feeling glad to be me, I have been reflecting on what is happening when I, and my world, get turned upside down. It looks like I am adopting a new attitude. It seems that these recurring dilemmas, as predictably unpredictable as they may be, are all part of a process that seems to be ripening me.

The idea that I am being ripened appeals to me. I know that soon I am going to fall off the tree. I know that despite all of my illusions, protestations and elaborate projects and schemes, the end is coming. I've stopped worrying about it. But, I am still curious. So the idea that I am being ripened, that I could be the seed pod for some as yet undefined new life form, intrigues me.

Now bear in mind, as I am this minute, I am only speculating. I don't really know anything. But, I keep imagining death as a form of transition, a shift from one form to another. In my mind, seeing death as a form of transition has a lot of explanatory value. Mainly, viewing things this way makes the ordeals, the inconveniences of my life, the little broken edges, have more dignity. These recurring challenges are not a sign of my incompleteness; instead I am being ripened. Maybe I am being prepared, ripening like a wine grape in the sun, steeping like a good cup of tea, evolving like a caterpillar being chrysalized. The thought that even death is a part of evolution, that I could, once more, be becoming something else, fills me with a feeling that I am going deeper into the familiar, instead of being cast away, dried out, useless, and done.

Thinking this way also helps me appreciate the difficulties that keep arising. They may actually be Nature's way of shaping me into a new form, one that I cannot imagine but can intuit. I know I do better, I play the hand dealt to me, am more creative in my responses to Life, when I am anticipating becoming. I may not know where I am heading, may not have any idea about how I'm going to get anywhere, but I have a sense that I am moving, ripening, changing, becoming something else.

This may be sheer delusion, certainly I have no science to back it up, but it still serves me. It seems to me that no matter what I believe, no matter how sophisticated I am with the scientific method, I still have to come to terms with the great inscrutable mystery of death. And, it also seems to me that how I come to terms with death determines how I come to terms with Life. I live according to the way I envision death.

Ripening offers me a chance to participate, not like I alone hold the key to my fate. I am prepared to be alone, to take responsibility for this life, actually, I think ripening demands it. But, ripening, becoming, implies yet another stage, in another, I would say, greater context. I seem to be part of some larger, as yet unknown ecosystem. If this is true, and in my current imagination it is, then there is this strange other, that I am part of, but that is unknown. I am simultaneously the new seed arriving and the old ecosystem receiving it. In my mind, I am being prepared to quicken a greater wholeness.

Death, in this line of thought, isn't the end of the line, it is some kind of timely ripening. As the caterpillar entering the chrysalis, or a pupa becoming an adult, there is a change of states. The timing is semi-predictable, and the general direction is assured. Despite the Second Law of Thermodynamics, the energy in the Universe doesn't seem to be running down; instead the Universe seems to confound us by conserving, even increasing its energy. Death may be another expansion of the Universe.

Ripening is a mysterious phenomenon for me. For instance, it seems to happen by virtue of a combination of circumstances. There seems to be something inside that matures. And, while that is happening, there also seems to be something outside that provides the necessary stimulation. Ripening, to me, is a co-creative process. This thought thrills me. Maybe, by ripening, accepting the unacceptable turns on this thrill ride of life, going into the darkness of Mystery, and dying as I live, I get a little closer to the source of all this complex stimulation.

If this is true, wow, am I glad to be alive and to get to die! If it is a delusion, a fantasy of my own making, then I'm merely glad I had imagination enough to create an interesting way of life.

I hope you do too.

DAVID GOFF, b. 1948, had a brain aneurysm in 2013. As a result of his stroke, and the onset of a rare brain syndrome, he nearly died and ended up permanently disabled. This experience had a transformational effect on David, which made him "Lucky," and cued him into how radically connected all things are. He blogs at *The Slow Lane*, conducts a monthly radio program called *Growing An Elder Culture*, and publishes books. He is a regular contributor at changingaging.org.

Subjective Age: *I'm just as old as I feel (sixty-eight), I think it important for me to note. I couldn't have the insight, sensitivity, and courage it takes to write what I do if I felt somehow younger than I am. I know that many people report otherwise, but I don't.*

The Crowd Inside Me

Gary Soto

Let's say for the sake of play that there are three people inside me: the boy lifting weights in a garage; the teenager with three guitar chords in his heart; and the young man painting minuscule hearts on a first girlfriend's thumbnail. This is all conjecture, of course, a way to keep my mind busy, a little creative wrangling on a day when I don't have much to do. I could wash the car, or sweep the garage, or watch my wife baste a chicken with large artistic strokes before sending it into the oven.

After forty years, however, I've tired of this game, a poet who used to lick the pencil to keep the tip moistened. I should favor history like, for instance, Erasmus. According to my mental notes, he left Italy for England in 1509. He sailed by single-masted ship, its hull loaded with barrels of wine, then was ferried by carriage—or perhaps, he rode a durable horse, certainly not a donkey. He would have been too smart to splay his bottom on a burdened beast, he a scholar with six languages at his disposal, a speed-reader who absorbed what he read in a logical manner. He settled in London, with King Henry VIII for his patron, and kept quiet during those years when heads were being lopped off and spiked for viewing on the London Bridge. This much I know about the saintly Erasmus.

I'm not a historian who scribbles marginalia on the pages of first-edition books. At the moment, however, I'm musing over an incident in which the trustees of the York Minster (the second-largest cathedral in England) debated the scandalous nature of an image of Mary breastfeeding the baby Jesus—an image painted on the ceiling. In truth, the portrait was difficult to make out unless you craned your head straight up, like a duck swallowing a small fish. Posed in such a manner, a viewer could eye the soft heaven of Mary's right breast, with Jesus clawing for the latch of a serviceable nipple. In 1910—a prudish period, one would think—this image of the blessed mother feeding her son so provoked a few congregants that the trustees voted on its whitewashing. One enlightened trustee suggested a partial paint job: over Mary's upper body. An artist could then supply an image of Jesus with a bottle in his mouth.

I can just imagine the others' reaction to this idea: "By Jove, we have it!" Thus Mary's breast was stained to match the fabric of her dress and a large baby bottle painted in place—after all, even Jesus needed his nourishment. None of the church members was troubled by this alteration; at the time, there was no Breastfeeding Association of Great Britain.

In the 1960s, however, when a new generation of trustees stood under the painting, gawking upwards, they were baffled by the presence of the baby bottle—did these exist in the time of old Bethlehem? Embarrassed by the decision of the previous administration, and recognizing the ridiculousness of the scene, the trustees again commissioned artists. Mary's breast returned, perhaps even fuller than before, while the baby bottle was booted into a recycling bin. If the painted Jesus could have spoken, he might have said, "Now we're talkin.'"

Again, I'm no historian. I habitually disrespect facts, though this bit of York Minster history is very much true. I'm a poet with three people inside me, none with spiritual rumblings. I have had to work with this gang of three for forty years. Recently, however, I added a fourth figure—an elderly gentleman, one sock black and the other dark blue, his sweater buttons in the wrong holes. This new person will ignore the other three, all loudmouthed youth who live by the senses of taste, touch, and smell—not unlike, I guess, the baby Jesus. The old guy won't do much but tinker in his garage and rake the hand-shaped leaves of the sycamore tree. He'll find solace on a public bench in Oakland and return home with grass in his pant cuffs. That's the best he'll do, an adventure in the wilds of an unkempt park where one afternoon he is bullied by teenagers: "Come on, pops, go down to the liquor store and hook us up with some cold ones."

The old guy mulls it over: drinks—that would be nice.

He has it together enough to say, "Okay, I'll buy if you fly," then corrects his verbal gaffe. "Oh, silly me—I mean you buy and I'll fly." The teenagers hustle away, afraid of the lunatic; they light up on a faraway bench, whiffs of good shit scenting the air. They stare back in the direction of the old guy and mutter under their breath, "Checkered pants with red socks—hell no."

"I'll die before I get that old," one claims. And in Oakland, this is often what they do.

GARY SOTO, b. 1952, is the author of more than forty books for young people and adults, including *Buried Onions, Living Up the Street, A Summer Life, Neighborhood Odes*, and *You Kiss by th' Book*. His output is undeniable, his readership also undeniable as his books have sold nearly four million copies. The Gary Soto Literary Museum is located at Fresno City College. He lives in Berkeley, California.

Subjective Age: *Age-wise, I am somewhere between five and sixty-four, depending on my appetite for sugary cereal and my rare moments of forgetfulness.*

Slaying St. George

Susan Troccolo

I can't remember now if it was potatoes or carrots, but I remember the feeling at the time: "God bless my hands," I whispered. "Thank you for my hands." It was the end of a muggy summer day, the first time I had cancer. I hadn't been doing anything, but I was weary to the bone. I stood at the kitchen sink—vegetable peeler in hand—and I watched my hands move without me. It was such a simple scene: my hands, the sunshine streaming in the window, and the red geranium in its pot on the windowsill. I was six weeks into treatment and simple was bliss; simple was all I wanted.

For a while, I watched from somewhere outside myself. My fingers shook ever so slightly, and lavender blue veins stood out from under my pale skin. Then there were those little brown liver spots that I used to notice on other people, three of them on my right hand. When did they show up? All of a sudden, tears formed, big soft tears like pillows propped up in the corners of my eyes, and just as suddenly they sank below the surface. I laughed a little under my breath because this seemed to be my new existence: a watery, salty existence with tears and laughter bubbling out dozens of times a day. Like a well, I spurted out water whenever the pump was primed by some observation of simple magic.

Now it was my hands that had my gratitude—the way they just did their work when everything else was on strike, the way they knew how much pressure to apply, the way they didn't ask for anything in return. Hands connected to the whole by delicate bones and ligaments; cells and nerves efficiently performing the ordinary business of doing whatever is necessary. I was aware of my body as friend, something to be grateful for—like feet that you walk on all day or eyes that take in the world's colors. Why is it that I had to become so sick to appreciate them?

It was in November the previous year that I was diagnosed with thyroid cancer. My young physician was making a name for herself, just a few years out of med school and zealous about regular checkups. She was moving competently around the examining room, with her short-cropped shiny hair and inquisitive eyes, wearing black opaque stockings and sturdy shoes. When she found the lump, she went into a kind of trance as she felt around my throat. It was so tiny, she said, she almost wasn't sure it was there. But ultimately she was sure, and that meant a series of needle biopsies, which indicated the tissue was malignant. I went through these unpleasant biopsies in my own kind of trance, believing myself to be invincible and ready for any challenge. Like St. George fighting the dragon, I saw myself as a feisty and victorious contestant in the upcoming battle.

When my husband Patrick and I lived in Italy, one of my favorite places to go was the Bargello in Florence. There was something about the simplicity of the place and the exquisite sculptures that drew me back and compelled me to sit for hours. In the big central room of the three-story fortress, there is a niche with a statue of the young St. George preparing to do battle with the dragon. George is handsome and resolute. His jaw is set for the fight and he holds his sword upright in front of him—prepared, vigilant, and magnificent. Twenty yards away and off to the side, there is a statue of St. John the Baptist, looking no more than twelve years old. Where George is in full armor, John is nearly naked except for the torn animal skin loosely wrapped across his hollowed chest and loins. The bones of John's neck and shoulders stand out and his feet are like claws grasping the earth. Yet in those starved eyes there is an incredible fire—it looks like nothing on earth could stop him.

I used to sit on a bench in front of both statues so that they were juxtaposed and almost superimposed one above the other. As I sat surrounded by this imagery signifying for me the Active Way (St. George slaying dragons) and a more Contemplative Way (St. John alone with his faith), I felt awe for human strength and all its variations. I wondered, without any particular focus at the time, where my courage resided. If put to the test, would I respond more like one than the other?

At the moment I received my diagnosis, I became St. George. This first time (I would receive a diagnosis eighteen years later and my reaction would be different), I was ready for the fight. I was strong and tough. I'm not sure how I chose St. George, but my experience with cancer has changed me and continues to teach me, making me a little less afraid of dying, and consequently less afraid of living. It has allowed me to befriend my own body, which is darned handy when you are looking at fifty and sixty. And it has given me the courage to look at myself as I age and accept the whole package. I'm not saying I like it all, but I've integrated the parts better—I've seen myself disintegrate, become invisible, and still survive. For a while, I was forced to watch the world go by from the river bank, and then, when I was able, I climbed into my little boat and shoved off into the flowing river again, this time at peace with myself.

I was just like a lot of people when they get a diagnosis of illness. I thought, "You found it, now take it out and let me get back to my life." I had just started a new business and was full of energy and plans for the future. Adopting a take-charge, active approach, I spent the weeks before the surgery reading about my condition and how to take care of myself. I even contacted a lawyer and created a durable power of attorney for health care, assuring that no one could put me on life support if something happened during the surgery.

I realize now that despite my outward display of courage, I maintained a distance from my feelings. I knew that this body was mine to care for— I never put the responsibility on someone else. I was trying so hard to be prepared, but I was not confronting my fear, the fear of mortality.

A week before I was scheduled to have my thyroidectomy, my doctor began to talk to me about how we'd get rid of any cancer cells that remained after surgery. She said that in a few months I would be given radioactive iodine to target any remaining thyroid cells, but before that it would be necessary to purge my body of regular iodine, which is required for thyroid cells to produce thyroid hormone. This purge—which would require me to forego foods high in iodine—would take several months, during which I would not be permitted to take any replacement for the hormone I was about to lose. Unfortunately, my doctor never told me which foods to avoid.

Something about this new information terrified me. I thought I knew what was going to happen; the prognosis was good. No one had said anything before about this gradual loss of strength lasting months. I was prepared to get stronger after surgery, not weaker. As my doctor calmly talked to me about the changes—yes, I would feel exhausted; yes, there would be a radical change in metabolism, the thyroid does control many functions in the body after all—I grew more furious. I found myself wanting to slap her calm little face.

I was staring at the prospect of a slow descent into someone I didn't yet know. I was imagining a gradual decline of vitality and spark until I felt slow and fat and depleted and used up in some kind of involuntary purgatory, a dress rehearsal for old age. I wanted anything but the slow, crummy feeling of going downhill and not being able to do anything about it. Anything but pasty dry skin and broken fingernails, bowels that wouldn't move and brain cells that wouldn't either. Anything but something I couldn't control. Just when I was feeling powerful and independent, I would be weak and in need of people and their help. I would be out of the flow of activity, sick but not really sick—not able to do things the way I always did them; not able to keep talking, keep charming, keep up the show. I felt the way you feel when a twenty-year-old calls you "Ma'am" and you know they don't see you, because to them you are old. You are invisible. And I was terribly afraid of invisible.

Patrick tried to understand what I was feeling. He told me, "Think about what a special time this can be for you—time just to heal, time when you don't have to do a thing but relax and be yourself."

Relax...be myself...How exactly do you do that? I know it may sound funny, but I was panicked at the prospect of spending a summer doing nothing. Afraid it might turn out that I was nothing. I was rushing to fill up an emptiness even before it was empty. And not yet able to understand that emptiness can be the beginning of a new life.

When the time came for the surgery, Patrick drove me from our home in Palo Alto to Mount Zion Hospital in San Francisco. Like most of us, I hate hospitals; even the best hospitals are germy, noisy, inhospitable places. I know people are doing their best, but by definition a hospital is a repair factory, and you are next on the assembly line. It has always disconcerted me that nurses and technicians keep coming in and out, asking many of the same questions over and over again. Then there is the matter of those terrific little gowns you get to wear. I have always been tempted to escape from my room and streak bare-assed down the halls, shouting to the other inmates, "Join me, friends, get out while you still can!"

You don't even get to keep your wedding ring these days, so it's just you in your birthday suit with your designer gown and those crinkly paper booties. No props—nothing that makes you any different from any other patient in her birthday suit. Because of all the cold sterilized metal and plastic tubes, you don't feel connected to the Earth in a hospital. But you reason that this is the modern medicine part and that you need it. The rest of the healing—the long quiet days, the building up again, the listening to what your body really needs—that comes later, in the long days when you are alone.

As I lay on the gurney looking up at the white lights in that antiseptic, pea-green, pre-op room, I tried to still my beating heart. I tried not to take myself so seriously that I would miss the chance to laugh and feel my life. There was piped-in Muzak—some unholy rendering of Up with People covering the Rolling Stones—sung with relentless good cheer. I joked with the anesthesiologist about it and we agreed that we would much rather be listening to Motown. Then, as luck would have it, the song changed to Motown and we started to sing out loud. Just me and the handsome, soft-spoken anesthesiologist who smelled of pine boughs. He said he would be there the whole time. I said I was counting on it. He suggested that I stop wiggling to the music while on the table because I was pulling out the tubes.

Do you remember how it is when you go on vacation? Not a traveling vacation, but one of those where you just go somewhere and stay for a while. It takes time for the layers and layers of tired to wear off and float up into the sky, like pieces of campfire ash in the wind. Unwind is the word people use. That word creates a funny image of coming apart at the seams, or of becoming a skein of yarn in the paws of a kitten until you are in strands all over the floor. Presumably you are the same stuff you were before, just strewn out over the armchair, across the kitchen linoleum, and around the legs of the piano. You are the same color, made from the same fiber, but you surely don't roll as fast.

I began to unwind after the red scar across my neck stopped hurting and I could swallow without a grimace. I began to unwind when the initial rush of visitors and phone calls stopped, when the get well cards stopped arriving, and when Patrick stopped calling six times a day from work. I began to unwind one voluptuously lazy day when the radio was off and the dog was asleep at my feet and the dark lawn chair was getting hot in the sun and I was starting to heal. But my body was looking for something higher octane, some metabolic starter fluid—and couldn't find it. I had no energy for anything other than lying on that lawn chair. I was beginning to feel what it is like to not have a thyroid gland.

I decided that I had truly turned a corner when I began to make to-do lists with only a few items on them. Going shopping for dinner became my big event of the day. After having breakfast outside and walking the dog around the block and reading the paper and pulling a few weeds, I began to contemplate the trip. Sometimes, I would ceremoniously produce a pad of paper and sit down to make out the shopping list. One day, after several minutes of thinking about what I wanted to eat, I had a revelation. I could go to the market and buy whatever looked and smelled good. Even when we lived in Italy, I had shopped daily because I had to, not because I understood the concept of eating seasonally. So off I went at a snail's pace to commune with the chard and the cantaloupe and to see who spoke up first and issued an invitation to dinner.

Going shopping like that gave me energy. I could pull my vigor from the foods around me—from the shiny purple eggplant, from the juice-red strawberries with their pretty green topknots. And because I was feeling so invisible to the world, having little or no energy to interact with anyone, I behaved like I was invisible. I grazed like a goat on produce in the store—a green bean here, a berry there. Now when I eat food right from my vegetable garden, wiping off the dirt and popping things into my mouth, I think the attraction to growing my own food was nurtured during those days in the aisles of that market. For the first time, food was real to me. It was as direct as milk from a mother's nipple.

As the weeks went by, I began to have powerful and disturbing cravings. I felt as though I was starving to death, even though I ate everything in the house. My body was looking for something that it used to have and it made me feel unsteady and crazy to be without it. One afternoon at the market, I walked through the aisles like a robot, eyeing all the counters with analytical intensity. Finally, I settled on asparagus, a whole pound of shrimp, and fresh peaches. I don't even like asparagus! The following day, I made an appointment at a spa near our house and selected a seaweed wrap. I had never had a seaweed wrap before, but suddenly it seemed like a good idea. By the next day, I felt renewed and almost back to normal.

The next time I saw my doctor, she scolded me, explaining that by selecting foods so high in iodine and by steaming myself like a tamale in warm seaweed (which is loaded with iodine) I had set my purge back by at least a week. The goal was to get the iodine out of my body; I was not supposed to be finding natural ways to bring it back in.

Without understanding the nuances of the treatment, I had used food to make myself feel good again. What I had done was in conflict with my doctor's plan, but it taught me a valuable lesson: If I paid enough attention, I was capable of integrating my body's own wisdom with mainstream medicine.

But I learned other things too, important things for planting the seeds of compassion in myself. I learned—quite simply—what I will need as I grow old. I discovered that I'll need beauty and stillness, and some intelligent conversation from the heart. I'll need music, books that make me think, and flowers. I'll need big people and little people and animals coming to visit. Most of all, I'll need the tiniest piece of a garden on which to drop a few seeds, water them and wait for the magic of life.

So the days melded together, and gradually St. George retreated to other battlegrounds. His armor had worn thin. He seemed a little foolish trying to take on the great world. The saintly John did not emerge as a viable alternative either. My new muse is a hybrid creation, one who loves both solitude and the fray, imagery from the medieval cloister and the Internet. Now I trust myself and make my own way in the world, stumbling and getting back up again.

It has been many years since the cancer. The doctors will tell you that if you survive without a recurrence for five years, you can call yourself cured. I've never had any doubt about being cured, although I can't tell you why I feel so sure. Maybe because I've felt the disintegration, experienced the invisibility when you are so tired and sick that no one (outside of those who love you) can see you. I have peeked into the future and seen myself old and decided I can live with that. God knows I don't want it anytime soon. But the terrors are gone. I will like that old woman when she comes. She is not an adversary; she is quirky and joyful in a quiet sort of way—she sings with anesthesiologists.

SUSAN TROCCOLO, b. 1950, chronicles the humor and poignancy of aging on her blog, *Life-Change-Compost*. She is the author of *The Beet Goes On: Essays on Friendship* and *Breaking New Ground*. At fifty-five, Susan planned her own birthday gig with a jazz quartet, BBQ, and danced barefoot on the grass. She remembers thinking: *"Now we are getting somewhere."* Susan lives with her husband and their border collie in Portland, Oregon.

Subjective Age: *Since fifty-five was so great, I've decided to stick with it.*

All Grown Up at Last

Barbara Neely

Dear Boomers:

Welcome to sixty-five—and be glad you've arrived. If this were 1911, given the life expectancy back then, you'd more likely be about to have a funeral than a birthday celebration. Of course, every generation creates aging in its own image; now it's your turn. Here are three things I've observed since sixty-five that you might find useful.

1. At sixty-five you are a distilled and aged version of who you've always been: you, only more potent.

As a part of my sixty-fifth birthday, I skimmed my journals from my forties forward—from this vantage point, I consider my pre-forty years part of my childhood. My entries reminded me that the heavy load of fears and foibles I'd once strapped to my back—all those childhood traumas, heartbreaks, disappointments and misconceptions that kept me in a near-perpetual state of self-criticism—had diminished. By sixty-five, this trunkful of angst could fit into a small change purse. Now, as I turn seventy, the change purse is so tiny it gets lost on my desk or left in my jacket pocket for weeks on end, unmissed. It would be nice to report that I was able to ditch my emotional baggage through meditation and sheer willpower. But what really happens, I think, is that—if we're lucky—we grow into ourselves. We become more nuanced, more able to see the shades of gray, the thing beneath the thing. And we have less room for self-defeat, less patience for the useless and unnecessary. So we begin unloading our bags of woe, bit by bit. It's as if the unconscious mind knows that the clock is ticking and we don't have a moment to waste on being anyone other than the person we genuinely are.

2. Sixty-five is as good an age as any to say yes to everything that isn't harmful to you or others. Rewards follow.

If you dream of learning Swahili or taking a walking tour of Paris, go for it. If you can still fit into those hot pants and are still inclined to wear them, it's strictly your call.

One of my throwback urges, as a self-taught author, was to explore what could be taught about writing. So I entered a university MFA program. There were days when I felt as if I'd been thrown into the kiddie pool. But from this experience came many rewards: a stint working with middle school writers, a couple of semesters volunteering as a reading-writing facilitator for a group of adult women and plans to use my new degree to start a program for adult learners in collaboration with community centers and other groups. I hadn't anticipated any of this at sixty.

3. Ignore others' definitions of who or what you should be at sixty-five and beyond. Run your own show, and be on guard against internalized ageism.

One of your generation's most sterling qualities has been its belief in itself. You didn't always get it right, but you fought for what you believed in. Just as you redefined what it meant to be young and socially engaged, I expect (and hope) you will redefine what it means to be post-sixty-five. I urge you to include a resurgence of the kind of sociopolitical activism that has brought us to a place where women's equality is no longer a total oxymoron and a family of color occupies the White House. I look forward to your doing your thing once again.

Remaking seniorhood in your own image won't be easy. Someone will try to make you feel bad about not dyeing your hair, or about dyeing your hair. Someone will insist that you are too decrepit to do whatever they hope to exclude you from, or what they want you to shut up about.

Worst of all, there will be days when you will look in the mirror with astonishment, if not horror. Get over it. One of my solutions is to look in the mirror more often, smile at the lovely lady and hope I look as good as she does when I reach her age.

BARBARA NEELY, b. 1941, is the author of the Blanche White mystery novels, the first of which won the Agatha, the Macavity, and the Anthony —three of the four major mystery awards. Neely's short stories have appeared in anthologies, magazines, and journals. She is currently writing a series of short stories, a novel, a play, and a monologue. Neely is also a proud board member of The Colored Girls Museum in Philadelphia.

Subjective Age: *I've graduated into agelessness, so I don't have a subjective age. But if I had to choose one, it would be sixty-five: old enough to let my freak flag fly with gusto and wise enough to know when to furl it.*

THE
7Os

The Changing Contract

Charles Handy

It was a day laden with romance, of anxiety mixed with joy. It was our wedding day. We had made promises to each other, raised glasses, cut a cake and waved goodbye to assembled guests. We were on our way.

To what? We had never sat down and talked about it, about what it would be like, who would do what and what would be the priorities. We were good together. We would go on being good together. No need to spoil it all with plans and job descriptions as if it was a business. Being fifty years ago, it was just assumed that my career would have priority, would determine where we would live and how we would live. She, Elizabeth, would have the main responsibility for the home, and for the children when and if they came. Whatever interests and talents she would develop, and there were to be many, would have to be fitted into her domestic priorities and my life. I assumed that she thought so too. I don't remember asking her.

Looking back, it was incredibly selfish of me, particularly as my career took me into ever more absorbing areas, from business to academia to the Church. What added to the problem was that each job came with less, not more, remuneration than the last. That left Elizabeth to fill the growing financial gap, which she always and valiantly did, running her own interior design business and later leasing and letting out a succession of small apartments, all whilst still managing the home front.

As one result, I never gave her any money to buy food or household necessities. She took care of all those out of her earnings, leaving me to look after the regular outgoings, the mortgage, the utilities, the repairs and, of course, the booze. That was unusual. My father had given my mother a regular monthly allowance, which she was expected to account for. I remember her agonizing over her accounts, trying to remember what she had spent on what. A frequent item seemed to be SPG, which I took to stand for the Society for the Propagation of the Gospel, a missionary charity dear to my parents' hearts, until my mother confessed one day that it stood for Something Probably Grub!

In that respect we had moved on, or society had. I was not the boss in the home, even if I was still the main anchor of our lives outside it. Yet, once again, we never formally negotiated these arrangements. They just emerged as circumstances dictated. I am ashamed, now, at how little I contributed to the domestic scene, leaving early in the morning in our only car, returning late in the evening after the children had gone to bed, letting my wife take the children to school on her bicycle, to do all the shopping and housework and still find time for her work. But we were both the children of our time and that was the widely understood pattern of marriage among our friends and colleagues.

Why did we not discuss it more formally, I wonder? We had made that set of vows and promises to each other in front of a bunch of our friends and relatives, a contract to love and care for each other, but the detailed specifics of what and how had never been spelled out. The necessary appendix to the formal contract had been omitted. Like almost everyone else, we made it up as we went along. As we did so, we began to realize that we each had different notions of what that appendix should contain. Because we had never spelled these out, unspoken resentments smoldered and occasionally flared up.

The truth is that every relationship is based around an implicit contract, a balance of expectations. Unless these are spelled out, misunderstandings are inevitable. Moreover, the contracts need to be fair to each party. Many years earlier, in the course of my business career, I had to negotiate a contract with a Chinese agent in Malaysia. We agreed on the terms, shook hands and shared the traditional glass of brandy. I then took out the official company contract form for him to sign. He was indignant. "What is that for?" he said angrily. "Don't you trust me? The contract will only work if both of us get what we want out if it. A signature should be unnecessary. In fact, it makes me suspect that you think you have got a better deal than me and want to lock me in to it."

I persuaded him that it was only a company formality, but I took his point. I have never forgotten it. If both parties don't feel the deal is fair it won't stick, in business or in relationships.

We would have avoided much unhappiness had I remembered my Chinese contract experience, if I had made a series of deals as we went through life, deals that gave both of us enough of what we wanted to ensure that the contract worked. That original Chinese contract was also time limited. It had to be renegotiated in due course. So it is with those implicit marriage contracts. Circumstances change. Jobs change. Kids grow up. People die or fall ill.

So it was for us. When I was fifty I ran out of jobs. There were none that I wanted that might want me. Too early and too poor to retire, I became a self-employed writer and lecturer. The freedom was exciting but the income precarious and I found it embarrassing to ask for it. My wife came to the rescue. She became my agent and business manager and was very good at it. So good, in fact, that I got both busier and richer. Until the day when she in effect gave in her notice. Her life, she said, had become submerged in mine. She had recently graduated with a degree in photography after five years of part-time study, and now wanted to fulfill her dream of becoming a professional portrait photographer. My life was now in her way, even if it had taken her most of the first fifty years of her life to get there. Largely my fault of course.

This time we did sit down to a proper contract negotiation. We agreed to split the year in two. For the six summer months her work would have priority in our diary, with my providing some background support. I would concentrate on research and writing and take on no outside commitments. The winter months would be free for my speaking engagements, with her help in organizing them. Furthermore we decided to split the cooking and catering, with each doing half, she in our London apartment, I in the country cottage. We were fortunate in that we were both independent workers, the children had left home and we were free to organize our lives as we saw fit.

That contract lasted for over twenty years. They were fruitful and enjoyable times. Then circumstances changed again. I was approaching seventy-five, a time when I was required by law to convert my savings into an annuity. That meant that I did not need to earn as much as in the past. I had a pension of sorts. At the same time our children belatedly began to produce grandchildren. I had not realized how rewarding, but also how time-consuming, these little people can be. Clearly, life had to change once more. This time it was going to be more like what people think of as retirement, in that paid work no longer dominated our two lives, but retiring was not how it felt. We were busier than ever, but differently. A new contract was needed.

First there was our work to consider. Since we no longer needed so much money-making work we could afford to do more voluntary work in addition to a continuing rota of lectures and exhibitions. We began to combine our skills and interests on a number of joint pro bono projects, making photo documentaries for voluntary organizations. No longer did we split the year in two because we now worked together. Then there were the grandchildren. We needed to make time for them, partly to give their parents time off. That was good work, but it was assuredly work and work we did together. Living now on a fixed and probably declining income we also needed to simplify our way of life, downsizing and discarding instead of accumulating. So much that we had once done now seemed unnecessary, even pointless. Life moves on and leaves a lot behind.

It was important, therefore, that we took time to reflect on how best to use the remaining years in our life, now that ambition was pointless and achievement meant something different than worldly success. People turn philosophers as they age, wondering what the purpose of it all is, whether it was all wasted effort, what is still left to do. Energy may be declining but you hope that wisdom, or rueful experience, has increased. These last years are precious years and we needed to make the most of them. The new contract needed careful thought.

I have long seen the shamrock, the three-leafed Irish plant, as an import-ant symbol, three leaves combining to make a whole. I have used it in a variety of contexts but now I wanted to use it to describe how it might define our purposes at this stage in our lives. The three leaves would be Body, Mind and Spirit. Together they would make for a fulfilling life, the whole shamrock, with Money providing the stalk, the essential support that we would be stupid to ignore. There had to be enough money, but money was always going to be the means and never the end, never the point.

The Body is crucial. When the body crumbles everything stops or changes. We resolved to eat less and exercise more. Easier to say than to keep to, but we try. To have regular check-ups was another resolution. Troubles spotted early are more easily dealt with. Body and Mind interact. An active Mind both needs and makes a healthy Body. There is much research that shows how work keeps one fit. A recent study by the Institute of Economic Affairs found that those who described themselves as fully retired, doing no active work, were forty percent less likely to describe themselves as having very good health compared with those still working. More worrying, the chance of a diagnosed medical condition rose by sixty percent if you were not working, and depression by forty percent. Work exercises the Mind.

Work also provides us with a social network, or rather several of them. That is important to the Spirit. The Chinese have a saying that happiness is having something to work on, someone to love and something to hope for. These three ingredients are, to us, what makes life worth living. It gives us a purpose, a purpose which for us is increasingly focused on the next generation and our hopes for them and their descendants, both in our family and wider. Life without others seems meaningless, so we have resolved to give as much time as we can to seeing old friends and family. Loneliness is the new poverty of the developed world. We are determined that we shall not suffer from it but we have to invest in others if we are going to matter to them.

Of course, we are the fortunate members of a fortunate generation. Many will envy the apparent ease of our lives, although it did not seem easy at the time. Not everyone will have the freedom to make the choices we did. But whatever our circumstances we all have choices. If we are lucky enough to be in a relationship those choices have to take account of the other person. And they need constant revision as our lives change. Otherwise they won't work. We learned that the long way, often the hard way. But it was worth it. I sometimes say, half seriously, when others are talking of their second or third marriages, that I, too, am on my third marriage. But, in my case, they have all been to the same woman, and that has made all the difference.

CHARLES HANDY, b. 1932, is a leading business thinker, social philosopher, writer and broadcaster. He has had a varied career, starting out as an oil executive and later becoming a professor and then the voice of Radio 4's *Thought for the Day*. Charles has been married to his wife Elizabeth for more than fifty years. They have two children and four grandchildren.

Subjective Age: *I am chronologically eighty-four but most days I feel about sixty-four. After standing at some wretched reception for over an hour I begin to feel my real age. Still, I am playing tennis, badly, and I am still rushing around the world speaking to polite audiences—I am off to California tomorrow.*

A Country for Old Men

Edward Hoagland

More and more I've been concluding that by middle age most people in this country have sculpted their lives so they'll land about where they aimed to. The few who genuinely aspired to be rich or famous will probably become so for a spell, and those who wished for comfortable stability will find themselves with tradecraft competence, a web of friendships, grandchildren. The pleasures of versatility are their own reward for "well-rounded" folk, much like committing a couple of decades to the responsibilities of raising kids. You acquire traction and smile lines, with perhaps a well-grooved marital banter. Two by two, Noah's Ark is said to have been boarded—pairings being the easiest equation for many of us to handle, after all. And in an era of chaotic governance and commonplace mendacity and meltdown, the ambition to excel seems a bit stunted. Hoe your own row is more the message than grabbing for a brass ring, though self-expression can become as crosswise as the old children's game of pick-up sticks. While the country splits, compounding its fractures left to right, we accommodate ourselves to zany loads of debt, outlandish overcrowding—trading trains for planes, for example, till both are drastically less fun and the roads alternatively an anthill, as blue-collar as well as white-collar families look for a hideaway, a second home.

In pick-up sticks the player plucks colored sticks singly from a pile of forty dropped helter-skelter on the table, down to the last, but without ever displacing any he isn't immediately after; if he does, the other player takes over, himself attempting to score. It resembles negotiating traffic, or the ballet of the sidewalk, threading throngs. Pedestrians finesse potential collisions by swinging slightly sideways, smiling distantly, parting the phalanx by body-language adjustments. There's nature; and then for phenomena like crowds, our second nature.

Homey imperatives such as steering kids through school, wage haggling, and good-neighborliness keep us from obsessing about what may be unraveling elsewhere: that plus our widened sense of travel—Florida, Calabria, Patagonia, Indonesia. There can be a knockabout anomie to shuttling around, and the density of our egos remains a problem, the clamoring holler to build McMansions. People wished to flaunt their first million, nibbling holes in any town, and our tribalism historically has wanted the other guy clamped underneath a heel, not just to stay in his own valley. Though tribalism lies in shards in this global epoch, the shards are still sharp, when you consider that nearly 3,000 New Yorkers, dying in an act of war earlier in this decade, received a thousand times as much attention as the five million or so killed in Congo's wars.

A cross-stitch of mercenary and sexual greed has marked the opening of the new century, plus a flight toward cyber-reality, which is to say the notion that I think, therefore I am. Such an idea has seemed absurd to me since I was in college, taking a first philosophy course but spending part of each day outdoors, where the seethe of life still swamped merely thinking about it. It continues to, on every library or movie or chat-room screen. We are dragging our anchors, whatever they happen to be—landscape or literary, folklore or ethical. Dick Tracy, Natalie Wood, and Babe Ruth morph into Sweeney Todd, Britney Spears, and Barry Bonds. The new fluidity, air-conditioned, unhinged from nature, cracks open opportunities for entrepreneurial idealism as well as greed, perhaps, in response to rolling famines, flood zones, mud zones, and the scalped forests and subsiding aquifers. Youngish activism rather than rootless self-exploration. The dwindling contexts that we operate in—whether it's water tables, tree cover, religious deference, historical reference, family continuity—makes for a kind of Queen of Hearts croquet, where the wickets, balls, and mallets all dash around in goofy, friendly-fire exchange. When Biology eventually has her say it may no longer simply be something, like cancer, we fight against; there may be hell to pay; the gamble is how much we can destroy without triggering an abyss of consequences. Extinctions—do they matter more than aesthetically? A warming climate? We truly don't know what's about to become the bottom line of that. And will the damage remain as constrained as along an avalanche track, or be multiplex? You might as well ask Thomas Jefferson or Johnny Appleseed, outdoorsmen both. If they thereupon sniffed the wind and looked for birds—What happened? Is no space left?—and you showed them instead the marvels inside a digital box, would they feel reassured that democracy had worked?

It has in the sense that I don't know a lot of older Americans who didn't get just about what they genuinely sought. Most of course set the bar pretty low—from modesty, timidity, inconsistency, indifference—or else were pursuing normalcies like love and family, children, friends and sports, which good humor can obtain without one doing too well on exams or achieving the stratospheric business success that risks a Humpty Dumpty fall. Life is going to go okay when rapport serves as well as sleepless ambition and if the person can weather the occasional divorce or job loss. Indeed, we seem to be engineered for it, and our setting the bar customarily low explains why human nature, human history, don't significantly improve. Yet by not expecting much, most of us age with considerable contentment—I've been noticing lately at senior-center lunches and church suppers—and even die with a bit of a smile, as I remember was often the case during a year I worked in a morgue in my twenties.

EDWARD HOAGLAND, b. 1932, is an author best known for his nature and travel writing. He has published over one hundred short stories and essays and has been included in nearly as many collections. Hoagland, the recipient of two Guggenheim Fellowships, was elected to both the American Academy of Arts and Letters and the American Academy of Arts and Sciences. He has published five books in the past six years, which may set a record.

Subjective Age: *Physically, I'm an octogenarian but mentally, for some inexplicable reason, I seem to be still in my prime.*

Into the Seventies

Gloria Steinem

Updating *Doing Sixty* almost a dozen years later is a way of talking with a previous self. Indeed, I wish I'd taken stock this way at a younger age—sort of a metaphysical version of cleaning for company, then wishing you'd done it before—but this feels especially crucial now that I know more every day, yet come ever closer to the unknown.

Even mentioning the unknown is a change. Well into my fifties, I had ignored aging in a way that was great for activism. At sixty, I was thinking about aging and leaving the center of life. At just past seventy, I'm conscious of the time I have before leaving it altogether; not at all the same thing. Even if I live to be a hundred, as I have every intention of doing, I will have less than thirty years to go: the same time I spent working on *Ms.* magazine, fewer years than I've lived in my current apartment, and about the same time I've been wearing my favorite pair of blue jeans.

To put this another way, aging feels like a process of the body, the concrete, the comparable, the mind. Making death real for even a millisecond feels like a mystery of the heart.

I'm not presuming that my experience is the same as yours. Everything that makes us unique—belief, culture, health, companionship, economics, hope, heredity—creates different paths on this universal journey. What I say here may be really helpful or really not. But I do have infinite faith in talking to each other. After all, we are communal creatures who must mirror each other to know who we are. Every living thing ages and dies, yet humans seem to be the only species that thinks about aging and thinks about dying. Surely, we are meant to use this ability, especially in a country that suffers so much from concealing aging and dying as if they were the last obscenities.

In retrospect, I realize that I, too, was in the Olympics of denial, yet some part of me needed to know the stages of life. Perhaps because I switched roles early and became the caretaker of my loving and sad mother, or because I didn't measure time by the usual periods of marriage, parenthood and the kind of career you retire from; perhaps because I didn't see a death early in my small family, or because I got so good at escaping into books and imaginary futures—for all these reasons, the central years of adulthood seemed as if they could stretch on forever.

I used to joke that I thought I was immortal and this caused me to plan poorly. Of course, part of me knew this was no joke. Now that distance allows me to see patterns, I notice that I've always been trying to figure out these secrets.

At twenty-five or so when I came to New York to be a writer, I fell in love with Muriel Spark's *Memento Mori*, a little gem of a novel about a group of friends in London who are all connected by careers, marriages and affairs. Because they are now over seventy, gossip that once focused on work or sex has centered on who is losing which faculty. Each person has specific fears about aging and death, so we watch as each fearful imagining comes true.

I bought copies to give to my friends because I knew we had something to learn here. The message begins when a threatening phone caller announces to one character at a time, "Remember, you must die." Most of the friends respond with fear, outrage, even calls to Scotland Yard, but there are two exceptions. A woman novelist, disdained by the group because she is barely able to remember if she had her tea, yet envied because her writing is being rediscovered by a new generation of readers, infuriates her friends even more by insisting that her caller was "a very civil young man." For the first time, we realize the various voices were each friend's personification of Death.

Then there is a retired inspector, asked by his friends to help find this caller or group of callers, who delivers the message: "If I had my life over again, I should form the habit of nightly composing myself to thoughts of death. I would practice, as it were, the remembrance of death. There is no other practice which so intensifies life. Death, when it approaches, ought not to take one by surprise. It should be part of the full expectation of life. Without an ever-present sense of death, life is insipid. You might as well live on the whites of eggs."

I wanted to be exactly like the inspector or the novelist.

I sensed that I would be profligate with time until I admitted it had an end—not just for other people, but for me, too. Nonetheless, in my heart, I didn't believe it for a minute. Life stretched before me without end. I lived in the future. I wasted time.

Change seems recognizable only after it's happened, like putting one's foot down for a familiar stair—and it's not there. It had taken a lot of living, plus time to metabolize that living, plus seeking out role models of great old women, plus realizing that my body knew how to age even if I didn't, to realize that the "endless" central years of life were over. A whole new and unimagined country lay beyond.

I don't know if the inspector and the novelist could have learned their wisdom earlier. But for me, it was only after I'd become an old lady myself that I lost the habit of imposing my sentimental interpretation on old people. Only after I knew I needn't have children myself could I see them as short people and potential friends. Only after I'd connected with both ends of the spectrum did I understand why, as Native American and other ancient cultures tell us, the very young and the very old have more in common with each other than with people in the central years. Both are closer to the mystery.

With another decade of perspective, I see that long years of ignoring the calendar and living outside the generational loop may have finally found a deeper use. They weren't so realistic at the time, but combined with a new sense of mortality for balance, they yield some valuable lessons. All come under the general heading, "Time is relative":

• As you may have noticed when taking a new journey, the way there seems very long, yet coming home by the same route seems much shorter. That's because newness stretches out our experience of time, but familiarity shortens it. From this, I've learned a kind of intimate version of Einstein's Theory: If time is relative, doing new things actually makes us feel we've lived a longer life.

- I used to think that generations had to do only with age. Parents were always parents, children were always their children even after they grew up, and that was that. But over the years of the women's movement, I've noticed that daughters who grew up with feminism in the air and water are often older than their own mothers who did not. Because the daughters were encouraged to use their own will, find their own talents, they are grown-up in a way that wasn't encouraged in an earlier generation. Even when their mothers find their talents later in life, go back to college, or otherwise blossom into a life once denied them, the daughters are immensely proud of their mothers, but as if they were their children. In other words, generations are relative, too.

- The valuing and naming of time is also relative, thus we speak of a passage like menopause in terms of loss. In fact, what women lose in those menopausal years is everything we needed to support another person. What we keep is everything we need to support ourselves.

- My inability to plan had little to do with living in a hazy future, and more to do with a lack of power and control. By my forties, I'd realized that planning ahead was one of the most reliable measures of class. Rich people plan for several generations forward; poor people plan for Saturday night. By that measure, even women born into powerful families are often lower class. They give control of their lives over to husbands, children, community, society.

In those years, I thought the sole answer was for women to take more control of our futures, and for men—especially powerful men—to learn the flexibility and spontaneity that women in general and the poor in particular have overdeveloped into an art form. Both are still goals; everything is about balance. But I realize now that the art of living in the present is not so much controlling time, it's losing track of time.

This is most likely to happen when we surrender to something we love to do: not because it's a demand, or an emergency, or an inability to do anything else. Seeking out what we love so much that we lose track of time when we're doing it—that goes beyond Einstein's theory and puts us into his life. He loved his work so much that he had to be careful while shaving; otherwise, he cut himself when a spontaneous idea struck.

That is a hint of the timeless Now.

GLORIA STEINEM, b. 1934, is a feminist writer, lecturer, and political activist. She is a co-founder of *Ms. magazine* and the Women's Media Center and the author of eight nonfiction books. Her essays and articles have appeared in dozens of anthologies and nonfiction collections. She was a contributing editor to *The Reader's Companion to U.S. Women's History*, and her 2015 memoir, *My Life On the Road*, was a bestseller.

Dogs, Cats, and Dancers: Thoughts about Beauty

Ursula K. Le Guin

Dogs don't know what they look like. Dogs don't even know what size they are. No doubt it's our fault, for breeding them into such weird shapes and sizes. My brother's dachshund, standing tall at eight inches, would attack a Great Dane in the full conviction that she could tear it apart. When a little dog is assaulting its ankles, the big dog often stands there looking confused—"Should I eat it? Will it eat me? I am bigger than it, aren't I?" But then the Great Dane will come and try to sit in your lap and mash you flat, under the impression that it is a Peke-a-poo.

My children used to run at the sight of a nice deerhound named Teddy, because Teddy was so glad to see them that he wagged his whiplash tail so hard that he knocked them over. Dogs don't notice when they put their paws in the quiche. Dogs don't know where they begin and end.

Cats know exactly where they begin and end. When they walk slowly out the door that you are holding open for them, and pause, leaving their tail just an inch or two inside the door, they know it. They know you have to keep holding the door open. That is why their tail is there. It is a cat's way of maintaining a relationship.

House cats know that they are small, and that it matters. When a cat meets a threatening dog and can't make either a horizontal or a vertical escape, it'll suddenly triple its size, inflating itself into a sort of weird fur blowfish, and it may work, because the dog gets confused again— "I thought that was a cat. Aren't I bigger than cats? Will it eat me?"

Once I met a huge, black, balloonlike object levitating along the side-walk making a horrible moaning growl. It pursued me across the street. I was afraid it might eat me. When we got to our front steps it began to shrink, and leaned on my leg, and I recognized my cat, Leonard; he had been alarmed by something across the street.

Cats have a sense of appearance. Even when they're sitting doing the wash in that silly position with one leg behind the other ear, they know what you're sniggering at. They simply choose not to notice. I knew a pair of Persian cats once; the black one always reclined on a white cushion on the couch, and the white one on the black cushion next to it. It wasn't just that they wanted to leave cat hair where it showed up best, though cats are always thoughtful about that. They knew where they looked best. The lady who provided their pillows called them her Decorator Cats.

A lot of us humans are like dogs: we really don't know what size we are, how we're shaped, what we look like. The most extreme example of this ignorance must be the people who design the seats on airplanes. At the other extreme, the people who have the most accurate, vivid sense of their own appearance may be dancers. What dancers look like is, after all, what they do.

I suppose this is also true of fashion models, but in such a limited way—in modeling, what you look like to a camera is all that matters. That's very different from really living in your body the way a dancer does. Actors must have a keen self-awareness and learn to know what their body and face are doing and expressing, but actors use words in their art, and words are great illusion makers. A dancer can't weave that word screen around herself. All a dancer has to make her art from is her appearance, position, and motion.

The dancers I've known have no illusions or confusions about what space they occupy. They hurt themselves a lot—dancing is murder on feet and pretty tough on joints—but they never, ever step in the quiche. At a rehearsal I saw a young man of the troupe lean over like a tall willow to examine his ankle. "Oh," he said, "I have an owie on my almost perfect body!" It was endearingly funny, but it was also simply true: his body is almost perfect. He knows it is, and knows where it isn't. He keeps it as nearly perfect as he can, because his body is his instrument, his medium, how he makes a living, and what he makes art with. He inhabits his body as fully as a child does, but much more knowingly. And he's happy about it.

I like that about dancers. They're so much happier than dieters and exercisers. Guys go jogging up my street, thump thump thump, grim faces, glazed eyes seeing nothing, ears plugged by earphones—if there was a quiche on the sidewalk, their weird gaudy running shoes would squish right through it. Women talk endlessly about how many pounds last week, how many pounds to go. If they saw a quiche they'd scream. If your body isn't perfect, punish it. No pain no gain, all that stuff. Perfection is "lean" and "taut" and "hard"—like a boy athlete of twenty, a girl gymnast of twelve. What kind of body is that for a man of fifty or a woman of any age? "Perfect"? What's perfect? A black cat on a white cushion, a white cat on a black one . . . a soft brown woman in a flowery dress . . . There are a whole lot of ways to be perfect, and not one of them is attained through punishment.

Every culture has its ideal of human beauty, and especially of female beauty. It's amazing how harsh some of these ideals are. An anthropologist told me that among the Inuit people he'd been with, if you could lay a ruler across a woman's cheekbones and it didn't touch her nose, she was a knockout. In this case, beauty is very high cheekbones and a very flat nose. The most horrible criterion of beauty I've yet met is the Chinese bound foot: feet dwarfed and crippled to be three inches long increased a girl's attractiveness, therefore her money value. Now that's serious no pain no gain.

But it's all serious. Ask anybody who ever worked eight hours a day in three-inch heels. Or I think of when I was in high school in the 1940s: the white girls got their hair crinkled up by chemicals and heat so it would curl, and the black girls got their hair mashed flat by chemicals and heat so it wouldn't curl. Home perms hadn't been invented yet, and a lot of kids couldn't afford these expensive treatments, so they were wretched because they couldn't follow the rules, the rules of beauty.

Beauty always has rules. It's a game. I resent the beauty game when I see it controlled by people who grab fortunes from it and don't care who they hurt. I hate it when I see it making people so self-dissatisfied that they starve and deform and poison themselves. Most of the time I just play the game myself in a very small way, buying a new lipstick, feeling happy about a pretty new silk shirt. It's not going to make me beautiful, but it's beautiful itself, and I like wearing it.

People have decorated themselves as long as they've been people. Flowers in the hair, tattoo lines on the face, kohl on the eyelids, pretty silk shirts—things that make you feel good. Things that suit you. Like a white pillow suits a lazy black cat … That's the fun part of the game.

One rule of the game, in most times and places, is that it's the young who are beautiful. The beauty ideal is always a youthful one. This is partly simple realism. The young are beautiful. The whole lot of 'em. The older I get, the more clearly I see that and enjoy it.

But it gets harder and harder to enjoy facing the mirror. Who is that old lady? Where is her waist? I got resigned, sort of, to losing my dark hair and getting all this limp gray stuff instead, but now am I going to lose even that and end up all pink scalp? I mean, enough already. Is that another mole or am I turning into an Appaloosa? How large can a knuckle get before it becomes a knee joint? I don't want to see, I don't want to know.

And yet I look at men and women my age and older, and their scalps and knuckles and spots and bulges, though various and interesting, don't affect what I think of them. Some of these people I consider to be very beautiful, and others I don't. For old people, beauty doesn't come free with the hormones, the way it does for the young. It has to do with bones. It has to do with who the person is. More and more clearly it has to do with what shines through those gnarly faces and bodies.

I know what worries me most when I look in the mirror and see the old woman with no waist. It's not that I've lost my beauty—I never had enough to carry on about. It's that that woman doesn't look like me. She isn't who I thought I was.

My mother told me once that, walking down a street in San Francisco, she saw a blonde woman coming towards her in a coat just like hers. With a shock, she realized she was seeing herself in a mirrored window. But she wasn't a blonde, she was a redhead!—her hair had faded slowly, and she'd always thought of herself, seen herself, as a redhead … till she saw the change that made her, for a moment, a stranger to herself.

We're like dogs, maybe; we don't really know where we begin and end. In space, yes; but in time, no.

All little girls are supposed (by the media, anyhow) to be impatient to reach puberty and to put on "training bras" before there's anything to train, but let me speak for the children who dread and are humiliated by the changes adolescence brings to their body. I remember how I tried to feel good about the weird heavy feelings, the cramps, the hair where there hadn't been hair, the fat places that used to be thin places. They were supposed to be good because they all meant that I was Becoming a Woman. And my mother tried to help me. But we were both shy, and maybe both a little scared. Becoming a woman is a big deal, and not always a good one.

When I was thirteen and fourteen I felt like a whippet suddenly trapped inside a great lumpy Saint Bernard. I wonder if boys don't often feel something like that as they get their growth. They're forever being told that they're supposed to be big and strong, but I think some of them miss being slight and lithe. A child's body is very easy to live in. An adult body isn't. The change is hard. And it's such a tremendous change that it's no wonder a lot of adolescents don't know who they are. They look in the mirror—that is me? Who's me?

And then it happens again, when you're sixty or seventy.

Cats and dogs are smarter than us. They look in the mirror, once, when they're a kitten or a puppy. They get all excited and run around hunting for the kitten or the puppy behind the glass…and then they get it. It's a trick. A fake. And they never look again. My cat will meet my eyes in the mirror, but never his own.

Who I am is certainly part of how I look and vice versa. I want to know where I begin and end, what size I am, and what suits me. People who say the body is unimportant floor me. How can they believe that? I don't want to be a disembodied brain floating in a glass jar in a sci-fi movie, and I don't believe I'll ever be a disembodied spirit floating ethereally about. I am not "in" this body, I am this body. Waist or no waist.

But all the same, there's something about me that doesn't change, hasn't changed, through all the remarkable, exciting, alarming, and disappointing transformations my body has gone through. There is a person there who isn't only what she looks like, and to find her and know her I have to look through, look in, look deep. Not only in space, but in time.

I am not lost until I lose my memory.

There's the ideal beauty of youth and health, which never really changes, and is always true. There's the ideal beauty of movie stars and advertising models, the beauty-game ideal, which changes its rules all the time and from place to place, and is never entirely true. And there's an ideal beauty that is harder to define or understand, because it occurs not just in the body but where the body and the spirit meet and define each other. And I don't know if it has any rules.

One way I can try to describe that kind of beauty is to think of how we imagine people in heaven. I don't mean some literal Heaven promised by a religion as an article of belief; I mean just the dream, the yearning wish we have that we could meet our beloved dead again. Imagine that "the circle is unbroken," you meet them again "on that beautiful shore." What do they look like?

People have discussed this for a long time. I know one theory is that everybody in heaven is thirty-three years old. If that includes people who die as babies, I guess they grow up in a hurry on the other side. And if they die at eighty-three, do they have to forget everything they've learned for fifty years? Obviously, one can't get too literal with these imaginings. If you do, you run right up against that old, cold truth: you can't take it with you.

But there is a real question there: How do we remember, how do we see, a beloved person who is dead?

My mother died at eighty-three, of cancer, in pain, her spleen enlarged so that her body was misshapen. Is that the person I see when I think of her? Sometimes. I wish it were not. It is a true image, yet it blurs, it clouds, a truer image. It is one memory among fifty years of memories of my mother. It is the last in time. Beneath it, behind it is a deeper, complex, ever-changing image, made from imagination, hearsay, photographs, memories. I see a little red-haired child in the mountains of Colorado, a sad-faced, delicate college girl, a kind, smiling young mother, a brilliantly intellectual woman, a peerless flirt, a serious artist, a splendid cook— I see her rocking, weeding, writing, laughing—I see the turquoise bracelets on her delicate, freckled arm—I see, for a moment, all that at once, I glimpse what no mirror can reflect, the spirit flashing out across the years, beautiful.

That must be what the great artists see and paint. That must be why the tired, aged faces in Rembrandt's portraits give us such delight; they show us beauty not skin-deep but life-deep. In Brian Lanker's album of photographs *I Dream a World*, face after wrinkled face tells us that getting old can be worth the trouble if it gives you time to do some soul making. Not all the dancing we do is danced with the body. The great dancers know that, and when they leap, our soul leaps with them—we fly, we're free. And the poets know that kind of dancing. Let Yeats say it:

O chestnut-tree, great-rooted blossomer.
Are you the leaf, the blossom or the bole?
O body swayed to music, O brightening glance,
How can we know the dancer from the dance?

URSULA K. LE GUIN, b. 1929, lives in Portland, Oregon. She has published twenty-one novels, eleven volumes of short stories, four collections of essays, twelve books for children, six volumes of poetry and four of translation. Le Guin has received many honors and awards, including the Hugo, Nebula and PEN/Malamud awards.

That Face in My Bathroom Mirror

Gordon Weaver

That is no country for old men.
—W. B. Yeats, "Sailing to Byzantium"

The male's awareness that one is aging—the certitude that one has aged—comes in small, but cumulative increments, starkly dramatized from time to time by epiphany-like shocks. The routine of morning ablutions, for example, is interrupted, without warning, by a freeze-frame glimpse of one's visage in the bathroom mirror, mid-shave or mid-rinse, wholly unanticipated. Who is that? Is that me? Indeed it is. Face it!

Women, by custom, may and do retard or mitigate such evidence in their vanity's glass—dyes and moisturizing lotions, cosmetics and cosmetic surgeries, chemical injections. But male pride, also by custom, requires a stoic survey of the evidences of the ravages of Time.

One's hair, once a crowning glory, has evolved into a ragged, thinning cap, the hairline having crept upward and backward. Glossy auburn richness has faded to a streaky, dingy gray. Is that me? The custom of masculine courage demands an honest attention to detail. Face it.

How came that sallow complexion (intensified by fluorescent lighting)? When did laugh lines degenerate into indelible furrows in the brow, alongside the mouth, at the eyes' corners? The nose is decidedly more prominent, as are the ears (from which sprout clumps of bristle as snowy white as one's whiskers). Lips once seductively plump have compressed to a thin, pale line more suggestive of anger than resolve. Yellowing teeth are longer. And eyes, once bright with expectation and delight, are now muddy, purging in sleep, as Hamlet said of Polonius, rheum, one's vision reliant on the assistance of ever-thicker bifocals. And one's throat has risen, dewlap seeming intent on swallowing the chin above.

Elizabeth I, in her sixties, termed by Raleigh "a woman surprised by time," had her palace mirrors removed, of course to no avail. Just so, one shuns reflective surfaces (shop windows, polished metal or wood) and expresses reluctance to be caught in candid snapshots, averts one's glance, feeling vaguely shamed, when producing a picture ID to board an airplane or cash a check. Family albums stay on the shelf, dramatizing as they do, year by decade, all that has been lost. Or, put another way, that went away. The supermarket checkout clerk, on the other hand, asks for no identification, simply ringing up the obvious geezer's senior discount. Time.

It is easier, for shorter or even longer periods, to ignore—if not forget—the gross remainder of one's corporeal self. But honesty, an aspect of courage for either gender, compels itemization:

One's skin, over hands, arms, torso, legs, shines an almost luminescent white, speckled randomly overall with (pre-cancerous?) wens. And the backs of those hands display nascent liver spots and the irremovable tobacco tinge on the first and second digits of one's smoking hand. And to flex a bicep is to invite at worst depression or, at best, comic ridicule. Joints: the creaking, knobby knees, the puckered gathering at elbows of something akin to medium-grade sandpaper, the dull ache that flares or persists across one's lower back. Buttocks—be grateful for small mercies!—have shrunk to hollows rather than ballooned. Long legs that once carried one with some grace and some speed on the hardwood court or playing field have morphed into fragile pipestems, horny feet and gnarled toes. The body, as Richard Pryor put it (or was it Ali?), should sue these legs for non-support.

Most any exertion, no matter how slight—bending to pick a pencil off the carpet, reaching high to change a light bulb leaning too far left or right—provokes an audible, unwilled grunt, followed by a stifled sigh of relief, and resignation. And one's height has diminished an inch, maybe two, this loss accentuated by an incipient dowager's hump. Visible in profile or full frontal, one's gut sags too low to be sucked up, what Farrell's Studs Lonigan called an alderman. Oh the gluttony, oh the drink!

Honesty. Consider within this too unsolid flesh.

One's breath is halt—oh the unfiltered Camels! The voice is scorched to a rasp after too many exuberant words. AM and PM hacking like a sick cat, wheezing like an asthmatic, are routine. A once cast-iron stomach, fond of hot spices, rich sauces, and every variety of meat, now grumbles and rumbles after even bland fare, sending forth an involuntary chorus of burps and belches ill-concealed behind a clenched fist. And oh the fits of farting, near-impossible to suppress in polite company! Satisfactory defecation is now a daily goal and ordeal. A bladder once capacious necessitates a bathroom stop before even short-distance travel, a ritual one remembers imposed by parents in childhood. The urgent need to urinate rouses one from sleep often enough to suggest (knock wood!) a failing prostate or (knock again) the onset of diabetes.

Do be honest! One's member is no longer consistently erect upon waking. Viagra and like supplements tempt, but the caution that erections lasting more than four hours should be reported to one's physician (as well worthy of informing the Guinness Book of Records?) puts paid to such notions. Still there are pills (cholesterol, blood pressure), and over-the-counter nostrums (Tums, Maalox, Alka-Seltzer, Pepto Bismol).

And as with the body, so goes the mind.

The quality of sleep has degenerated. Instead of the solid six-eight hours, slumber is broken into larger or smaller bits and pieces; micturation signals through dreams in which nature's call is loud and clear, narratives placing one in frantic search of a lavatory that never materializes, or pissing a stream accompanied by an electric buzzing and vibration; with no discernible cause, one wakes suddenly and fully, the prospect of further sleep improbable at best. Dawn's first light in the bedroom window gives notice it's over for yet another night. Utterly gone is the ability to crash hard, sleep off a late-night carouse or recover from unaccustomed physical exertion.

And one's recurring dreams are now ridden with futility and fear. Again and again, one is stricken with paralysis when flight from danger is called for. Weapons misfire, strength fails, answers to profound questions elude. Now, in place of the usual bizarre violent action or randy sex, dreams are peopled with faces and names not consciously recalled for decades: childhood friends, grammar school teachers, old army buddies, long-dead relatives come from the grave to mystify and tease and torment. And what of the frequent dreams in which one has committed unpardonable sins or crimes, the fear of exposure lingering for moments after the shock

THAT FACE IN MY BATHROOM MIRROR | GORDON WEAVER

of waking, dissipating to a foolish gratitude that none of this was real?

What source, save for aging, explains the loss of restorative sleep? To sleep, as the Bard had it, perchance to dream; but the raveled sleeve of care is not knitted up.

Out and about in the quotidian world of wakefulness, one enjoys longer or shorter spans of forgetfulness, untroubled by the facts of life, the fact of aging. But as in the bathroom mirror, come moments not to be denied, unbidden, unprovoked—or so they seem.

The aged are everywhere, in the aisles and at the Piggly Wiggly checkout. They annoy, irritate. "Why must that frail granny pause her cart directly in one's path? Why must that wizened gramps take so long to write a check with trembling hand? Why does that doddering ancient back up his car without looking behind him first? Does that scrawny or semi-obese septuagenarian not realize how absurd her too-red or too-black hair coloring looks? Does that shuffling codger not know his spider's legs, purple-veined, are pathetic in walking shorts?" On senior-discount day, the canes, walkers, and motorized chairs abound.

In the midst of one's arrogance and intolerance, a discomforting insight floods one's consciousness; these pensioners are one's peers! How, the question strikes one, am I attired, coifed? Does my gait betray me? Is there a tremor in my digits as I pluck at bills in my wallet? Am I one of them? Indeed. Face it.

And though there are palliatives for the body, pills for cholesterol and blood pressure and constipation, aspirin regimen, periodic upgrades in prescription eyeglass lenses, no relief exists to ease the chaos that assaults one's mind.

Senior Moments are scary. There are times you can't recall the title of a favorite poem or the name of a former colleague. Does noun-failure signify something truly sinister just over the horizon? A list of the day's errands is worthless if one forgets to pocket it before leaving to shop, and worthless, when pocketed, if one neglects to consult it, finds it still in that pocket after returning home.

Worse is the realization that curmudgeonly scorn threatens to become a permanent mindset toward the surrounding world. Politics, local, national, international, are swamps of corruption, nests of vipers, theaters of the absurd, asylums of the insane. Culture is Big Business in a mask. What once gave joy now annoys and angers. Art is pretense and self-indulgence and exhibitionism. One's neighbors not yet past the bloom of youth are utterly uninteresting and unattractive. How came contemporary fashion and music and literature to be so superficial, so blatantly stupid, effete, and hollow? Why have civility, manners, and style disintegrated? One cannot even ogle the nubile, indulge a propensity for the fleeting pleasure of thought-lechery, without feeling shameful, a classic Dirty Old Man.

A retreat into one's past—nothing in the present suffices, a future unimaginable—fails to console. Examined from an aged man's perspective, successes now seem trivial, failures monumental. Regret is a nagging companion; what was foolishly attempted, what wrongly pursued, what wholly undone. Like Charlie Brown at bat, why didn't I swing, why did I just stand there? The past is just that: past. Children are grown, rightly and totally embedded in their own lives. One will never know grandchildren too young who live half a continent away. And there are too many already dead in the past, family, friends, the celebrated and the obscure.

Reading the daily obituaries is a fixed routine. How old? Of what cause? An acquaintance? A morbid habit one cannot seem to break.

And when one looks squarely into that bathroom mirror, what's behind that worn face? A vision, a glimpse of the dark at the end of the tunnel.

Face it.

GORDON WEAVER, b. 1937, is a retired English professor and the author of four novels and ten story collections. He lives in Pewaukee, Wisconsin.

Subjective Age: *I am in denial about crowding eighty—do people really live that long!?!—since, subjectively, I'm in the midst of puberty.*

On Not Wanting Things

Jane Miller

My favorite sweater, brown and from Gap, is unraveling, on its last legs, in its death throes. I can't quite throw it away, or not until I'm sure it's absolutely beyond help, so I wear it to write in and to go swimming, usually with a dark, long-sleeved T-shirt under it to disguise or anyway mitigate the holes in its elbows. I'm wearing it now. It needs elbow replacements, as I've needed knee replacements. But if I were to go to the department that sells leather patches to sew on its elbows I'd have to do something about the ragged sleeve ends that I roll up out of the way, and then these improvements would entail doing something about the neck and the bottom of the sweater, and so on and on. It needs, as I need, a clinic where all its drawbacks can be attended to at the same time, where someone could weigh the pros and cons of keeping it alive or letting it go: give an official verdict. Perhaps I would then be able to discard it or give myself over to its total renovation. Or even buy a new one.

This business of not wanting new things is beginning to unnerve me. I have lots of horrible old clothes with all too much wear left in them. They're relics from when I went to work every day, and I stopped doing that twelve years ago. So, though I'm nowhere near the position of King Lear's poor, bare, forked animal, I'm not quite far enough from being one of those old women whose clothes are fairly clean and tidy, but unimaginably out of date—several really serious sartorial decades out of date. I try to believe that my old flared jeans are back in fashion, that a granddaughter or two might be taken in. But they won't be. My flared jeans are subtly and disastrously different from anything they would consider wearing, and they're not quite 'Vintage' either.

Luckily, perhaps, my clothes were never very fashionable in the first place, though now I come to think of it I had some wonderful high brown boots that cost me £6 in the early '60s. I wore them to go to New York to stay with my sister Rachel, when we were both pregnant with babies who are now at least forty-five. Jonathan, my sister's husband, introduced these two enormous sisters to people we met as Jane and Rachel Miller, without explaining that we weren't both married to him and bearing his children simultaneously. What happened to the boots? They went with a long brown coat and a white sheepskin hat that made me imagine or hope that I looked a little like Anna Karenina.

It goes against nature not to want new clothes: I used to want them badly and all the time. I remember in the war that once you'd spent almost the whole of a season's clothes coupons on an item of school uniform you'd be lucky to squeeze in a blue rayon dress with cap sleeves and a pair of heavy brown walking shoes; and these with tap dancers' metal segs affixed to toe and heel to stop you wearing them out too fast. So I grew up dreaming of clothes and later made some for myself from paper patterns: proper dresses with belts and zips and darts and buttonholes, and once an elaborate strapless evening dress with bones in it that I made for going to balls at university and never wore. I bought some beautiful black velvet jodhpurs in the '60s and a little later two skin-tight dresses with flared skirts designed by Mary Quant or Biba, that made you look as if you might be going skating.

My four granddaughters would rather shop than do anything else in the world, and one of them wondered especially idly the other day whether it might be possible to do a PhD in shopping, and of course it would. While I can hardly bring myself to go into a shop these days! If I do, I become instantly restless and despairing. There is nowhere to sit, nothing to want and absolutely nothing to buy. I congratulate myself when I actually manage to buy something, relieved that it is still possible, that I am able to part with money in exchange for something I didn't have before and don't need. When I get home with my new treasure I invariably discover that I already have several versions of the thing I've just bought: a black polo-necked sweater, Converse trainers, and so on. I have a page at the back of my diary for noting down things I've bought, and so far this year I've bought nothing for myself except two toothbrushes, some cough linctus and yesterday (what a triumph!) a suitcase on wheels. I went on an expedition the other day in my brown suede Converse trainers with yellow cut-out stars, in the hope of finding another pair just like them. But shoes like mine have long since gone out of fashion, and I came back empty-handed.

When I do manage to buy something, the pleasure I get from it is mainly in the thought that it will 'see me out,' that this might be the last pair of socks, the last shirt, the last sweater I will ever need to buy. I am definitely on my last car. And far from feeling cast down by that thought I am restored by it to smugness and warmth, like some cozy, hibernating Beatrix Potter character, Mrs. Tiggy-Winkle, perhaps, sensibly squirrelling away (if hedgehogs can be said to do that) for the winter ahead. The job's done, time has been saved, and I am braced for all weathers, floods, earthquakes and terrorist attacks.

And there was I, worrying that I don't want things any more. I do seem to want to stay alive, though it's hard to imagine a long life stripped of all covetousness. I might stop wanting breakfast, for instance, or my bed, or company of any kind. There must be things I want, just as there were things Rupert Brooke loved. Perhaps I should list them as he listed his best things. Except that the things I want are not really on the cards. They're things like a swimming pool under the basement of my house, some decent teeth and going to India every year on a magic carpet rather than in a Virgin airplane. And I don't really even want those things much. I feel about my house rather as I feel about my clothes. Apart from its own swimming pool, it lacks for nothing that I can see. Yet most of the houses in the street where I live undergo nearly total renovation every other year or so. The changes are often so radical that the owners have to move out for months while the builders move in. As a result of my neighbors' most recent thoroughgoing transformations, I too have had several bits of my house painted, inside and out. I find myself doing little sums about how old I'll be before anyone is likely to point out that it needs painting again.

. . . .

What I'm laboriously getting round to, I suppose, is the fact that the main thing I don't want any more is sex. This is a relief, but also a surprise. And I wonder whether desire for things and people, covetousness, longings, are all aspects of narcissism, or rather, whether they are all feelings related in some way to pleasure in one's self. If I had known when I was young that a time would come when I would get no pleasure from inhabiting my body or looking at it, and no excitement at the thought that it might be admired and even desired by someone else, especially if delectably adorned—or entirely unadorned—I suspect I would have thought it not all that worthwhile continuing to be alive. Something like that, no doubt, sends my delectable granddaughters on their shopping sprees. It's true that when I had such feelings of pleasure and sheer interest in myself they were spasmodic, and often frail and challenged. They were, after all, precisely the part of one's being most vulnerable to dips and depression, to losses of confidence. But they were there constantly, if only as memory and hope. Without wanting things and without feeling that there was something potentially attractive and, yes, desirable, about one's clearly otherwise unremarkable self, it would have been hard to be in the world, to enjoy it, to love and like other people, to long for them, to face the future with avidity and energy. It can't be a coincidence that one should be stripped of desire and of being desirable and desired more or less in one fell swoop. Rather a good arrangement, really. But if it makes for peace, it also feels like an absence, a removal of one significant way of being in the world, perhaps even a loss: though perhaps not a loss of any greater significance than the loss of a front tooth.

Presumably people do go on living quite comfortably without narcissism, self-love, vanity? But without libido? Because I can no longer detect it in myself I suddenly realize what people mean by 'libido.' Not just desire, but a sort of greedy and even competitive energy. That's what I don't have any more. I always thought 'desire' an embarrassing word: I knew perfectly well what it meant, but I couldn't bring myself to use it. If it contained some kind of swooning, blissful, heavenly sensation, it also had something barbaric and grasping about it, a fierce fury to have what one wanted in the teeth of opposition and of what other people wanted. And has it just disappeared? Has the heart grown old?

Something very like desire is indeed missing now, altogether gone: so much so that I can hardly remember having such feelings, and I have to work hard to create some simulacrum of them in myself in order simply to pass muster as an adult female human being and avoid causing dismay to my nearest and dearest. But far from regretting the absence of such feelings, I am happier, easier, lighter without them. I was often buoyed up by sensations of longing and wanting. They gave potential excitement to my waking up, to a new day, a new week, a new year. But all that wanting was distracting, contradictory, laced with tripwires and danger. It entailed competition, fear of failure, risk, jealousy, embarrassment.

So there are real gains in being shorn of it. I was sometimes so busy wanting things, people, love, praise, that I stopped looking at things, didn't notice trees and birds and buildings, as I do now. I forget people's faces these days and can't remember what they were wearing when I last saw them. Forgetfulness, no doubt, but also inattention, lack of interest. If there are gains in all this, and there are, it is also excluding and strange having to adjust to the disappearance of sex as a preoccupation when there is so much of it still going on in the world, visibly as well as invisibly. There are women of my age who have boldly, and usually shamefacedly, confessed to wanting sex now, preferably with a beautiful young man. I see the point of the beautiful young man, but none at all in the sexual act, though I'm greeted on most mornings by emails inviting me to enlarge my penis or purchase quantities of cheap Viagra, and my communicants, whose names change with each message, tell me they are nice girls, who just want to be my friend. Could they imagine that for me those messages are simply a daily reminder of what I don't want any more?

I remember how warmed I could be just thinking and dreaming about sex, never mind wanting and having it. I also remember laughing at a friend of mine who seemed to regard sex as a bit like Ovaltine, good for sending you to sleep. And then I remember realizing, probably quite late and in my twenties, what power it had over you and having to think all over again about everyone I knew in the light of that belated discovery. How troublesome we have all found its sheer force and insistence and how carefully we've disguised our interest and excitement. And how hopelessly it inclined one towards some people and not others, often regardless of their manifold charms or disadvantages. Now I am detached and curious, and I have rather solemnly to remind myself that various kinds of inexplicable human behavior may well be provoked by untrammeled or over-trammeled sexual feeling of one kind or another. I read about love and attraction and people being in the grip of feelings they can't control, and I recognize what I read as you might recognize the general layout of a town you visited years ago or the rough storyline of a novel you read in your teens. Every now and again I read about very, very old people falling in love and looking forward to a rejuvenated sex life. I am astonished. I hear too that there are people as old as I am who go in for Internet dating, and that it's possible for them to find far more suitable mates online than they would if they left it to catching someone's eye at a party or on a bus.

It seems—when I think about it now—that as a young woman I was required to insert and contain my thoughts and feelings about sex within a curiously particular set of rules and regulations, which were never clearly articulated, were hard to make out, but also hard to resist. I remember feeling that my job was to reflect and even to act out a role created for me by the fantasies of strength and domination that any young man was bound to feel he ought to possess and exhibit; and that, by and large, my dreamy foreshadowings of what sex would be like were to be dismissed as thoroughly beside the point. There was, above all, a rash of D. H. Lawrence at the time. His novels were read by some of my male contemporaries as injunctions to have as much sex as possible. Nothing much was specified as to what this actually meant or why it was such a good thing, though as a friend of mine pointed out to me recently, Lawrence seems to be suggesting in *Lady Chatterley's Lover* that there's nothing like a daily dose of buggery for awakening and activating a woman's sexual desire. The question of possible conception was simply ignored (though I suppose buggery could be said to address this problem, if a little circuitously), perhaps because D. H. Lawrence himself was probably infertile.

This aspect of the times coexisted with other unclear, indeed unspoken, instructions. I knew that my parents had married because they thought my mother was pregnant. This, as it happened, turned out not to be the case, and I was born towards the end of their first year of marriage. Yet my mother quite often suggested that it would be better not to have sex until I was married, and both my father and my grandfather warned me at different moments about the intentions of the young men I was likely to meet at university—from, it seemed to me, some personal knowledge of what such young men were likely to be up to. Perhaps we all move into new kinds of anxiety when we become parents. Almost all the young women I knew in my college had affairs with men, sometimes serially, and in one or two cases with several at the same time, thereby occasioning farcical scenes, in which we all cheerfully collaborated, with young men whisked in and out of cupboards and boiler rooms in order to avoid detection or ugly scenes. The young women who didn't have lovers were thought likely to be lesbian or religious or strange in some way, or just resting. So we were liberated and thought of ourselves as liberated: a claim that seems to me both astonishing and mysterious when I consider it now. What did I think I knew that earlier generations had not known? And who had liberated me and from what?

I am also amazed at how patiently we waited to be approached and chosen by men rather than approaching and choosing them, how meekly we undertook to guard, all on our own, against having babies, without any help from men, and how uneasily yet apparently willingly we— or perhaps I should say I at this point—consented to this inequality and imbalance in the interests of remaining trouble-free, popular and desired by men, who were in the vast majority at my university. We could easily have done a Lysistrata, denying ourselves *en masse* to these lusty Lawrentian undergraduates. You resisted or you succumbed, and when you succumbed you didn't discuss what you were doing with the person you were doing it with, nor did you talk much about it with your women friends. All this, I think, in the interests of what would now be thought of as 'cool,' but also, of course, out of the most intense embarrassment, uncertainty, confusion, which I think of in hindsight as, collectively, the most powerfully determining array of feelings I experienced in those days. I have ever since thought of myself as hopelessly, but also shyly and uneasily, seduced by male desire and by the elaborate justifications that flourish in the world for its constant and free expression. So that over the years it has become difficult, if not impossible, to know whether fitting in with all that—as its object but also as its apparent champion—made it impossible to consider what I really wanted for myself. There was certainly a mismatch in my case between my apparent sophistication and my actual control or understanding of what I was getting into, physically, emotionally, even socially, and how this would affect my future life.

Not only do I think that in most respects my experience was very like that of my contemporaries, in this country anyway. I think that most young men and women are swept along by the narrative about sex that prevails among their contemporaries in the crucial years, their late teens and early twenties, and probably also by some form of resistance to what their parents have counseled on the subject or demonstrated in their own lives.

So I did not feel terror but perhaps I should have done. I trusted to an alien rhetoric, I sometimes think, that was deaf to my experience and interests, and which could not accommodate my sexual feelings and needs or even allow me to consider them at all seriously. Accepting sex as above all natural, securely protected from the artificialities and contrivances of everyday life, was essential to all this, the sine qua non. From Lawrence we learned to skirt the dangers of 'sex in the head,' so that the worst thing of all was to think or talk about sex. To protest would not only have been to argue with D. H. Lawrence, it would have been to defy nature. The deal, though, the reason why I and other young women put up with all this, was because we were flattered and excited by men's desire for us. I feel now that if I was taking foolish risks and putting myself outside any safe place where such matters could be helpfully and generously discussed, I had only myself to blame. And I was relatively chaste compared with some of my friends. But I was exposed to the possibility of finding myself in a situation of extreme intimacy with the person least able to help me sort out my contradictory feelings about what was going on, precisely because of the way his feelings were implicated too.

I've almost never heard of anyone enjoying their first sexual encounter. Most of us, however, survive it, though perhaps less and less often with the person involved in that first, doomed episode. Perhaps I am being unfair to my young self just because I no longer recognize the emotions and the longings which guided me then, and because I am sometimes as much in the dark about that young woman in the late 1940s and early 1950s as I am about my granddaughters today and their burgeoning sixteen-year-old selves.

JANE MILLER, b. 1932, first worked in publishing, then as an English teacher and finally at the London University Institute of Education. She retired as Professor Emeritus in 1998 and subsequently wrote *Crazy Age: Thoughts on Being Old*, "as a way of convincing myself I really am old."

Losing Ground

Gail Godwin

The nurse who is going to appraise me for a "cutting-edge" home care policy is due at one, but when I return home from errands at twelve thirty, her Explorer is parked in the driveway. "I started early in case I got lost!" she calls brightly, sliding down from the driver's seat to help me with my packages. She is a vigorous woman in her prime with a thick mane of blond hair, dressed in loose, colorful clothes.

She accepts a glass of ice water, and we take adjacent seats at the dining table. She unpacks her briefcase and lays out papers. She takes my blood pressure sitting (127/80) and standing (126/90), writes down all my medications (I have lined them up so she can copy right off the labels), and then asks a long list of questions:

"Do you: have frequent headaches, spells of dizziness, stomach pains? Need help climbing stairs, going to the bathroom, shopping? Of course I can see you don't. I've been watching you move, but I have to ask anyway."

Her name is Theresa. ("With an 'h.' Take out the 'h,' you take out the heart.") She's a home care nurse herself, works five cases at a time, and conducts these interviews for the insurance company on a part-time basis.

At her request, I offer up my own list of imperfections: pacemaker since 2003 for skipped heartbeats; mother, maternal grandmother, and grandfather had heart disease.

"What about your father?"

"Oh—ah—suicide." Feeling the need to qualify: "But otherwise he was in excellent health."

"Now, some of these questions will seem silly to you, but bear with me. What is your complete name? Address? What state are we in? What is the date? Repeat this series of numbers after me." Next come multiplications, additions, and subtractions, done in the head.

"Now I'm going to show you a series of ten flash cards. On each card there's a word. I want you to make a sentence with each word. Then in ten minutes I'm going to ask you to recall as many of those words as you can."

CHIMNEY. "The chimney is on the house."

TABLE. "The table is in the dining room."

HARP. "The harp is in the dining room."

SALT. "The salt is on the table."

If I can keep all the words under the same roof—even better, think of them all in the same room, I can remember them as part of a picture/story.

FLOWER. "The flower is in a vase on the table."

TRAIN. "We hear the train passing outside."

RING. "The ring is on my finger."

MEADOW. "The meadow is outside the window."

CARPET. "The carpet is under the table."

BOOK. "The book is on the table."

During the ten-minute waiting period, Theresa and I talk about the gambling aspect of these long-term home care policies. "You want to die at home with your familiar views and no horrible institutional lighting and no one taking away your individuality," I say, "but when you're imagining this future, you can't quite get your mind around the fact that you may be much altered from the you who is now projecting this future. You may be blind and unable to see any views or be disturbed by the institutional lighting. You may be gaga enough not to care where you are—or even to know you are an individual. But now you feel that if you can just qualify for the policy and get to stay at home, you'll go on being yourself and everything will be all right." I tell Theresa how antsy my Robert got each time he was in the hospital. "If he could just get back home, he felt, he would be safe." I also tell her about my mother's promise to God: "If he would keep her out of a nursing home, she would do everything she could to help the people in them while she was still able to wield some clout, which she did."

"And did he keep his part of the deal?" Theresa is eager to know.

"Yes."

Theresa tells me a bit about her life. Like me, she was in her early twenties when her father committed suicide. Her mother died at forty-nine from undiagnosed kidney cancer. Her husband divorced her after thirty years of marriage, and it hurt. But she believes that everything that happens to her, no matter how painful, has a reason. Whenever she starts fretting about what might happen, she makes an effort to "change her flow of thought." It's possible, she says, but you have to work hard at it. She is fifty-six and has five visits to homes per day. She does what nurse things have to be done and coordinates the whole home care plan for each patient. She loves her work.

It would be nice to have someone like Theresa coming here every day in that vaguely imaginable future in which I am, in some vaguely imaginable way, homebound. ("Now, Gail, you need to stop fretting about that right now and change your flow of thought. It takes work, but you can do it! Meanwhile, how about a cup of tea?")

The ten minutes are up. I visualize the scene I have created. First the CHIMNEY on the house, the TABLE on the CARPET in the dining room. The vase with the FLOWER, and the BOOK and the SALT and the RING on the finger of someone at the table. And the MEADOW and the TRAIN passing by outside. "How many is that?" I ask.

"That's nine. You're doing really well."

"I can't get the tenth. I give up."

"Well, if you're sure, it's—HARP."

"That damned harp! Who keeps a harp in the dining room?"

"But you did exceptionally well. Believe me, you really did."

It turns out she has left her mother-in-law in the Explorer. "But you should have brought her in," I protest. "She could have been sitting on the terrace all this time."

"No," explains Theresa, "we're not supposed to do that during the interview. But I'd like to bring her in now."

She returns with a tiny, vibrant lady in an ankle-length black skirt, black stockings, and elegant embroidered jacket. ("Theresa bought this for me. She has such good taste.") She praises the house in what sounds like an Irish accent, but no, she's English, met her American husband in Plymouth on D-Day, was married for sixty years. "He was wonderful, and I miss him terribly. I'm broken-hearted that my son isn't married to Theresa anymore, but she will always be my daughter."

"Do you need to go to the bathroom, Mother?" Theresa asks.

"Already taken care of!" the old lady replies, mischievously swiveling her eyes toward the woods outside.

I walk them out to the Explorer. "We're going to come back to Woodstock and take you out to lunch," the old lady tells me.

Theresa gives me a hug. "You did really, really well, Gail. You are a great lady. No one would ever guess you were seventy-one."

. . . .

The insurance agent calls me in November. I have been turned down for the policy. A representative of the famous company has read through my medical records for the last five years and decided I was not a good risk. "You fall into that category of people who take too good care of themselves," explains the agent, hoping to comfort me. "And the more you keep track of yourself with your doctor, the thicker the paper trail. I'm really sorry about this. Hey, I wanted you to get that policy. That's how I make my living."

First bubbles up the incredulous outrage. The first examination I have ever failed! If I apply to another company, I will have to check the "yes" box next to "Have you ever been turned down for a long-term home care policy?" My record is ruined, and this faceless representative (probably gets a bonus every time she/he roots out a risky applicant) doesn't even know me, hasn't seen the agile way I bop up my front steps laden with packages. Damn it, I got nine out of ten of the memory words, and Theresa says that's exceptional. I just finished a 550-page novel. I lift weights at my gym. I watch my diet.

And so on, staring out the window, until I pass over into what I recognize as the "losing-ground place" in my psyche. I first found myself in this place at the age of eighteen and have been there many times since. It is a place I have learned to pay close attention to.

It is a still, dreary landscape, open and lonely. You look all around you, feel the dry mouth and the pang in your chest, mark your position. You note that you are not in the slightest moved to cry or get drunk or curl up in a ball and seek oblivion. Alertness is all, and you hold on to it for dear life. Alertness is its key attribute. You sense that if you were to stop paying attention you could lose yourself. Though the place is somber, there is plenty of air here; if anything, it's super-astringent. And something else is here with you that you might as well welcome because it's all you have. That something else is your fate, as it stands at the moment, with all the other people in it, and you are fixed in its crosshairs.

Many years after that first time, I would come across this passage in a 1954 letter from Dr. Carl Jung to his good friend Father Victor White:

> A "complete" life does not consist in a theoretical completeness, but in the fact that one accepts, without reservation, the particular fatal tissue in which one finds oneself embedded, and that one tries to make sense of it or to create a cosmos from the chaotic mess into which one is born.

I would note the similarities between Jung's regard for his "fatal tissue" and mine for my losing-ground place. But when I was eighteen, I had never heard of Carl Jung. Currently there was no wise person available to me, though there had been several in the past.

We were living in a tract house in Glen Burnie, Maryland, a suburb of Baltimore. There were about two hundred identical houses in the development, which ran alongside a busy highway. Inside our house were my seven-months-pregnant mother; my stepfather, who had been transferred from chain store jobs six times in four years; my two-year-old half sister; and myself, just graduated as salutatorian from Woodrow Wilson High School in Portsmouth, Virginia. Because of our many moves occasioned by my stepfather's transfers, I had attended six high schools in four years: ninth grade at St. Genevieve's, in Asheville, North Carolina, on the full high school scholarship I had won in eighth grade (and forfeited when we left town at the end of ninth grade); tenth grade in Anderson, South Carolina, where my little sister was born; eleventh grade split between Norview High in Norfolk, Virginia, and Woodrow Wilson in Portsmouth; twelfth grade divided between a first semester at Woodrow Wilson, three weeks in a high school in Louisville, where our family lived in a hotel while my stepfather and his latest boss quickly discovered they were not compatible, then the last two months at Glen Burnie High—and finally back to Woodrow Wilson for graduation.

And now summer was beginning and everyone but me seemed to have a future. My mother was expecting her next child in August. My step-father was starting over in another W. T. Grant store with a brand-new boss he had not yet alienated. That morning I had received a letter from Mother Winters, my eighth-grade teacher at St. Genevieve's, one of the wise figures in my past. She congratulated me on being salutatorian of my class in Portsmouth, asked about my plans for college, and brought me news of some of my classmates at St. Genevieve's. "Pat has received a full scholarship to Duke, Carolyn will be going to Radcliffe, Stuart and Lee to St. Mary's in Raleigh, Sandra to …"

Here I stopped reading and underwent my first losing-ground experience:

You look all around you, feel the dry mouth and the pang in the chest, mark your position.

My position. At that time I couldn't hold all of it in a steady glimpse. If I had tried, it might have defeated me. I might have despaired and harmed myself or somebody else. Fifty-three years later, I find it hard to focus steadily on that juncture in my life. In many ways it was the worst of all because I had so little experience or means of escape. Over the course of my writing life, I have lifted pieces from that time and doled them out to this or that character to deal with. But never all the pieces. I won't reveal all the pieces now, only give a broad narrative summary of the situation.

I was eighteen, good-looking, and smart. I loved learning and was dis-ciplined in my study habits. I had developed a persona to get me through our family's frequent moves. This persona was more extroverted than I; she pretended to far more security than I felt. I became a pro at embellishing and editing my history. Whenever I entered a new school, I "went out" for things I knew I was good at: the school paper, the drama club, paint-ing posters and scenery, entering extramural speech competitions—and, of course, getting high grades. I dated lots of boys, was cagey and "hard to get" until each got exasperated and moved on—usually just as I had begun to appreciate him.

That was the outside of things. Inside our various rented domiciles other dramas were playing out. We were not free people. Our embattled breadwinner was frustrated and angry most of the time. There was no money for us except what he doled out of his wallet. There was no going anywhere except where he drove us. All too frequently the mother and the older daughter were backhanded or knocked to the floor for challenging him. The breadwinner "loved" his stepdaughter, who was twelve years younger than he. He confided this to her in unctuous undertones during "drop-bys" to her room. She would wake to find him kneeling beside her bed, his hand taking liberties.

The mother had shed her former confident self. I had come to consciousness knowing a woman who arrived home on the 10 p.m. bus after her wartime job on the newspaper, a woman who taught college and in her spare time typed out love stories she made up in her head and sent off to an agent, who sent back checks for $100. This powerless woman seemed more like someone I was visiting in prison. Only I was in prison with her. She suffered because there was no money to send me to college; she who had earned a master's degree in English! She made phone calls to a private college in Baltimore to see if I could go as a day student. The registrar said a partial scholarship might be arranged, given my academic record, but where was the rest of the money to come from? There was no "rest of the money," my stepfather reminded us, as though we were dim-witted. He suggested I take a year off and find a job, "maybe in sales work," and save up for the college next year. He added magnanimously that I could continue to live under his roof free of charge.

That's the way the ground lay, that summer morning in Glen Burnie, when the girl sat cross-legged on the bed, the letter from her old teacher clutched in her fist; Pat to Duke, Carolyn to Radcliffe, Stuart and Lee to St. Mary's…

This is your life, but you may not get to do what you want in it.
I can't see a way out of this. Things will not necessarily get better.

That's the kind of language that speaks to you in the losing-ground place, whether it happens to be oppressive living conditions you lack the means to escape from, the crushing realization that someone you love does not love you back, a sudden falling off in health, the loss of prestige in your profession, the death of someone who did love you back—or being turned down for a health insurance policy that would enable you to "die at home"—a code phrase for remaining in control until the end? Or maybe even for cheating death altogether?

. . . .

. . . a distinct sense of loss, a flavor in the mouth of the real, abiding danger that lurks in all forms of human existence . . .

That's Joseph Conrad describing the sensations of the commander of a stranded ship in *The Mirror of the Sea*. Marking one's position in the losing-ground place has been richly chronicled in the literature and religions of the world. In Buddhism—of which I also knew nothing in 1955—the practice of "mindfulness," of bringing your mind completely to bear on whatever confronts it, is considered a form of prayer.

In the novel I just completed, two old nuns are being driven back to their retirement house from doctor visits, and one says to the other, "There was a sentence this morning in that Prayer for Holy Women: 'In our weakness your power reaches its perfection.' What do you think it means, Sister Paula?" Sister Paula thinks for a minute and then replies, "I think it means you have to admit you can't save yourself before you're fully available to God."

In 1955, God was undergoing some very slippery changes in my psyche. He was no longer the comforting heavenly father who was always aware of me, and he had not yet expanded into the "mystery beyond my ken" that I could finally feel comfortable with. All I could be certain of, that long-ago summer morning, was that I could not save myself.

But something else did, something already in place in the "fatal tissue" in which I was embedded—my earthly father, who had spent most of my life being unaware of me. I had sent him an invitation to my high school graduation, though I hadn't seen him since I was a child. Mother said not to expect him to show up, but he did. He and his new wife and his brother drove from Smithfield, North Carolina, to Portsmouth for the ceremony. After that, we began to correspond. Finally, at the age of fifty, he had achieved a stable, though all-too-brief, respite from his troubled life. He had stopped drinking, had married a widow with a prosperous brother-in-law, and was making good money in the brother-in-law's car dealership. He wrote that he would like to know me better. Could I spend a vacation at the beach with them? The vacation turned into my going to live with them in Smithfield and boarding at Peace College in Raleigh. When I was a junior at UNC-Chapel Hill, he killed himself.

> At every age, in every person, there comes a partial imprisonment, a disabling psychic wound, an unavoidable combination of circumstances, a weakness that we cannot banish but must simply accept.
> —Helen M. Luke, "King Lear," Old Age, 1987

When my mother was seventy-five, she divorced her second husband and moved to a condominium. It was her first experience of living alone. She had gone straight from her parents' house to a college dormitory and from there to share her first husband's itinerant life until they parted ways and she set up house with her widowed mother and young daughter until in 1948 she married an ex-GI who was taking her college English class and lived under his various roofs for thirty-nine years, raising their three children.

"How wonderful it is not to have anyone around to tell me what to do," she wrote in her meticulously kept diaries in the new condominium, which she called "The Happy House." She had just begun her forty-eighth notebook at the time of her death. In high school, she had used her diaries to keep secrets from others in a tiny, illegible script. Now she taught herself calligraphy in order to be fully readable. She intended to account for her days and nights in a form meant to be shared. She faithfully caught up if she missed a day. What is remarkable about this record of her two years of independent life is not just the fullness and scope of her activities but how every person on the diary pages comes across as a fully rounded character: each woman and man she regularly visited in nursing homes all over the county; every good-hearted slogger and canny power grabber on the many committees she joined or chaired; the battered women she met and drove to Helpmate shelters. ("Only a year ago, I was where you are now," she told one young woman whose husband had blacked her eyes and dislocated her shoulder. "If I could get out at my age, so can you.")

After I was turned down for the home care policy and had the losing-ground moment, I went into a depression. All I desired to do was sleep. I couldn't find anything I wanted to read, until I remembered my mother's diaries. I fetched them from the file cabinet in the hand-sewn slipcases she had made for them, two at a time, before she mailed them off to me. I had read them while she was alive. I had told her they should be published for their sharp observations and character studies and social history, but she'd said some people might be hurt or offended. Nevertheless, she assented to their being included in my archives at UNC-Chapel Hill, her own alma mater. Now, as I devoured them addictively during three weeks of deepening winter, my curiosity about my future, whatever it turns out to be, revived. Her voice coaxed back to life a fascination for the "fatal tissue" into which I happened to be born. Surely I can do no less with my materials than has been done for me.

On the next-to-last day of 1989, my mother died at the age of seventy-seven, two years into her rich independence, when her car went off the interstate and crashed. Her doctor thought it most likely that her heart had at last given out and that she had never felt the impact.

GAIL GODWIN, b. 1937, is an American novelist, short story writer, and librettist. She is the author of three National Book Award finalists and the bestselling novel, *A Mother And Two Daughters*, which sold over 1.5 million copies. Godwin has been awarded grants from the National Endowment for the Arts and the John Simon Guggenheim Memorial Foundation. In her most recent book, *Publishing: A Memoir*, she reflects on her forty-five years as a working writer. Godwin is currently completing her twentieth novel.

Subjective Age: *I am somewhere between fourteen and eighty.*

After Aging

Walter Cummins

What comes after aging? Most likely the finality of the Monty Python dead parrot sketch: 'E's kicked the bucket, 'e's shuffled off 'is mortal coil, run down the curtain and joined the bleedin' choir invisible!

Considering that alternative, getting old isn't so bad. But it's out there—the inevitable farm waiting to be bought. One of the existentialists—Martin Heidegger, I believe—said something to the effect that a person really doesn't get in touch with his existence until he fully understands that it's not enough to say, "One dies," but that it must be, "I will die."

Sure. But me? I know many people who have died, been close to a number and actually been present at the moment of death. Still, I get up every morning, drink a cup of coffee, read the headlines and the comics, clean the litter box, check my email, and perform the rest of my daily rituals as if I'll be doing them forever. A somewhat rational being, I know it can't go on indefinitely. I can't go on. But Heidegger would be disappointed in me. I don't live with the overriding consciousness of my non-being. Yet I think about it from time to time.

OBITUARIES

When reading the morning paper, somewhere between the Mets box score and the editorial page, I scan the obituaries to see if anyone I know or know of has left us, an occasion to shake my head and tell my wife, "Guess who died." And I also check the ages of the deceased.

On one recent day, among the four full pages of obits, sixty-two names, I mentally sorted the dead into three categories. Donna was forty-four; John, forty-seven; Todd, fifty-five; poor Calvin, only seventeen; and, even sadder, Joseph, only two and a half. These and others make up the group younger than I, strangers I have the perverse satisfaction of outliving.

Benedict was ninety-five; Marie, eighty-eight; Carmine, eighty-six; Joe, ninety-four; Florence, ninety-three. This group gives me a certain amount of comfort, the expectation of possible years ahead. If Benedict and Florence can do it, why not me?

What brings me up short are all those in my age range: Doris, seventy-four; Vincent, seventy-three; Audrey, seventy-three; Martin, sixty-five; Elizabeth, sixty-eight. There I'd be—Walter, seventy-nine, my ended life summed up in five or six column inches, a handful of people shaking heads and tapping the arm of a partner. "Guess who died." Then the paper discarded for recycling.

PHOTOS

Our northern New Jersey daily often prints photos with obits, pictures provided by the family, the subject usually smiling at an age years younger than that at which he or she ceased to be. It must be the way loved ones want to remember them, not gaunt and gasping as they were on their deathbeds.

That's usually the way it is with other people—friends from the past, acquaintances, celebrities. The image in our memories is fixed in time, how they looked in their prime. For us their identities are static, and we're often shocked to see them different, the classmate you last saw when he was twenty now an elderly man. But in our relationships with ourselves we're always in process, our state at the moment what matters most, our understanding of who we are, the past like a novel we once read, most of it far less vivid than the book on our nightstand.

In my wallet I carry a university ID with a picture taken around twenty-five years ago. On the rare occasions I've looked at it in the past, I've thought to myself that I hadn't changed all that much. My glasses are different, tinted aviators long out of style now. But recently I decided to compare that photo with the very recent mug shot on my credit card. That certainly turned out to be a reality check. No doubt about it. I've been transformed into an archetypal aging male.

GYM

I work out, try to make it a priority to spend time at the gym at least three days a week, a ritual I started about ten years ago. Most of my life

I'd never been one for systematic exercise, probably a reaction to my uncoordinated youth, when if I did get into a pickup baseball game, I'd end up in right field with a 50-50 chance of catching the rare fly balls that came in my direction. Then there came a time when men my age were advised to keep in shape.

My start was tentative, just time on a treadmill, a bit embarrassed to be in the midst of all those student athletes decades younger, women with cute tattoos on the smalls of their backs who could run for hours on the treadmill next to mine, bulky guys with thick biceps bearing images of chain links and elaborate crosses who hoisted heavy barbells high over their heads. Me wondering what would happen if I raised the pace on my machine above four miles an hour.

Now I'm on the elliptical trainer, tugging on the weight machines, pushing back on the head and neck extender, no longer thinking that this is no country for old men, no longer wondering if the young, taking a break from being in one another's arms, consider me a paltry thing, a tattered coat upon a stick.

Some days, especially during summer break, most of the men in the gym are geezers like me, a couple looking as if they were retired drill sergeants, bald heads tanned and gleaming. On such days old men have taken over the country, pumping and stepping and lifting in their defiance of mortality.

DIET

I'm fortunate to have a wife with long experience as a medical writer who is nutritionally informed and wants to keep me around. Over the time of our marriage, she's informed and reformed me. We eat healthily, with zero tolerance for trans fats, while minimizing saturated fats and opting for whole grains, yogurt, fresh salads, green vegetables, fruits and nuts. Salt and mayonnaise are anathema to me.

I take vitamins and supplements too, every morning like clockwork: a multiple, calcium with more D, 81-mg aspirin, beta-sitosterol, omega-3, glucosamine/chondroitin. I'm working at it to keep my joints lubricated, my bones firm, my triglycerides in check, my circulation whooshing along.

BLOOD

But like my late parents and siblings, I have a tendency toward high blood pressure, mine medicated as soon as it reached 140 over 90. After trying various combinations, my doc settled on HCTZ (the standard diuretic that keeps me going and going day and night) and a generic ACE inhibitor. They work, keep my pressure artificially normal.

Feeling the call to some version of public service, I started donating blood several decades ago, in total gallons of it. That's how I realized my blood pressure was rising, when the nurse checked me. The first couple of times I assumed it was an aberration, then saw the doctor, who checked me sitting up and lying down and fifteen minutes later. I'd reached a stage in life where I needed pills.

Even medicated I was still able to donate—that is, until I fainted. Not at the blood center but that evening after a potluck dinner with a group of friends. The blood center had called lamenting severe shortages, people in need, even for my mundane O-positive. I considered the donation an excuse to eat a Twinkie, a concoction of sugary pulp I don't even like. Drink plenty of fluids, the nurse advised. Avoid alcohol for two hours.

My intention was to drive home and relax with chilled glasses of flavored seltzer. But a half mile from the blood center, the "Check Engine" warning flashed, followed by a message about a brake light problem. I ended up spending the afternoon sitting in the dealer's service area listening to the inane cellphone conversations of the woman next to me. That should have been a clue that this wasn't going to be my day.

After several hours of conversation and sampling the food—including a glass of white wine, now that far more than two hours had passed— I was standing at a kitchen island listening to a man explain the talks he gave at mathematical conferences when I realized I couldn't think of a single intelligent comment to make, not that I'd have much to say about advanced math in the best of circumstances. But this felt odd, my mind bogged down in mental sludge. Within seconds I was drenched in a cold, clammy sweat, suddenly nauseous.

When I opened my eyes, I found myself sitting cross-legged on the floor, a young woman I had never seen before taking my pulse. She was, I soon learned, the daughter of a guest, an emergency medical technician who lived two houses down and had gotten there in a flash during the time I had been unconscious. About a minute, according to those hovering over me. "I'm going to throw up," I announced; someone handed me a plastic pan, and I did. My wife began applying wet paper towels to my forehead, and cold water ran down my shirtfront.

"I think we should call the rescue squad," the EMT daughter told the huddled group. They nodded, seconding the motion. So, despite my protesting that it was just my lack of fluids, I ended up in the hospital for several days, my heart continuously monitored, my carotid arteries checked with a Doppler test, my ticker evaluated with an echocardiogram.

I was fine, released after great expense to Medicare. But my doc told me to stop donating blood, assuring me that I had given my share, and, besides, I was a man my age.

HOSPITAL

Every time I visit someone in the hospital and see the friend or relative stretched under a white sheet, a plastic ID looped around a wrist, needles in each arm, drip bags suspended behind them, machines blipping, I get the sense of otherness. The person has been transformed into an object to be poked and tested and wheeled about by medical professionals. Strangers performing procedures on you. Volition is gone and, with it, the dignity of being a functioning person. After each visit, I wondered how I would feel when I became the patient.

Until my fainting, I hadn't been in the hospital for decades. At ten I had pneumonia, at sixteen an ear infection, conditions that would be treated at home with drugs these days. In my thirties, I spent a couple of days in for tests. Now here I was delivered by the local rescue squad, lifted from gurney to bed, all the time thinking, This is a mistake. I don't belong here. I want to go home.

In fact, I was only a few days from a flight to Europe and felt compelled to give that information to anyone who tended to me—doctors, nurses, technicians, the women who delivered meals. Even though I had to wear a gown, I kept my pants on, my socks, too, poised for a quick getaway. Fortunately, the last nurse assigned to me had just returned from a trip to the Amalfi coast. We chatted about places, and she sympathized, got me released right after the echocardiogram results cleared me.

Of course, it's quite likely that I'll be a real patient someday, too sick to resist, the nurses grim, my doctor asking if I had prepared a living will.

NURSING HOME

That prospect is even scarier than the hospital. I've visited in bad ones and good ones. In the bad, the residents were lined up in wheelchairs outside their rooms, eyes closed, chins on their chests as if they were drugged, as they probably were. The place smelled of disinfectant and urine. In the good—good in the sense that it cost a great deal, didn't smell and had a location in a very affluent town—when you walked down the hall, you saw many of the residents comatose in their beds, white hair wispy, pale flesh brittle, jaws dropped. Those awake were aligned in front of blaring TV sets gaping at programs so far removed from the state of their existence that they could have been beamed from Mars. Or they might be in a dayroom where chipper entertainers were trying to lead group sings of turns like "I'm Looking Over a Four-leaf Clover," all sound emanating from the people at the piano, a few toothless mouths barely moving.

In my limited experience, by far most of the residents were women. Aged males must be kicking off before they reach that state. Lucky them.

SYMPTOMS

With my blood pressure under control, my doc tells me I'm in good shape for a man my age. How long can that last? Every once in a while I get a pain in my gut or a tightening in my chest. I've had them before, and they've always gone away. A bug in my system, heartburn, gas. But someday I'll have a pain, a throb, a clutching that will be for real. It may be a harbinger of a long decline or a sign of sudden termination. Like all aging men, more likely soon than later, I'm going to die.

WALTER CUMMINS, b. 1936, now finds himself ten years older than he was when he wrote "After Aging." During the intervening decade he survived cancer, which became another subject to write about. In addition to essays, he has published more than 125 short stories and seven collections. He still writes, co-edits a literary press, and teaches in an MFA creative writing program. His goal is to hang around.

Subjective Age: *I think I am on the cusp of maturity.*

THE
8Os

The Overtone Years

William Zinsser

The number eighty-eight, referring to the number of keys on a piano, hovers in our collective memory. I remember a character in a Dick Tracy comic strip named 88 Keys, and I've listened to honky-tonk pianists who call themselves "Mister 88" or who "tickle the 88s."

As anyone who ever played a piano knows, the eighty-eight-note keyboard is our universe, bounded by the highest note that the ear can comfortably enjoy and the lowest note that a crazed Russian composer might compose. To venture beyond the wooden frame that encloses those eighty-eight notes would be to fall off the earth.

Earlier this fall, if asked my age, I could say that I was just as old as the number of keys on a piano. Then, on October 7, I wasn't. I had outlived the standard Western keyboard and the largest piano. But then I was told that Bösendorfer, the Austrian manufacturer of sumptuous concert grands, makes a nine-foot, six-inch model that has nine extra keys at the low end of the scale. I was saved! I had entered the Bösendorfer years.

Those nine extra bass notes almost never get played. But they give the piano a deeper and darker tone because their "strings," which are made of wire, are longer and thicker than the longest strings on a standard piano. They therefore generate overtones, which produce resonances with compatible notes of higher frequency farther up the scale.

So the Bösendorfer years are overtone years. That's as it should be— old age is mostly overtones. Older people have long since played all the necessary notes and musical forms: the joyful capriccios at the birth of a child or the graduation of a grandchild, the somber Bach fugues at the inevitable visits of disappointment and death. We are left only with the overtones of those long-gone events—their endlessly overlapping echoes and vibrations.

As a fourth-generation New Yorker I live with overtones wherever I go. I pass the apartment where my parents lived to their own old age, and the *Herald Tribune* building where I had my first job, and the office where my wife came out of the Midwest to work for *Life*, and the various places where our children went to school and where we all went to church on Sunday. Those places send sympathetic ripples across the decades— intermingled memories of happy and productive times.

Today my city has been dimmed by glaucoma; the landscape is hazy. But my shoes still know the way. Every morning I walk from my apartment to my office, skirting long-familiar potholes and Con Edison excavations, and when I arrive I go to my computer, formerly an Underwood typewriter, as I always have. There I am anchored in my craft. The irrelevancies of the world close down around me and I'm alone with my materials, as the painter is finally alone with his canvas and the potter is alone with her wheel. I now write this column mainly from personal experience and remembered detail, not from external sources. I turn on my computer and I listen for overtones.

WILLIAM ZINSSER, b. 1922, was an American writer, editor, and literary critic. His book *On Writing Well* had sold over 1.5 million copies by the time of his death in 2015 and is widely respected as one of the essential texts on the art of writing. He taught writing at Yale University, Columbia University, and The New School, and was a regular contributor to *The American Scholar.*

Somewhere Towards the End

Diana Athill

One doesn't necessarily have to end a book about being old with a whimper, but it is impossible to end it with a bang. There are no lessons to be learned, no discoveries to be made, no solutions to offer. I find myself left with nothing but a few random thoughts. One of them is that from up here I can look back and see that although a human life is less than the blink of an eyelid in terms of the universe, within its own framework it is amazingly capacious so that it can contain many opposites. One life can contain serenity and tumult, heartbreak and happiness, coldness and warmth, grabbing and giving—and also more particular opposites such as a neurotic conviction that one is a flop and a consciousness of success amounting to smugness. Misfortune can mean, of course, that these swings go from better to bad and stay there, so that an individual's happy security ends in wreckage; but most lives are a matter of ups and downs rather than of a conclusive plunge into an extreme, whether fortunate or unfortunate, and quite a lot of them seem to come to rest not far from where they started, as though the starting point provided a norm, always there to be returned to. Alice's life swung in arcs far more extreme than most, but still I feel it may have followed this pattern. I suppose I think it because I have seen other lives do that, and I know that my own has done so.

Not long ago a friend said to me that I ought to be careful not to sound complacent, "because," he added kindly, "you are not." I believe he was wrong there, and that I am, because complacent (not to say smug) I certainly started out during a happy childhood wrapped warmly in my family's belief that we were the best kind of people possible short of saintliness: a belief common in the upper levels of the English middle class and confirmed by pride in being English, which I remember deriving from an early introduction to a map of the world. All those pink bits were ours! How lucky I was not to have been born French, for example, with their miserable little patches of mauve.

This tribal smugness was not, of course, a license to rampage. Like all such groups, ours had its regulations which one had to observe in order to earn one's place among the Best. Apart from all the silly little ones about language and dress, there were three which went deeper: one was supposed not to be a coward, not to tell lies, and above all not to be vain and boastful. I say "above all" because that was the rule against which infantile rumbustiousness most often stubbed a toe: "you are not the only pebble on the beach" might have been inscribed above the nursery door, and I know several people, some of them dear to me, who still feel its truth so acutely that only with difficulty (if at all) can they forgive a book written in the first person—about that person's life.

I soon came to see our tribal complacency as ridiculous, and can claim that I never slipped back into it, but the mood it engendered is another matter: it was based on nonsense—on wicked nonsense—but it was sustaining, it made one feel sure of oneself. I was robbed of that mood (by being rejected, more than by seeing through class smugness and imperialism, though that must have modified it a good deal), and such a deprivation—the smashing of self-confidence—whatever its cause, makes a person feel horribly chilly. Now, however, having become pleased with myself in other ways, I recognize the return of the comfortable warmth I knew in early youth. If this is smugness, and I can't help feeling that it is, then I have to report that I have learned through experience that, though repulsive to witness, it is a far more comfortable state to be in than its opposite. And comfort one does need, because there's no denying that moving through advanced old age is a downhill journey. You start with what is good about it, or at least less disagreeable than you expected, and if you have been, or are being, exceptionally lucky you naturally make the most of that, but "at my back I always hear/Time's wingèd chariot hurrying near," and that is sobering, to say the least of it. For one thing, it's a constant reminder of matters much larger than oneself.

There is, for example, the thought quite common, among us who are old: "Well, thank god I shan't be here to see that!" Try as you may not to brood about global warming, there it is, and it doesn't go away because I shan't see much of it, or because, having no children, I don't have to worry about their experience of it . . . All that happens when I try to use that for comfort is the looming up of other people's children. I suppose there is a slight relief in the knowledge that you, personally, will not have to bear it, but it is unaccompanied by the pleasure usually expected from relief.

And that capaciousness of life, the variety within it which at first seems so impressive—what does that do after a while but remind you of its opposite, the tininess of a life even when seen against the scale of nothing bigger than human existence? Thought of in that light the unimportance of the individual is dizzying, so what have I been doing, thinking and tapping away at this and that? I too, as well as my dear disapprovers, ask that question—though with a built-in expectation, I must admit, of justification.

Because after all, minuscule though every individual, every "self" is, he/she/it is an object through which life is being expressed, and leaves some sort of contribution to the world. The majority of human beings leave their genes embodied in other human beings, others things they have made, everyone things they have done: they have taught or tortured, built or bombed, dug a garden or chopped down trees, so that our whole environment, cities, farmland, deserts—the lot!—is built up of contributions, useful or detrimental, from the innumerable swarm of selfs preceding us, to which we ourselves are adding our grains of sand. To think our existence pointless, as atheists are supposed by some religious people to do, would therefore be absurd; instead, we should remember that it does make its almost invisible but real contribution, either to usefulness or harm, which is why we should try to conduct it properly. So an individual life is interesting enough to merit examination, and my own is the only one I really know (as Jean Rhys, faced with this same worry, always used to say), and if it is to be examined, it should be examined as honestly as is possible within the examiner's inevitable limitations. To do it otherwise is pointless—and also makes very boring reading, as witness many autobiographies by celebrities of one sort or another.

What dies is not a life's value, but the worn-out (or damaged) container of the self, together with the self's awareness of itself: away that goes into nothingness, with everyone else's. That is what is so disconcerting to an onlooker, because unless someone slips away while unconscious, a person who is just about to die is still fully alive and fully her or himself— I remember thinking as I sat beside my mother "But she can't be dying, because she's still so entirely here" (the wonderful words which turned out to be her last, "It was absolutely divine," were not intended as such but were just part of something she was telling me). The difference between being and non-being is both so abrupt and so vast that it remains shocking even though it happens to every living thing that is, was, or ever will be. (What Henry James was thinking of when he called death "distinguished," when it is the commonest thing in life, I can't imagine—though the poor old man was at his last gasp when he said it, so one ought not to carp.)

No doubt one likes the idea of "last words" because they soften the shock. Given the physical nature of the act of dying, one has to suppose that most of the pithy ones are apocryphal, but still one likes to imagine oneself signing off in a memorable way, and a reason why I have sometimes been sorry that I don't believe in God is that I shan't, in fairness, be able to quote "*Dieu me pardonnerai, c'est son metier*" (God will forgive me. It's his job), words which have always made me laugh and which, besides, are wonderfully sensible. As it is, what I would like to say is: "It's all right. Don't mind not knowing." And foolish though it may be, I have to confess that I still hope the occasion on which I have to say it does not come very soon.

DIANA ATHILL, b. 1917, had a distinguished career as a book editor. She also won the National Book Critics Circle and Costa Biography Awards for her memoir *Somewhere Towards the End*. Her other books include *Instead of a Letter, After a Funeral, Stet,* and *Alive, Alive Oh!,* which contains Athill's *Guardian* piece on entering a care home at ninety-two. In January 2009, she was presented with an OBE. She lives in Highgate, London.

Our Last Drive Together

Frederick Buechner

It was while my mother was staying with us in Vermont that the fatal phone call came. It was from Incoronata, the woman who for years had been her factotum and mainstay in the New York apartment that she rarely left except for occasional visits to us or trips to the doctor or the hearing aid people who were always selling her new models, none of which, she said, were any damn good.

Incoronata must have spent hours working herself up to it because I'd barely lifted the receiver when she dropped her bombshell. She said she was quitting. She said she'd had all she could take. She said there was nothing more to say. And then she said a good deal more.

She told me my mother said such terrible things to her that I wouldn't believe it if she repeated them. She said she had to work like a slave and never got a word of thanks for it, let alone any time off. She said her live-in boyfriend threatened to walk out on her if she stayed on the job a day longer because in her present state she was giving him ulcers. She was getting ulcers herself, she said. And no wonder. She said she had left the key to the apartment with one of the doormen because she would not be needing it again to let herself in. And that was that. She said she was on the verge of a nervous breakdown.

I could feel my scalp run cold at the thought of my mother's reaction and said everything I could think of to make Incoronata change her mind. I told her my mother was devoted to her no matter what terrible things she said. I told her the whole family was devoted to her. I told her that when people got old and deaf and started falling to pieces, they said things they didn't mean and then felt awful about it afterward. I said I didn't know how my mother could possibly manage without her, how any of us could. I said we would give her a raise and see to it that she got more time off. But by then she was so close to hysterics I don't think she even heard me.

So I changed my tactics and begged her at least to stay on till we could find somebody to replace her, at least to be there when we got back from Vermont to help my mother unpack and get resettled. But if she did that, Incoronata said, she knew my mother would find some way to make her stay, and with her nerves the way they were she simply couldn't face it. So there was nothing more to say, and we finally hung up.

The question then became how to break the news to Kaki, which was what her grandchildren called my mother as eventually all of us did. To have told her then and there would have been to ruin the rest of her visit for all of us, so we decided to wait till I had managed to find somebody else to replace her and then not breathe a word till we had gotten her back to her apartment where there would be another Incoronata waiting to welcome her and she would simply have to accept the new state of things as a *fait accompli.*

My brother Jamie, who lived in New York too, came up by bus to help with the historic drive back. There was the usual mound of luggage piled out on the lawn—the suitcases with bits of brightly colored yarn tied around their handles to identify them, the plastic and canvas carry-alls, the paper shopping bags from Saks and Bonwits stuffed with things like her hair dryer, her magnifying mirror, extra slippers, and so on. There was the square Mark Cross case she kept her jewelry in and the flowered duffel bag with her enormous collection of pills and assorted medicines together with a second like it which was full of all the things she needed for making up her face in the morning. She said it was all of it breakable so for God's sake not to put anything heavy on it and to be sure to put her long black garment bag in at the very end so it could lie flat on top of everything else and her best clothes wouldn't end up a mass of wrinkles.

We put her white plastic toilet seat extender behind her on the back seat like a wedding cake in case she needed it on the way. She kept her straw purse on her lap with things she might want during the journey like her smelling salts and Excedrin and the little flask of water in case she started to choke. She also had me put a can of root beer in the cup holder because she said root beer was the only thing that helped her dry throat. The final thing was to get Jamie to stuff her little velvet, heart-shaped pillow in behind the small of her back because she said he was the only one who knew how to do it properly.

She had one of her many chiffon scarves around her neck to keep off drafts and another one, just for looks, tied around her melon-shaped straw hat with her crescent-shaped diamond pin to hold it in place. For shoes she wore her usual suede Hush Puppies with crepe soles to prevent her from slipping and kept her cane within reach at her side. Before we started off I told her not to forget to fasten her seat belt, but she refused. She said she sat so low in her seat that the strap went across her face and almost knocked her dentures out, and that got all three of us laughing so hard I was able to click it into place without her even noticing.

Driving with Kaki was one of the best ways there was of visiting with her because with no other noises to distract her I could speak in my normal voice, and that meant that not only could we speak the kinds of things that can't be shouted but could do it like the old friends we were instead of the caricatures we became when almost nothing I said got through to her. Heading west through the rolling green farmland, I began to think of her again as the hero she had been all through my childhood when it seemed there was nothing she couldn't do, no company she couldn't charm, no disaster she couldn't pull us all through like my father's death in a garage filled with bitter blue fumes when I was ten and Jamie going on eight. I remembered how proud I was of how much younger and prettier and skinnier she was than the mothers of any of my friends and how I loved being with her. I remembered the new life she had made for us in Bermuda in a pink house called the Moorings on the harbor across from Hamilton where Jamie and I could catch fish much too beautiful to keep and where we lived until 1939 when the war broke out and we had to go home.

At sixty miles an hour she seemed as mobile as I was, and I couldn't imagine her ever again having to hand herself across a room from chair back to chair back groaning that her knees bent the wrong way like a stork's and she had no balance and couldn't imagine what in God's name was wrong with her. What was wrong with her, of course, was that she would be ninety on her next birthday, but if ever I tried telling her that, she would put her hands over her ears and close her eyes tight shut. Sometimes she would scream.

Jamie was dozing in the back seat next to the toilet seat extender, and all was peaceful until she complained that the sun was getting in her eyes and giving her a terrible headache. She had her dark glasses on, but she said they were no damn good so I pulled her sun visor down, and she said any fool could see she was too low in her seat for that to be any damn good either. She told me to stop at the next service station we came to and get her a piece of cardboard or something to cover her half of the windshield. I explained if I did that I wouldn't be able to see the road properly, and she said she couldn't believe a man would treat his own mother the way I did.

Her next step was to take off the chiffon scarf she had around her neck and get Jamie to tie it on from behind like a blindfold. That seemed to work at first, but then she said she needed something heavier so he took off his jacket and draped it over the melon-shaped hat and the chiffon scarf. We said it made her look as if she was being kidnapped by terrorists, and she said we could laugh all we wanted, but as for her she failed to see the joke.

Not long afterward she said in a muffled voice that she was having trouble breathing. If it led to a heart attack, she supposed that would give us another good chuckle. But by this time we weren't driving into the sun anymore, so Jamie took off her various wrappings, and for a while she didn't say anything until we hit a stretch of rough pavement. Each time the car gave the smallest jounce, she sucked her breath in through her teeth like a hissing radiator. It was like me, she said, to pick out the worst road I could find when I knew what it did to her back.

It was toward the end of the journey as we were barreling down the Hudson River Parkway toward the 79th Street exit that she told me she had to get to a bathroom in a hurry. I told her there was no way in the world we could find her a bathroom where we were, but if she could just hold out about twenty minutes longer, we would have her home. She told me she never dreamed that the child she'd almost died giving birth to would treat her like a dog the way I did, and it was at that point that I found myself having fantasies. I could pull the car over to the side of the road and just leave her there with all her belongings including the seat extender. I could move to another country. I could grow a beard and change my name.

She did hold out, as it happened, but by the time the doorman had helped her out of the car and into the elevator, she was in such a rush she didn't even notice that it wasn't Incoronata who opened the door to let us in. When she eventually came out of the bathroom, she still had her hat on her head with one end of the chiffon scarf trailing out behind her, and it was only then that she noticed that the person who was offering to take it off for her was a total stranger.

As briefly and calmly as I could, I explained what had happened to Incoronata, and to my surprise she didn't explode the way I'd been dreading but just stood there in the hallway looking old and dazed with her skirt pulled crooked. Incoronata's replacement, whose name turned out to be Sheila, was under five feet tall, and it wasn't until she had helped her lie down on her bed and taken her shoes off that Kaki spoke to her for the first time.

"Get me a root beer out of the icebox," she barked and then, before Sheila left the bedroom, "That dyed hair doesn't fool me for a minute. She's seventy if she's a day. And if you think I'm going to have a dwarf taking care of me, you're out of your minds."

Kaki's bedroom was where she spent the last few years of her life, rarely leaving it except when Jamie and his wife came for supper. She had pasted gold stars on almost everything—the headboard of her bed, the picture frames, the lamp shades, the covers of books. Her chaise lounge was heaped with pillows, and there was a pile of magazines on the carpet beside it and a fake leopard-skin throw at the foot. There was her bow-fronted antique desk that she loved telling she'd bought out from under the nose of a childhood friend who would have killed for it, and the dressing table where she used to do her face the first thing every morning until she took to having the powder and lipstick and eyebrow pencil and what have you brought to her on a tray while she was still in bed.

The glass-topped green bureau was loaded with colognes, hairsprays, eye drops, cough syrup. There was a jar of almonds that she had read kept you from getting cancer and a bowl of M&M's that she said gave her energy. A number of pictures hung on the peach-colored walls including a watercolor of the Moorings with its whitewashed roof and the blue harbor beyond it. She said she'd never been so happy anywhere else. There was a framed piece of needlepoint she'd done with the word "JOY" on it and several ladybugs for luck. She kept her bedside telephone under a quilted tea cozy and beside it a little covered china dish for her teeth at night.

It was in this room that early one morning she died in her sleep. Little pint-sized Sheila was the one who phoned Jamie the news. He said that when he got to the apartment shortly afterward, she told him she had put one of Kaki's best nighties on her and the ribboned pink bed jacket that was her favorite. She had washed her face and hands and brushed her hair. When he turned to go in and see her, Sheila went and busied herself with something in the kitchen.

Kaki was lying on her bed with a fresh sheet pulled up all the way over her. He said that for a few moments he thought he would pull it back to have one last look at her face and then didn't. He just stood at the window for a while staring down at 79th Street three stories below. The windowsill felt gritty to his touch. He noticed that one of the muslin curtains needed mending.

When the long black vehicle with side curtains pulled up at the awninged front entrance, he found himself remembering an exchange he and I had had with her once. She had told us for God's sake not to let them carry her out in a bag when the time came, and we had told her we wouldn't. Instead, I said, I would take her under one arm and Jamie would take her under the other and together we would walk her out between us, which had gotten all three of us laughing the way we did in the car when she said the seat belt strap almost knocked her dentures out.

Down below he could see the undertakers talking to the doorman. He went back and stood by the bed for a few moments, then reached down under the bottom of the sheet and pinched one of her toes.

"They're coming," he said.

FREDERICK BUECHNER, b. 1926, is an American writer and theologian. He has been a finalist for the Pulitzer Prize and the National Book Award, and has been awarded eight honorary degrees, from such schools as Yale University and the Virginia Theological Seminary. In addition, Buechner has been the recipient of the O. Henry Award, the Rosenthal Award, the Christianity and Literature Belles Lettres Prize, and has been recognized by the American Academy and Institute of Arts and Letters.

A Mosquito Bite, a Coma, and a Reckoning

Morley Torgov

Time and again, people of the cloth love to finger-waggingly remind us (as though we needed reminding) that we enter this world with nothing and we depart this world with nothing. But what about the time and space between the two nothings? What are we to do with a lifetime of accumulating hard assets and harder experience?

Lawyers offer us last wills and testaments; scientists offer theories and statistics; the clergy offer prayer. All to little or no avail. Life continues to be a daily craps game. Man plans and God laughs. Only one thing is certain: Something totally random is bound to occur and, for sure, the dice ain't gonna come up lucky seven.

In my case the craps game came to an abrupt halt one Sunday in August last year. The cause: a mosquito bite—unseen, unheard, unfelt—that left me with a life-threatening case of West Nile virus.

I survived (no, this piece is not written posthumously). Unfortunately, however, my ability to render a full account of what followed that might be of service to modern medicine is hindered by the fact I was comatose during the crucial first couple of weeks of the three months and two days I spent in hospitals.

Family and friends, knowing this, nevertheless have urged me to write of this experience, arguing that whatever I recall might be instructive because of the rarity, while at the same time helping me make some sense of it for my own benefit. If nothing more, they insist, it may make clear the reasons for my ongoing recovery.

Take, for example, the matter of genes. "You must have inherited good genes," people tell me. Good genes? Me? My mother died at the age of thirty-four of what was, back in the mid-1930s, incurable kidney failure. My father, who would have captured gold at the Olympics if smoking were a competitive sport, died of lung cancer at sixty-nine. True, my maternal grandfather, a long-time resident of Winnipeg, lived to almost 101, but genes in Manitoba's capital tend to stay frozen solid year-round. No way could a single one of them have come loose and drifted as far as Sault Ste. Marie at the time of my birth there eighty-five years ago.

So "good genes" is out.

"You must have been a good fighter," some people suggest. That's doubtful. How can a person who is unconscious be a good fighter? Besides, good fighting requires a history of regular physical exercise and athletic activity, all of which I had managed successfully to avoid, as one avoids syphilis and all 500 concertos of Antonio Vivaldi, throughout my life. As for the prospect of mortality, it's a "given" that I have always faced with unconcealed cowardice. The "courageous battles" newspaper obituaries lie about will never be reported about me.

A good fighter? Not a chance.

Some say I was lucky. All right, let's consider luck. With apologies to Rick in *Casablanca,* of all the bodies in all the world, this mosquito had to land on mine. You call that luck? The insect—not I—is the one that played craps and won.

Finally, people tell me that, in order to survive, I must have had faith, an idea I rejected instantly with a dismissive "Yeah, right!"—that is, until I thought about it. Then I decided that, yes, I did have faith after all: faith in a battalion of dedicated nurses, doctors, occupational therapists, speech and cognitive therapists, physiotherapists, dietitians, orderlies and lab technicians. These people taught me how faith works.

Faith is a process of abandoning.

First, you abandon Pride. You quickly accept the idea that your body is really just a hunk of meat with convenient apertures (some natural, some man-made) through which numerous plastic tubes can deliver good stuff or extract bad stuff.

Modesty—or Privacy, if you prefer—is next to go. This became essential when, one morning, I was unable to give myself a shower and was obliged to submit, in a state of complete nudity, to being showered by a comely nineteen-year-old nursing student. I prayed my body would behave itself. (It did.)

Embarrassment, too, must be stored for the duration. Your body refuses to abide by rules drummed into you in early childhood. Every time you press the button by your bed to summon help, you appreciate something that, as a two-year-old, you couldn't possibly have understood: The role of a caregiver is as close to messianic as a human being can get.

Say farewell also to taste buds, which, without your express consent, have gone on an extended leave of absence. After weeks on a feeding tube, I was deemed ready for my first real meal. This turned out to be spaghetti Bolognese with side orders of squash and mashed broccoli—a combination which, if served in Rome, would bring down the government of Italy (yet again!).

So all these things were jettisoned, thrown overboard to lighten my distress and heighten my faith. And after fifty-three days at St. Michael's Hospital, followed by forty-two days at Bridgepoint rehabilitation hospital, look at me: I can walk a forty-foot straight line frontwards, sideways and backwards!

I must mention my family and friends again. They are the ones who had faith, the kind the people of the cloth preach about. Thank God!

MORLEY TORGOV, b. 1927, practiced law in Toronto from 1954 until 2012. He has written eight books, two of which received the Stephen Leacock Medal for Humor. His essays have appeared in various anthologies including *About Men and Family Portraits*. He was awarded the Order of Canada in 2015 in recognition of his contribution to Canadian literature. Torgov is at work on additional books in the Inspector Hermann Preiss mystery series.

Subjective Age: *Post-Viagra, post-Cialis, I am well into my dotage.*

Being with Someone Dying

Ram Dass

I sit with people who are dying. I'm one of those unusual types that enjoys being with someone when they're dying because I know I am going to be in the presence of Truth. I was with my mother and later my stepmother when they were dying. I am deeply grateful for those experiences.

My mother was dying in early February, 1966, in a hospital in Boston. I was sitting at her bedside. By then I had been working on understanding my own consciousness for some years. She was sort of resting. I was in kind of a meditative mode, just being spacious and aware and noticing what was happening as the relatives and doctors and nurses came into the hospital room and said, "Gertrude, how are you doing?" I listened to the cheery tone of the nurse. I realized that my mother was surrounded by a conspiracy of denial. I watched people coming into the room, all the relatives and doctors and nurses saying she was looking better, that she was doing well, and then they would go out of the room and say she wouldn't live out the week. I thought how bizarre it was that a human being going through one of the most profound transitions in her life was completely surrounded by deception. Can you hear the pain of that? One woman came in and said, "The doctor just told me there's a new medication that we think will help."

Nobody could be straight with her because everybody was too frightened—all of them, everybody, even the rabbi. Mother and I talked about it. At one point, when nobody else was in the room, she turned to me and said, "Rich?" I'd just been sitting there—no judgment, no nothing, just sitting—and we just met in that space.

She said, "Rich, I think I'm going to die."

I said, "Yeah, I think so too."

Imagine what that must have been for her to just have somebody affirm what she knew. She couldn't get anybody in the entire constellation of her friends, relatives, doctors, and nurses to validate it for her.

She said, "What do you think it's going to be like, Rich?"

I said, "Well, of course, I don't know. But I look at you, and I can see your body disintegrating. It's like a house burning. But you are still there, and I figure when the building burns, it will go, and you'll still be there. It seems to be the way you and I are connected isn't really defined by this body that is disintegrating, because you sound just like you've always sounded. I feel like I've always felt. Yet this body is decaying before us.

"I think the way that you and I love each other, I just believe that love transcends death." That was a very touching connection for us.

Later I was with my stepmother, Phyllis, when she was dying of cancer. Phyllis was sixty-nine, and my father was eighteen years older. When they got married, I gave away the bride. We were good buddies. Now she was dying, and my role was to be with her and help her through this process.

She and I had been to the doctors together, and we had done the whole thing of getting all the reports and dealing with all the emotions. Phyllis was a very tough New England lady, a wonderful, grounded, poker-playing woman. She was argumentative and willful, just fun.

She had a stiff-upper-lip way of living life, and she was approaching her death the same way. My job wasn't to say, "Hey, Phyllis, you should open to this." That wasn't my moral right. My job was just to be there with her. So I would lie on the bed, and we would hold each other, and we would just talk. We would talk about death and what we thought it might be like and all, but she was still being very strong.

The pain of the cancer was intense, and over time it finally wore away her will. A moment came, maybe four or five days before her death, when she gave up.

In our culture, giving up is seen as a failure. Everybody says to keep trying, keep trying. The result is we sometimes surround dying people with a kind of false hope that comes out of our own fear.

With Phyllis, I was just open, and she could ask whatever she wanted. I didn't say, "Now let me instruct you about dying," because she wouldn't have accepted that. But then she gave up. At the moment she surrendered, it was like watching an egg hatch. A new being emerged that was so radiantly beautiful and present and light and joyful. It was a being that at some deep intuitive level she knew herself to be but never had time for in her adult life. She opened to this being, and together we just basked in its radiance. At that moment she had gone into another plane of consciousness. We were together talking, but the pain and the dying process had just become phenomena. She was no longer busy dying; she was just being, and dying was happening.

Just to complete this story, to tell you how extraordinary this transformation was, right at the last moment she said, "Richard, please sit me up."

So I sat her up, I put her legs over the bed, and her body was falling forward. So I put my hand on her chest, and her body fell back. So I put my other hand on her back, and her head was lolling. So I put my head against her head. We were just sitting there together. She took three breaths—slow, deep breaths—and she left.

If you read the ancient Tibetan texts, you read that when conscious lamas leave their bodies, they sit up, they take three breaths, and they leave. Who was Phyllis? How did she know that? What was that about? These are the mysteries that we live with.

My dear friend Deborah was dying at Mount Sinai Hospital in New York. She was a member of the New York Zen Center, and every evening her friends from the center came to her hospital room to meditate. Doctors entering this hospital room were surprised to find it lit by candles and filled with the fragrance of incense and the deep peace of people in meditation. In this busy big-city hospital, this group of people meditating had redefined the metaphor for dying. You can create your universe anywhere you are. A hospital is merely a collective of beings who share a certain model about what it's all about. Each night her doctors entered the room more gently.

Curing a disease of the body is not always an option, but healing from the soul level is always possible. In working with those who are dying, I offer another human being a spacious environment with my mind in which they can die as they need to die. I have no right to define how another person should die. I'm just there to help them transition, however they need to do it. My role is just to be a loving rock at the bedside.

When Wavy Gravy, the clown prince of the Hog Farm commune, talks to children about dying, he tells them to shed their body like taking off a suit of old clothes and to go for the light that will take you to God, your friend.

Working with the dying is like being a midwife for this great rite of passage of death. Just as a midwife helps a being take their first breath, you help a being take their last breath. To be there fully requires being deeply grounded in compassion and love. Compassion, in this instance, is just both of you becoming who you are together—like the right hand taking care of the left.

In *Guided Meditations, Explorations and Healings*, Stephen Levine says:

> Death is an illusion we all seem to buy into. . . But death, like any-thing that catches the heart's attention, can bring out the best in us. We have seen many people as they approach even the confusion around death, go beyond that dismay and become one with the pro-cess. . . They deepen the work they perhaps took birth to complete. They are no longer someone separate, someone "dying consciously." They are merely space within space, light within light.

See in the dying person only that which is eternal. Then you will be able to communicate as souls.

When you are with someone who is dying, *be there* with them. All you have to give is your own being. Be honest. Meditate and become aware that the pain or confusion is, and here we are, in quiet equanimity. We all have limits of tolerance. Stay as clear and conscious as possible as someone nears death. Open to the unexpected. Open and stay centered. If you remain centered, your calm presence helps to free all those around you. Go inside yourself to that quiet place where you are wisdom. Wisdom has in it compassion. Compassion understands about life and death. The answer to dying is to be present in the moment. To learn to die is to learn how to live. And the way you do that is by living each moment—this one, now this one—just being here now.

The moment when the soul leaves the body is palpable and deeply profound. To share consciousness with a person who is dying, to be with them and help them die consciously, is one of the most exquisite manifestations of service. It is one role you may want to try out.

RAM DASS, b. 1931 as Richard Alpert, is an American writer and spiritual teacher. He is the founder of multiple organizations dedicated to service and spiritual well-being, and the author of fifteen books. Ram Dass is best known for the monumentally influential *Be Here Now*, which champions present-centeredness and joyous living and has sold over two million copies. The documentary *Fierce Grace*, about his 1997 stroke, demonstrates his philosophy in action.

Old Age

Penelope Lively

"The party's nearly over," says a friend and contemporary; she says it a touch ruefully, but gamely also. We have had a party; we've been luckier than many. And we are attuned to the idea of life as a narrative—everyone is. Just as the young Afghan knows his story has only just begun—and he is hell-bent on seeing that it continues—so we take a kind of wry satisfaction in recognizing the fit and proper progress, the shape of things. The sense of an ending.

The trajectory of life, the concept of universal death, conditions our thinking. We require things to end, to mirror our own situation. The idea of infinity is impossible to grasp. When I am invited to do so, watching one of those television programs about the expanding universe, with much fancy computerized galaxy performance on the screen, and sober explications from Californian astrophysicists, I can't, frankly. And what is intriguing is that they too, while evidently accepting the concept in a stern professional physicist way, seem also to have an ordinary human resistance. Last time, two of them said "mind-boggling," reaching helplessly, it seemed, for that most jaded cliché to account for something that is beyond language. They couldn't find words for it; neither can I.

I have had much to do with endings, as a writer of fiction. The novel moves from start to finish, as does the short story; at the outset, the conclusion lurks—Where is this thing going? How will I wrap it up? How will I give it a satisfactory shape? You are looking to supply the deficiencies of reality, to provide order where life is a matter of contingent chaos, to suggest theme and meaning, to make a story that is shapely where life is linear. "Tick-tock"; Frank Kermode's famous "model of what we call a plot, an organization that humanizes time by giving it form." The need to give significance to simple chronicity: "All such plotting presupposes and requires that an end will bestow upon the whole duration and meaning." This is the satisfaction of a successful work of fiction—the internal coherence that reality does not have. Life as lived is disordered, undirected and at the mercy of contingent events. I wrote a novel recently which mirrored this process but tried also to make a point about the effects of the process, which seemed like having it both ways and was fiendishly difficult to do, and that served me right, but it was a chance to explore the alarming interdependence that directs our lives.

We have this need for narrative, it seems. A life is indeed a "tick-tock": birth and death with nothing but time in between. We go to fiction because we like a story, and we want our lives to have the largesse of story, the capacity, the onward thrust—we not only want, but need, which is why memory is so crucial, and without it we are lost, adrift in a hideous eternal present. The compelling subject of memory is for another section of this book; the point here is simply that we cannot but see the trajectory from youth to old age as a kind of story—my story, your story—and the backwards gaze of old age is much affected by the habits of fiction. We look for the sequential comforts of narrative—this happened, then that; we don't care for the arbitrary. My story—your story—is a matter of choice battling with contingency: "The best-laid schemes o' mice an' men . . ." We are well aware of that, but the retrospective view would still like a bit of fictional elegance. For some, psychoanalysis perhaps provides this—explanations, understandings. Most of us settle for the disconcerting muddle of what we intended and what came along, and try to see it as some kind of whole.

That said, it remains difficult to break free of the models supplied by fiction. "The preference for progress is a basic assumption of the Bildungsroman and the upward mobility story and an important component of much comedy romance, fairy tale," writes Helen Small in her magisterial investigation of old age as viewed in philosophy and literature. "It is also an element in the logic of tragedy: one of the reasons tragedy (certain kinds, at least) is painful is that it affronts the human desire for progress." We are conditioned by reading, by film, by drama, with, it occurs to me, long-running television soaps being the only salutary reminder of what real life actually does—it goes on and on as a succession of events until the plug is pulled; we should note the significance of *Coronation Street* and *EastEnders*. We want some kind of identifiable progress, a structure, and the only one is the passage of time, the notching up of decades until the exit line is signaled.

Helen Small has written also of the debate—usually between philosophers, it seems—about the concept of eternal life. Is death in fact desirable? A moot point indeed, and of course it depends on what sort of life you suppose—some kind of imagined eternal youth or the inevitable decline we all know, and do not love but recognize. Swift's Struldbrugs seem to me to have had the last word. And the very euphemism we use for death—an end—seems to reflect our fictional conditioning, our sense of an ending. It is appropriate, that end.

Appropriate in theory, though we view it without enthusiasm. The thing that most vexes me about the prospect of my end is that I shan't know what comes after, not just—in fact, perhaps least of all—in the grand scale of things but on my own immediate horizon: how will life unroll for my grandchildren? What will they make of it? I shall be written out of the story (like disposable actors in soap operas), and my story is hitched to many other stories. Every life is tangled with a multitude of other lives, again in a perverse mix of choice and contingency. You choose partners and friends; you don't choose those you end up working with, or living next door to. Either way, your story has wound in with theirs, and because of this you can be wrong-footed by your own existence. There is existence as it has seemed to you, and there are those other versions served up by other people. You think it was like this; your parent, child, discarded lover, professional rival, says no, the view from here is subtly different.

I shall never know the view from my grandchildren, which may be just as well. And the discordant aspects of any life are of course the stuff of fiction—the ambiguities, the contradictions. When it comes to reality, plenty are anxious to get in a preemptive strike by way of autobiography and memoir, especially those who have been on the public stage and are well aware that they are going to get a good going-over in due course; there can't be many politicians who have not spent their declining years honing their version of things before it is too late.

There is a vogue for "life writing" at the moment, both for publication and as private endeavors. I am all for it, partly because I gobble up other people's lives, as a reader, but also because it seems to me a productive personal exercise—to stand aside and have a look at your story and try, not to make sense of it, which may be too taxing, but to trace the narrative thread, to look at the roads not taken, to see where you began and where you have got to. An exercise also in solipsism, perhaps, but we are all solipsistic, and actually the exercise itself demands as well a measure of detachment.

There is one thing missing, of course, from personal life writing: that requisite ending. Tick without the tock. I would find that most unsettling, were I to attempt any sort of conventional memoir (which I shan't do); the novelist in me requires that tension between start and finish, the sense of a whole, of a progress towards conclusion. But I am quite at home with the idea of my life—any life—as a bit-player in the lives of others; that is the stuff of fiction, again, and the challenge of any novel is to find a balance for the relationships within the cast list, to make these interesting, intriguing, to have them shift and perhaps unravel over the course of the narrative. So that side of things is fine; fact and fiction nicely reflect one another. It is the search for an ending that is the problem.

Which takes me back to the prompt for this digression: the parabola between youth and age, and the way in which it conditions the view in winter. The winter of old age is not going to give way to spring, so the term is inept, but it suits the static nature of old age, the sense that things have wound down, gone into suspension. The party is nearly over, yes, and that euphemistic ending is somewhere just over the horizon, but in the meantime there is this new dimension of life—often demanding, sometimes dismaying, always worth examining.

PENELOPE LIVELY, b. 1933, is a British writer born in Cairo. She has written dozens of well-regarded books for children and adults; her most recent book is her 2013 memoir, *Dancing Fish and Ammonites*. Lively has received numerous awards, including the Arts Council Book Award, the Carnegie Medal, the Whitbread Award, and the Booker Prize. She is a Fellow of the Royal Society of Literature, as well as a member of PEN and the Society of Authors.

Death

Donald Hall

It is sensible of me to be aware that I will die one of these days. I will not *pass away*. Every day millions of people *pass away*—in obituaries, death notices, cards of consolation, emails to the corpse's friends—but people don't *die*. Sometimes they rest in peace, quit this world, go the way of all flesh, depart, give up the ghost, breathe a last breath, join their dear ones in heaven, meet their Maker, ascend to a better place, succumb surrounded by family, return to the Lord, go home, cross over, or leave this world. Whatever the fatuous phrase, death usually happens peacefully (asleep) or after a courageous struggle (cancer). Sometimes women lose their husbands. (Where the hell did I put him?) Some expressions are less common in print: push up the daisies, kick the bucket, croak, buy the farm, cash out. All euphemisms conceal how we gasp and choke turning blue.

Cremation hides the cadaver; ashes preclude rot. Neanderthals and *Homo sapiens* stuck their dead underground or in mounds. Pyramids sealed up pharaohs. Romans shifted by the century between incineration and burial. Commonly Hindus burnt dead bodies by the Ganges, in the old days performing *sati* by adding a live widow to the pyre. Cinders clogged the river, along with dead babies of families too poor to buy wood. Zoroastrians and Tibetans tended to raise corpses onto platforms for vultures to eat. My favorite anecdote of ash disposal is recent. After I finished a poetry reading, a generous admirer presented me a jar of her late husband's remains.

Myself, I'll be a molderer, like my wife Jane.

At some point in my seventies, death stopped being interesting. I no longer checked out ages in obituaries. Earlier, if I was fifty-one and the cadaver was fifty-three, for a moment I felt anxious. If the dead man was fifty-one and I was fifty-three, I felt relief. If a person lives into old age, there's a moment when he or she becomes eldest in the family, perched on top of a hill as night rises. My mother at ninety left me the survivor. Soon I will provide that honor to my son. When he was born, I was twenty-five and wrote a poem called "My Son My Executioner." A decade ago I went to the emergency room when I fell and hurt myself. It was no big deal. The resident doctor dropped by and we chatted. When I asked about blood pressure numbers, he said I had nothing to worry about. "How many years do you want to live anyway?" Without thinking I grabbed a number out of the air. "Oh, until eighty-three," I told him. On my eighty-fourth birthday I was quietly relieved.

In my eighties, the days have narrowed as they must. I live on one floor eating frozen dinners. Louise the postwoman brings letters to my porch, opens the door, and tosses the mail on a chair. I get around—bedroom, bathroom, kitchen, new chair by the window, electrical reclining (or lifting) chair for Chris Matthews and baseball—by spasming from one place to another pushing a four-wheeled roller. I try not to break my neck. I write letters, I take naps, I write essays.

The people I love will mourn me, but I won't be around to commiserate. I become gloomy thinking of insensate things I will leave behind. My survivors will cram into plastic bags the tchotchkes I have lived with, expanding a landfill. I needn't worry about my Andy Warhols. I fret over the striped stone that my daughter picked up at the pond, or my father's desk lamp from college, or a miniature wooden milk wagon from the family dairy. My mother approaching ninety feared that we would junk the Hummel figurines that decorated her mantelpiece, kitsch porcelain dolls popular from the forties to the sixties. Thus, a box of them rests in my daughter's attic. More important to me is this house, which my great-grandfather moved to in 1865—the family place for almost a century and a half. In the back chamber the generations stored everything broken or useless, because no one knew when they might come in handy. My kids and grandkids don't want to live in rural isolation—why should they?—but it's melancholy to think of the house emptied out. Better it should burn down. Remaining in the old place, I let things go. I shingle the roof, I empty the cesspool, but if a light fixture fails, I do without it. Maybe the next tenant will not want it.

I let the old wallpaper flap loose. Somebody will remove four hundred feet of bookshelves.

There are also bits of land I cherish. When Jane and I moved here, I found my great-grandfather's stationery, labeled "Eagle Pond Farm," and borrowed the name for our address. Last November a friend took me driving past Eagle Pond. It's obscured from my windows by the growth of tall trees, although the pond is only a hundred yards west, twenty-four acres of water. My land includes half the pond's shore. I titled books of essays *Seasons at Eagle Pond* and *Here at Eagle Pond.* Then I collected them as *Eagle Pond.* Then I wrote *Christmas at Eagle Pond.* Back in the day, Jane and I used a tiny, hidden beach, among oak and birch, to lie in the sun on summer afternoons and grill supper on a hibachi. We watched for mink and beaver, we saw the first acorns fall. In the years after she died I visited the pond rarely, and by this time it's long since I've even passed it by. When my friend drove me on its dirt road—an afternoon of bright autumn sunlight, the pond intensely blue with its waters choppy— I glimpsed the birches of our old beach and wept a tear of self-pity.

Of course we start dying when the sperm fucks the egg. (Pro-lifers dwell on this insight.) At my age I feel complacent about death, if sometimes somber, but we all agree that *dying* sucks. I've never been around when somebody, in the middle of a sentence or a sandwich, has the luck to pitch over dead. I've only sat beside two deaths, my grandmother Kate's and my wife Jane's. In both cases the corpse-in-waiting was out of it. Hours earlier each had slipped into Cheyne-Stokes breathing, when the brain stem is stubborn about retaining oxygen though the big brain has departed. Cheyne-Stokes is one long breath followed by three quick ones, then a pause. The brain stem holds on, in my experience, for as long as twelve hours. Because my grandmother's mouth drooped open and looked sore, a nurse spooned water on her red tongue. She choked as if she had swallowed the wrong way. I held her hand. I rubbed Jane's head until the long breath ceased. Least enviable are folks who die while alive, panicked as they rush, still conscious, from pink to blue. My father and my mother both died alive.

Beginning as a schoolboy, death turned me on, and for decades I practiced an enthusiastic morbidity. At home a whole bunch of great-aunts and -uncles took their turns at dying. At ten I enjoyed banquets of pre-cocious lamentation, teaching myself that Death had become a reality. In seventh grade I wrote my first poem, which explained that Death hunted you down, screeching through the night, until Death called your name. When I was fifteen, more and more practicing the poet, I decided that if I announced that I would die young, it would appeal to cheerleaders. I let it be known that I would die between pages seventeen and eighteen, not noticing that seventeen and eighteen are two sides of the same page. When I started writing real poems I kept to the subject, though death dropped its capital letter. I wrote cheerful poems—about farm horses or a family dog—and pointed out that eventually they all died. Who would have guessed? I wrote a poem, "In Praise of Death," that tried to get rid of death by flattery.

Except in print, I no longer dwell on it. It's almost relaxing to know I'll die fairly soon, as it's a comfort not to obsess about my next orgasm. I've been ambitious, and ambition no longer has plans for the future—except these essays. My goal in life is making it to the bathroom. In the past I was often advised to live in the moment. Now what else can I do? Days are the same, generic and speedy—I seem to remove my teeth shortly after I glue them in—and weeks are no more tedious than lunch. They elapse and I scarcely notice. The only boring measure is the seasons. Year after year they follow the same order. Why don't they shake things up a bit? Start with summer, followed by spring, winter, then maybe Thanksgiving?

I've wanted to kill myself only three times, each on account of a woman. Two of them dumped me and the other died. Each time, daydreams of suicide gave me comfort. My father presented me with a .22 Mossberg when I was twelve, but self-assassination by .22 is chancy. If I didn't aim it like a surgeon, I could spend the rest of my life on a breathing machine. My friend Bruno suggested an infallible method—to carry my gun into Eagle Pond, wading up to my knees, then plonk a long-rifle bullet into my head. I would drown if the shot didn't finish me off. Bruno gave sui-cide a lot of thought, and he took no chance with himself. In his Beverly Hills condo he pulled the pin on a hand grenade clutched to his chest.

By this time, even if I wanted to, I'm too frail and wobbly to walk into Eagle Pond.

In middle life I came close to dying of natural causes. When I was sixty-one I had colon cancer, deftly removed, but two years later it metastasized to my liver. A surgeon removed half of that organ and told me I might have five years. Both Jane and I assumed I would die soon, and she massaged me every day, trying to rub the cancer out. I went through the motions of chemo and finished writing what I was able to finish. Aware of my own approaching death, I was astonished and appalled when Jane came down with leukemia. Her death at forty-seven—I was sixty-six—was not trivial. Six years later I had a small stroke and my potential death felt matter-of-fact. A carotid artery was eighty-five percent occluded. Dr. Harbaugh removed a pencil-wide, inch-long piece of plaque during a two-hour operation under local anesthetic. I enjoyed hearing the chitchat of the white-coated gang. Now and then somebody asked me to squeeze a dog's ball, which tinkled to affirm my consciousness. I was disappointed when Dr. Harbaugh wouldn't let me take the obstruction back home.

In his "Homage to Sextus Propertius," Ezra Pound has his poet protagonist say, "I shall have, doubtless, a boom after my funeral." Particular circumstances contribute to the response, like death at a comparatively young age. When Jane died, obituaries reprinted her poems. I was interviewed about her. NPR rebroadcast her interview with Terry Gross. In India—Jane and I had visited—there were ceremonies in her honor in Bombay, New Delhi, and Madras. There were memorials in New Hampshire, in New York, at Harvard, and in Minneapolis. When her posthumous selected poems, *Otherwise,* came out on the first anniversary of her death, it quickly went into three hardback printings. Eighteen months later a paperback flourished, and her publishers have now added a *Complete Poems.* I love her work—but her books sold as they first did because of leukemia and her age. Eighteen years later she is reprinted in anthologies. Maybe she'll stick around.

My dearest old friend just died at eighty-nine. At least he died at home. I'm old enough to remember when everybody died in their houses, tended by family as Jane was tended. I was nine when I spent a summer at the farm while my grandmother's older sister lay dying in the parlor. Parlors in those days were reserved for special events—entertaining the pastor, funerals, weddings, and dying. (The parlor has become the television room.) Great-Aunt Nannie lay on a cot, blind, unable to turn over in bed, her back in continuous pain. She told my grandparents Kate and Wesley that the people of this house (Kate and Wesley) tortured her by making her sleep on a woodpile. She told Kate that she wanted to see her family, and Kate told her that she could arrange a visit from Kate and Wesley. When Kate and Wesley dropped by, Aunt Nannie was overjoyed. She died soon after I left for school, in September 1938, just before the New England hurricane. My mother got stuck coming back from the funeral.

Some fortunate people die in a hospice, which is tender but brief. I visited an old friend, James Wright, as he lay dying in a Bronx hospice, under warm and intelligent care—but the hospice found a bed only four days before he died. My first wife died in a New Hampshire hospice—admitted with six days to live. Some hospitals perform palliative care for the terminally ill. Others of us still die at home, like my father, Jane's father, and two aunts of mine. Jane could have died in a shiny hospital bed but chose home, as I will, if I can manage. In the same bed. These days most old people die in profit-making expiration dormitories. Their loving sons and daughters are busy and don't want to forgo the routine of their lives. One said he would *not* diaper his parents so he handed them over to women who diapered at the minimum wage. My friend Linda spent two of her college summers working at a place called Eternal Peace, on the three-to-eleven shift. After she fed the patients, she pulled out their teeth and put them in a jar. One night she could not get a woman's teeth out. She pulled and pulled and pulled. One tooth came out dripping blood.

Old folks' storage bins bear encouraging names. I've heard of an Alzheimer's unit called Memory Lane. There are also Pleasant View, Live Forever, Happy Valley, Pastures of Paradise, Paradise Pastures, Heaven's Gate, Peaceful Meadow, Summerglen, Paradise Village Estates, Autumn Wind, Fountain of Youth, Elder Gardens, Harbor Isle, Enchanted Spring, Golden Heirloom, Golden Dawn, Pastures of Plenty, Thistlerock Farm, Village Green, Green Village, Ever Rest, and Everest.

At such an address our elders pass away, or rest in peace, or meet their Maker, or leave this world, or buy the farm . . .

DONALD HALL, b. 1928, is a writer, editor, literary critic, and was the 14th Poet Laureate of the United States. He has written more than fifty books of poetry, memoir, biography, criticism and essays. Nominated for dozens of awards, he has been the recipient of a Caldecott Medal, the Robert Frost Medal, the Ruth Lilly Poetry Prize for lifetime achievement, and the National Medal of Arts.

Nearing 90

William Maxwell

Out of the corner of my eye I see my ninetieth birthday approaching. It is one year and six months away. How long after that will I be the person I am now?

I don't yet need a cane but I have a feeling that my table manners have deteriorated. My posture is what you'd expect of someone addicted to sitting in front of a typewriter, but it was always that way. "Stand up straight," my father would say. "You're all bent over like an old man." It didn't bother me then and it doesn't now, though I agree that an erect carriage is a pleasure to see, in someone of any age.

I have regrets but there are not very many of them and, fortunately, I forget what they are. I forget names too, but it is not yet serious. What I am trying to remember and can't, quite often my wife will remember. And vice versa. She is in and out during the day but I know she will be home when evening comes, and so I am never lonely. Long ago, a neighbor in the country, looking at our flower garden, said, "Children and roses reflect their care." This is true of the very old as well.

I am not—I think I am not—afraid of dying. When I was seventeen I worked on a farm in southern Wisconsin, near Portage. It was no ordinary farm and not much serious farming was done there, but it had the look of a place that had been lived in, and loved, for a good long time. The farm had come down in that family through several generations, to a woman who was so alive that everything and everybody seemed to revolve around her personality. She lived well into her nineties and then one day told her oldest daughter that she didn't want to live anymore, that she was tired. This remark reconciled me to my own inevitable extinction. I could believe that enough is enough.

Because I actively enjoy sleeping, dreams, the unexplainable dialogues that take place in my head as I am drifting off, all that, I tell myself that lying down to an afternoon nap that goes on and on through eternity is not something to be concerned about. What spoils this pleasant fancy is the recollection that when people are dead they don't read books. This I find unbearable. No Tolstoy, no Chekhov, no Elizabeth Bowen, no Keats, no Rilke. One might as well be—

Before I am ready to call it quits I would like to reread every book I have ever deeply enjoyed, beginning with Jane Austen and going through shelf after shelf of the bookcases, until I arrive at the *Autobiographies* of William Butler Yeats. As it is, I read a great deal of the time. I am harder to please, though. I see flaws in masterpieces. Conrad indulging in rhetoric when he would do better to get on with it. I would read all day long and well into the night if there were no other claims on my time. Appointments with doctors, with the dentist. The monthly bank statement. Income tax returns. And because I don't want to turn into a monster, people. Afternoon tea with X, dinner with the Ys. Our social life would be a good deal more active than it is if more than half of those I care about hadn't passed over to the other side.

I did not wholly escape that amnesia that overtakes children around the age of six but I carried along with me more of my childhood than, I think, most people do. Once, after dinner, my father hitched up the horse and took my mother and me for a sleigh ride. The winter stars were very bright. The sleigh bells made a lovely sound. I was bundled up to the nose, between my father and mother, where nothing, not even the cold, could get at me. The very perfection of happiness.

At something like the same age, I went for a ride, again with my father and mother, on a riverboat at Havana, Illinois. It was a side-wheeler and the decks were screened, I suppose as protection against the mosquitoes. Across eight decades the name of the steamboat comes back to me—the Eastland—bringing with it the context of disaster. A year later, at the dock in Chicago, too many of the passengers crowded on one side, waving good-bye, and it rolled over and sank. Trapped by the screens everywhere, a great many people lost their lives. The fact that I had been on this very steamboat, that I had escaped from a watery grave, I continued to remember all through my childhood.

I have liked remembering almost as much as I have liked living. But now it is different, I have to be careful. I can ruin a night's sleep by suddenly, in the dark, thinking about some particular time in my life. Before I can stop myself it is as if I had driven a mine shaft down through layers and layers of the past and must explore, relive, remember, reconsider, until daylight delivers me.

I have not forgotten the pleasure, when our children were very young, of hoisting them onto my shoulders when their legs gave out. Of reading to them at bedtime. Of studying their beautiful faces. But that was more than thirty years ago. I admire the way that, as adults, they have taken hold of life, and I am glad that they are not materialistic, but there is little or nothing I can do for them at this point, except write a little fable to put in their Christmas stocking.

"Are you writing?" people ask—out of politeness, undoubtedly. And I say, "Nothing very much." The truth but not the whole truth—which is that I seem to have lost touch with the place that stories and novels come from. I have no idea why. I still like making sentences.

Every now and then, in my waking moments, and especially when I am in the country, I stand and look hard at everything.

WILLIAM MAXWELL, b. 1908, was a distinguished American editor. As the fiction editor at the *New Yorker* from 1936 to 1975, Maxwell worked with many of the most prominent writers of the twentieth century. By the time of his death in 2000, he had also been lauded as a writer in his own right. Maxwell was the recipient of numerous writing awards including the National Book Award and the PEN/Malamud Award.

THE

90s

AND BEYOND

Astonishment

Jan Slepian

There are so many ways and words that can describe what it's like to be the age that we are. The terms creaky and cranky jump to mind, but they are just crumbs from the table. The main feeling I have is what I can only call astonishment. I, who once was fleet of foot, sound of limb, thick of hair, and smooth of skin, am now old and none of those things apply. It plain astonishes me that I am as old as I am. Yet, I must confess, that hidden to others, I still feel young in certain ways. I'm sure I'm not alone in this, and yet nobody ever told us that it was possible. There once was a brochure that we prepubescent girls were handed called "Marjorie May's Twelfth Birthday." There should be one for her eightieth. We have to learn about old age on the job, so to speak.

What astonishes me even more than my own age is to realize that my children, yesterday's adorables, are now middle-aged people with mortgages and creased skin. Worse yet, or even harder to believe is how old my friends' children are. I knew them when they were cuddly lap-sitters and now they're doctors, and the cop on the corner. Mind-boggling.

Things that I took for granted without a thought now astonish me. Old is evidently a time when you marvel at the ordinary. The world is round? Well, if that's so, and the earth is spinning, how come we don't fly off? And please don't tell me about gravity. Or take childbirth. There was a time when we were so busy list-making and feeding and tending that there was no time for this kind of awareness. Now the fact of childbirth seems a pure miracle. Astonishment is hardly the word.

I stand under the night sky and try to get my mind around the vastness of space, or the stretchiness and ruthlessness of time . . . or the fact that the trees know to shed their leaves and then grow them again . . . or that we humans can be so cruel and stupid and so noble and smart . . . or that we are alive at all. It's all astonishing.

JAN SLEPIAN, b. 1921, was the author of twenty-eight books for children and young adults. Married to mathematician David Slepian for fifty-nine years, she had three children and four grandchildren. In her early nineties, she wrote *Astonishment: Life in the Slow Lane* and *How to be Old: a Beginner's Guide*, both of which were adapted for the stage. Slepian subsequently wrote poetry, adding *Jellybeans in Space* and *The Other Shoe* to her books on old age. In 2016, shortly before turning ninety-six, Slepian died while taking a nap: exactly the death she wanted.

Subjective Age: *I am sixteen when I'm engrossed in a poem, but 120 when my muse appears to have abandoned me and I fear she will never visit again. Or when I've slept badly.*

The View from Ninety

Doris Grumbach

I am a self-appointed historian of those of my generation who are still living. Who are we? We are not easily discernible among the more than 300 million persons who live in the United States. We were born between 1908 and 1918, which makes us the oldest of the old, perhaps, even, the long-lost generation.

There are more of us still alive than anyone expected. We constitute a small tribe of one and a half million persons. The Census Bureau predicts that this number is growing rapidly. In one Quaker community of 430 persons, eighty-two are over ninety. But our views, habits, opinions, and characteristics are not often recorded, unless they are satirized or made the butt of cruel and, to some of us, humorless jokes.

There exists a vast literature about babies, children, teenagers, young adults, the middle-aged, the baby boomers, and the recently retired, aimed at helping the world to understand and sympathize with them. Very little that is trustworthy has been written about us.

My disadvantage as a historian is that, for the most part, I lack objectivity. For my information I must be self-reliant. My sole qualifications are that I am the right age—past ninety—and I believe (it may be erroneously) that I know something about myself and a little about my peers. My model for this assumption is the novelist E. M. Forster, who said that he constructed his characters out of what he knew about himself and what he guessed about others. What I know about myself comes from the limited memory of a New York City girl. What I presume to guess about others must come from what I have read about and been told.

If I were to speak in architectural terms, I would say that we are the country's ruins. So, my description of us and our time will not make entirely cheerful reading. Despite long and careful research I have not been able to discover dependable evidence for what literature often calls the golden years. I have seldom heard the phrase used by my contemporaries. More often it is spoken by younger people who are approaching their retirement. The actual proof for this euphemism is lacking.

. . . .

The years between the two wars, for my generation, were, to the pictures that remain in my mind, a rapid succession of dire events: the long, deep Depression showing men on soup-kitchen lines and the unemployed on street corners selling apples for five cents apiece. Hobos, as they were called, living in jungles of shacks and lean-tos under the bridges and in barren stretches of riverbanks.

We heard about world news on the radio and in newsreels, but it was all unreal and far away from us. But much closer to home and more immediate, the children and teenagers of those wretched years, especially those like me who lived in crowded cities, were subject to a widespread and deadly disease, infantile paralysis, called, in the worried conversations of their elders, polio.

My parents decided to send my sister and me to a Catskill Mountain camp to escape the risk of infection. They were not allowed to visit during the two months' period for fear of bringing the disease into the camp from the city. But, curiously enough, it was already there. One of my bunkmates, a twin named Rita, was sent home with weakness and a high fever and, I learned later, died almost before she could be treated.

I was spared the disease, but not the sight. The winter after camp I developed rheumatic fever, another common affliction of the time. I was taken for the month of February to Atlantic City; it was believed that the strong sea breeze would cure my fevers, swollen glands, and general debility.

One cold, windy day my mother took me for a walk up the boardwalk. I remember how my mother's face was almost covered by her veil and her hands and mine were kept warm by fur muffs. We came to a large, high clapboard house close to the ocean. My mother said it was the Children's Home for the treatment of polio.

In the lee of one of the house's wings I saw a torpedo-shaped metal structure on wheels. Out of one end was a child's head, wrapped in a woolen cap. I gripped my mother's hand, I remember, and asked what that was. She told me it was where they put children with severe polio. "It's called an iron lung," she said. "It breathes for them."

For a long time, until I heard that Jonas Salk had devised a vaccine, I had nightmares about being wrapped in metal like the child in Atlantic City, unable to move or escape. I did not feel sick, but I was nonetheless a prisoner of graphic fear.

When we were children there was another dreaded affliction. We often saw classmates with huge bandages behind their ears and were told they had had an operation for "mastoid," as they called it. Later there would be an ugly scar behind their ears. My friend Dolly, the daughter of the superintendent of our apartment house, and I used to put our hands behind our ears when we went to Central Park, for fear of catching the mastoids.

We never did.

. . . .

The images that remain in my mind from my college years are these: in 1936 many students stood on the steps of Main Building at New York University in Washington Square and took the Oxford Pledge: we would not to go to war under any condition.

The Square was the college's campus. In my senior year I remember sitting on a bench at the southern end, near tables of old men playing chess and checkers, and studying for finals. A madam (as I soon learned she was), from a house on a nearby street, sat down beside me and turned her handsome, highly made-up face to the sun. After a while she looked down at my book and asked me what I intended to do after I graduated. I said I was going to graduate school if I was fortunate enough to get a fellowship.

"And after that, what will you do?"

I said I had no idea. Then she told me about the advantages of pursuing her profession, the high compensation it provided, free housing, food, and drink, even medical care, in return for work "only at night" and in very comfortable surroundings in her MacDougall Street house—"my home," she called it.

I listened, fascinated by the details of her offer. She asked if I would like to see the house. Regretfully, I said no, I had a final exam that afternoon and needed to study before I took it. Several years later, when I had been fired from two jobs and was unemployed, I wondered if I should have taken her up on her offer.

Two years after we had sworn that solemn oath, war broke out in Europe and the president promised aid, under a lend-lease arrangement, to England. A draft was established for men over eighteen to join the Army. Suddenly the boys, now men, of my generation were called up, by number, and went off to camps to be trained for what was to become one of the bloodiest wars in history.

. . . .

Back then I corresponded with a fountain pen, filled by putting the enclosed little bladder into a bottle of ink and pumping. For special occasions, I used thin airmail paper that folded in on itself and cost five cents more in stamps than regular mail. Everything was written on top of the desk blotter and then blotted with a handheld roller. Even with this precaution there were often little spots of ink on the letter.

For manuscripts I used a clipboard that held lined white pads. It was only later that I resorted to a manual typewriter, which somehow seemed weak, effete, and almost cowardly to me. I was accustomed to the sight of my definitive handwriting.

. . . .

The long time—almost a century—during which my generation has lasted exists for us in faulty memories. The world has changed, progressed, as history would claim. We have been left behind or, perforce, we have changed a little. In the world in which we now find ourselves we are very noticeable for the differences between us and those multitudes behind us.

Of course there are those who claim there are some benefits: discounts at the movies, a front seat on the bus, special parking spaces, and widely available games of bingo, croquet, bocce, and shuffleboard, and the ulti-mate source of home entertainment, television.

But, diligently as I dig, I can find very few other advantages. I remember the story told of the novelist W. Somerset Maugham. In his late years he was asked to lecture on the virtues of being old. He came to the podium, stared at the audience for a few seconds, said: "I cannot think of one," and left the platform.

. . . .

When we were young, many of us went in for skinny-dipping. We would often pose undressed before a floor-length mirror. But now those pleasures are, of course, denied us. We find it necessary to cover up, the better to obscure evidence of decay and fallen flesh. The ideal garment for very old women is the total disguise of the Hawaiian muumuu, but any long dress with long sleeves and a high neck will serve. In bed we are partial to a long nightgown that provides coverage for our unacceptable anatomy. What once we unabashedly revealed, we now embarrassedly conceal.

. . . .

Even punctuation changes in very old age. Some years ago a few of my youthful letters written to a suitor were returned to me by his widow. I was dismayed to see in my careless scrawls a profusion of exclamation marks, which appear at the end of paragraphs and sometimes twice in the sentences that compose them. Why? I wondered. I concluded that I must have felt it necessary to be emphatic about my preferences, opinions, expectations, and dislikes to the person, especially to the person I was very fond of.

In old age the fervor went out of all those matters. The ardor-laden exclamation point has largely disappeared from my elderly letters. Dashes, yes, and many periods, but no !

. . . .

When I was young, many of us drank too much. We liked concoctions, colorful drinks, cocktails of every sort. They were characteristic of parties, they denoted liveliness and (it may be) the promise of a forbidden pleasure to come.

But now it is different. In my old age I have learned that straight alcohol, even in small amounts, may disorient me, cause me to lose fluency of speech and my footing. But I, and a small minority of my compatriots, still cling to the much-favored martinis of our younger days. I limit myself to one, and sip it very slowly. A fellow imbiber explained to me his faithful adherence to gin. He said the purity of that liquid still appealed to him, the subtle suggestion of, well, almost nothingness. He often quoted Cole Porter:

> . They have found that the secret of youth
> Is a mixture of gin and vermouth.

He told me about Dean Acheson, Harry Truman's secretary of state, who preferred martinis because, his son David reported, he "likes drinking something transparent after the murky transactions of statecraft."

. . . .

If it is true that the need of young people is always for more, then some of the very old seem to relish having less. I am aware that what little I have I will not need much longer. Some of those I know still cling to their possessions, it is true, but a few (I am one of those) enjoy giving away what once they valued. I feel satisfaction in letting go, stripping down, giving to friends and relatives, libraries and charities what during a lifetime I have collected and accumulated: books, furniture, art, and other beloved objects. My acquaintances slowly dispose of their collections: miniature lighthouses, stuffed bears, glass giraffes, snow scenes in paperweights, whatever.

In this gradual dispersal we few may feel we are preparing for the final, dark, unfurnished dwelling, what Emily Dickinson called "a house that seemed / A swelling of the ground." We will feel less regret because we have so little to leave.

. . . .

I remember fondly how I enjoyed spending and wasting time in my life. But the modern world seems always to be racing to save time. I do not trust mail that is displayed instantly on a screen by pushing a button. I object to the cult of instant obsolescence, which makes everything I use unrepairable. The shoemaker, the dressmaker, the tailor have almost disappeared because their individual activities take too much time. It is now cheaper and faster to buy new things. There is no replacement for most things I have cherished. The lovely Blackwing 602 soft-lead pencil with a removable and reversible eraser is nowhere to be found.

I am no longer able to shop in the small, friendly, one-product store: butcher, greengrocer, baker, dress shop, Thom McAn, the hatter, the dry-goods store. And that marvelous emporium distinguished only by price, Woolworth's, has long since gone out of business. Now I must be driven to an endless, tiresome mall (once the word meant a shaded walk but alas, no longer) where I am told much time will be saved because everything I could possibly want is under one roof.

I mourn the passing of the leisurely *Queens Mary* and *Elizabeth,* now replaced for most travelers by crowded, noisy, uncomfortable but very fast airplanes. The oven is used less often because the microwave is much faster.

"What does everyone do," I once heard an old person inquire, "with all that time we are now said to save?"

. . . .

I prefer black-and-white photographs to colored ones, which to my mind have a kind of violence, an excess, what I see as overemphasis. They strike me as bordering on, well, call it sentimentality.

Goethe called color "the suffering of light."

. . . .

The Puritans once termed themselves Separatists.

So are the very elderly, segregated from the general population, cut away from it by virtue of age, residence, state of health, outlook, and sometimes preference. To escape their separation they congregate at social events, as, of course, people of all ages do. In *Mrs. Dalloway* someone says that parties are held "to cover the silence."

. . . .

It is often remarked that the elderly live in the past. Of course we do. Even in its unreliable form it is almost all we have. But our past changed, oddly. Endlessly recounted stories have been emended, expanded, exaggerated. In time they are magnified into myth and finally assume the epic form of unreality.

I often resent the present, even neglect it, because, in most cases, it has become almost incomprehensible to me, its shape having become so different from what I once knew. And as for the future, I blot out, as quickly as I can, any thought of it.

But oh! The rapture of that invented past.

For the very old the most-often-traveled route to the past is invention. Memory is a slippery activity, the more untrustworthy the longer it is resorted to. It will omit, mistake, blunder, race ahead unreliably, and then fall behind and falter when everything factual deserts it.

Couples who have lived together for many years may widely differ about the same event in their past. The meretricious God of memory has worked his tricks on both minds. These different versions often end in fierce arguments about what really happened.

Perhaps the past is better left untold or unwritten. But if it is spoken about or recorded in writing, empty as it is of verifiable detail, it can do no harm. It can be best thought of as entertaining fiction.

. . . .

How reliable is the recent finding that happy, optimistic people tend to live longer than those who see the world, in A. E. Housman's phrase, "for ill and not for good"? The old are pessimists because they cannot conjure up the energy for optimism. A wise aphorist said: "Anyone who is not pessimistic in old age is not paying attention."

. . . .

When their families and old friends live at a distance from them, it is likely that the very old become attached to animals. Of course such affection is not limited to them. Edward Albee wrote a play about a middle-aged married man who falls romantically in love with a goat. There is a novel (written in 1976 by Marian Engel) called *Bear*, the story of a lonely young woman living in the Canadian wilderness who has a love affair with a huge brown bear.

Both stories suggest the unacknowledged varieties of human love. They stretch the limits of human affection to include other members of the animal kingdom.

My own preference is for cats. I chose them, it may be, for the feline's preference for quiet that matches my own. As cats age they move more slowly, and become companionable and tactilely satisfying. In this way, Leonard Michaels has said, they "make the world unreal," and Auden wrote that a cat "feels in us, and we in him perceive / A common passion for the lonely hour."

Like the old person who is often alone, my cat seems to sense that, when we are alone together, our solitude is good company.

. . . .

The artist Marcel Duchamp collected dust.

When his sculptor friend Joseph Cornell died, he left behind boxes marked the Duchamp Dossier. It turned out they contained a large collection of dust bunnies. Another artist friend, Man Ray, made a gelatin-silver print called Dust Breeding and may have given it to Duchamp. For them, dust might have seemed an emotional symbol.

After a lifetime of churchgoing, I now attend once a year: on Ash Wednesday. I am not able to explain this curious attendance custom to my more observant friends.

But privately I like to be reminded of the sentence in the liturgy for this day: "Remember thou art dust and to dust thou shalt return." The thought of returning to dust comforts me. I prefer to end as a silent, dry, colorless presence—somewhere.

. . . .

The usual picture of a very old person: crippled, almost bald, stooped, shaky, living in a crowded single room. Of course this dour picture is hardly universal. There are exceptions, mostly the fortunate few inhabitants living in expensive retirement communities. Good genes, moneyed upbringing and schooling, excellent health care, useful contacts with others of their class, seemingly secure marriages, longtime upscale housing, satisfactory children, permanent employment, and ample pensions, yes, and some amount of good luck, have helped them reach an untroubled old age. In their retirement they live in communities where their apartments or cottages are cleaned weekly, their meals and entertainment, books, and TV are provided, and their medical care scrupulously supplied down to the very end.

These communities are set in parks filled with great trees, gardens, meadows, and ponds, shielded from the outside world and from the noisy, critical young by long, winding roadways. Those of advanced old age often chose these pleasant places for their proximity to their children (sometimes to discover that these offspring do not visit as often as they had expected).

So, given all these similarities, the fortunate citizens of such choice communities tend to resemble each other. With a few, usually token, exceptions they are white, well-to-do, Christian, college-educated, professional, and heterosexual.

Most are also caring, amiable, polite, and cheerful. They participate in a multitude of activities. The bulletin board of one such place listed ninety active committees, including origami, Scottish dancing, a "laugh committee." Of course there were more serious ones: nature and bird walks, bus trips to the symphony, bridge, and such.

There is nothing bad or wrong about these provisions. But this small minority has often lost diversity, the interest of differences, even some of the charm and variety of the real world.

Such homogeneity can be—and often is, to put it perhaps unjustly—well, dull.

. . . .

It is not uncommon to see elderly couples, hand in hand or supporting each other, visiting famous ruins like Yucatan sites or ruined English churches or Tintern Abbey. Rose Macaulay in *The Pleasure of Ruins* explains why pleasure is to be found in such places. The parts are somehow more satisfying than the whole. Completeness leaves little room for fantasy or imagination.

Why is this so? Why are the old, like me, so fond of them? Ruins are not in themselves always beautiful. But like us they are the remains of what was once a more perfect whole. They have withstood imperfectly the destructive forces of time. There is a certain rightness, an inevitability, about their decline. They are my fellow structures, my companions over time.

Sadly, there are signs of restoration at some sites. Stones from somewhere else are brought in; the new cement that holds them in place is a jaundiced yellow. Hammers and machines disturb the silence of centuries. Midas Dekkers, in *The Way of All Flesh,* says: "The aim of restoring something to its former glory is as futile as it is human. A lot of glory is simply at its best if it's decaying."

The ancient places are a welcome relief from the contemporary sight of ugly "planned" communities, long malls, inhuman-scaled skyscrapers, faceless factories, "developments," and snaked-in-upon-themselves highways.

Having become a ruin myself, I identify with them.

. . . .

A very small minority of the very old think of themselves as solitary, but in a curious, contradictory way. Jay Parini, one of Robert Frost's biographers, described the poet as a loner who loved company. Edith Wharton claimed that her friend Henry James was a solitary who could not live alone, and Tadié wrote of Marcel Proust that he was "a recluse who was unable to live alone."

. . . .

For me, like most of the elderly, it becomes hard to make new friends. My time is short and my energies limited. Friendship is the result of long-term alliances. Even those alliances I do manage to form are delusionary. Proust said that friendship is no more than "a lie that seeks to make us believe that we are not irremediably alone."

. . . .

I knew an elderly couple, George and Mary, who lived together for seventy years. They lived identical lives, were rarely apart even for meals, and always traveled together. Only their chores differed, he doing the outside work, the driving, going to the office, she occupied with cooking, cleaning, laundry, and child care.

What kept them together for so long? A wondrous fact: during all these years they quarreled, endlessly. The unusual endurance of their lives and their marriage came from the strength of their disagreements. In their many homes and apartments, in the garden, in bed, in restaurants, during visits to friends, on their travels, they carried on their arguments and continued to disagree about every detail of their mutual lives. The very air around them seemed filled with the heavy clouds of disputation.

I attended the party to celebrate their seventieth wedding anniversary (they claimed they had met in the sandbox), surrounded by their children, grandchildren, great-grandchildren, and friends. They were presented an elaborate cake topped with many candles. It took some time for me to get my piece of cake because the two old celebrants argued vociferously and at length about who should hold the knife to make the first cut.

A few months after the party, George died, leaving Mary to join other survivors of her sex. The elderly widows often met at card tables, luncheons, on porch rockers, to reminisce about the past. Their conversation was full of sentimentally reiterated proper nouns, the first names of their departed husbands. Howard and Larry and yes, George, had become mythic figures. When George's widow spoke, the passage of time had whitened the stories she contributed to the general conversation. Often she was heard to say: "We were so happy. Never a cross word between us."

Oscar Wilde knew the truth about such revisions: "There is no such thing as a romantic experience," he wrote. "There are romantic memories and there is the desire for romance—that is all."

. . . .

In contrast to those few elderly who take pleasure in letting go of possessions, there are many more who are compulsive savers. There is a curious slant to this. They save useless things: silver foil, envelopes for their canceled stamps and places of origin, holiday wrapping paper and twine, bottle corks and tops. Their special fondness is for tiny wood, glass, and stuffed animals—teddy bears, pandas, giraffes, dogs and cats, and every other species.

Saving becomes for them an absorbing occupation that fills time, drawers, and shelves. After their death their survivors, in fits of annoyance, dispose of the beloved objects into the garbage, or to thrift shops where, it may be, a new generation of those growing old and delighted at the bargains such stores offer, add to their own collections of teddy bears, pandas, giraffes...

. . . .

Recently I was privileged to listen to a perspicacious old lady who had just returned from her sixtieth college class reunion:

"My classmates' conversation was almost entirely cheerful. There were many stories about their fortunate pasts, their children who were incredibly successful, and their grandchildren with unusual talents. I heard descriptions of trips made to spectacular, out-of-the-way places. I grew tired of it all.

"But I came upon a fellow I had known in college. We had once met at Sunday Mass at a Catholic church off-campus. He wanted to know if I still believed in immortality. Had I outgrown the teachings of the Church on that subject? I said yes, I had. I now thought the promise of life after death was, in someone else's words, 'a sloppy consolation.' I could not remember who had called it that.

"He laughed. Then he said: 'Recently, I came upon an interesting book by André Comte-Sponville, called, if I remember correctly, *The Little Book of Atheist Spirituality*.' Speaking of our old belief in immortality he said: 'We are already in the kingdom. Eternity is now.'

"We sat together in chairs apart from the high-pitched, self-congratu-latory talk and ceaseless laughter of our classmates. We said nothing more and both, I think, enjoyed our long silence. Then he said, to my delight: 'I read somewhere that silence also is conversation.'"

. . . .

A memorable remark on memory: My friend's mother reproved her daughter who had said, "Oh, Mother, you don't remember that." She responded sharply: "I know what I've forgotten."

On another occasion the same witty lady admitted that "I have lost my nouns," but had fortunately retained all her other parts of speech.

. . . .

"I am lonely only in company," an elderly woman told me. She said that her seclusion allows for frequent journeys into her interior self, for listening to music without interruption, for times of critical thinking about political and religious matters without the necessity of expressing an opinion. She finds herself reexamining old ideas that do not need to be verbalized but remain contentedly in her aging mind.

To these happy few for whom being alone is a boon, an additional gift, a blessing, silence is a healing salve after submitting to years of mindless prattle, pointless stories, and the unremitting autobiographical talk of their garrulous contemporaries. A Syrian monk, speaking of God, writes: "Many are avidly seeking, but they alone find who remain in continual silence." He goes on: "Every man who delights in a multitude of words, even though he says admirable things, is empty within." And he adds: "[Silence] brings a fruit that tongue cannot describe."

. . . .

In the middle of the last century many families were proud owners of a camera called a Brownie. It took what were called snapshots. The father of the family was most often the "taker." (He knew best how to operate the square brown, or sometimes black, box.) He "snapped" family members and friends on vacation, posed in front of monuments and famous sites, at holiday celebrations, anniversaries, birthdays. He documented historic events like the new car, the new dog, the new house.

Always, before the advent of a flash attachment, the pictures were taken out-of-doors, and almost without exception, everyone in those pictures was smiling, not so much an indication of their state of mind, perhaps, as the obedient response to the order to say "cheese."

Pictures had to be taken while the sun was out and situated over the photographer's left shoulder. Then, when the twelve or twenty-four frames were all used (the numbers appeared in a little box at the top of the Brownie), the yellow roll of film was removed carefully in a dark place to avoid exposure, and taken to the drugstore to be developed.

Many of the exposures turned out well, but some were blurred because the smallest girl had turned her head or someone has raised an arm at the moment the button was clicked or the hapless father had moved the box. The satisfactory ones were pasted, with four small white corners, onto the black pages of an album and labeled in white ink: "John, aged four, in his new sailor suit, July 7, '37."

For members of my generation much of our memory is restricted to these snapshots, to those invariably happy faces on apparently happy family occasions and at beautiful places. They remember these pictured celebratory victorious teams, the blissful vacationing couples feeding the pigeons in a sun-filled Roman square, the joyful graduating classes, the triumphant, straw-hatted fishermen holding aloft their catch for the benefit of the Brownie.

Nothing negative is recorded in these albums, no sad occasions, nothing puzzling or questionable behind these everlasting grins, no bitterness, hurts, no perpetual misunderstandings. Why, it must have been thought, waste these valuable black pages on the truth, even if, by chance, it had been caught in the sunlight over the photographer's left shoulder?

Afterthought: Joseph Conrad said that words "are the great foes of reality." Can the same be said of snapshots?

. . . .

The glossy covers of catalogs sent out by prosperous retirement communities to solicit new residents usually show current occupants working in their flourishing communal gardens or striding athletically through woods. Always there is one smiling brown face among them, and sometimes an Asian one to suggest (falsely, it may be) the diversity of its present members.

I once encountered a black, smiling old man, known for his quick wit, seated on a bench at the doorway of a retirement community. I stopped to question him.

"How are you?"

"All right."

"Why are you smiling?"

The old man's smile broadened. "I'm paid to sit here to look like a happy resident."

"Only a joke," he added.

. . . .

At the moment my contemporaries and I are on "holding ground," the maritime term for a place to anchor temporarily for the night. This haven will not serve for very long, the way childhood had seemed to and youth and maturity did. Old age is terminal, but still, I find the long habit of living hard to break.

The fortunate among us will die quickly. James F. Fries termed it "compressed vitality." But there will be the exceptions who will disintegrate slowly. A hip, a knee, a vital organ, one part at a time, unlike the old conveyance in Oliver Wendell Holmes's one-horse shay in "The Deacon's Masterpiece." That old carriage had served without a part failing or needing replacement for a century. Then, when it was one hundred years old, it collapsed, fell down, and died, all at once.

However death arrives, in installments or in one instant stroke, I regard myself as fortunate. I will be able to echo the last words of Lady Mary Wortley Montagu (who died in 1762):

"It has all been very interesting."

DORIS GRUMBACH, b. 1918, is the author of seven novels, six books of memoir, and a biography of Mary McCarthy. This essay is part of a larger memoir, *Downhill Almost All the Way*.

The Impossibility of Dying

Erving Polster

When I asked gestalt therapist Erving Polster to write about being in his nineties, he told me that macular degeneration now kept him from writing. He suggested that we talk instead; what follows is an edited version of our conversation. We began by discussing his use of the word "interruption" in relation to the deaths of his wife and daughter when he was seventy-nine.—*Nan Narboe*

. . . .

You spoke of Miriam and Sarah's death as an interruption, which is a much milder word than "catastrophe" and the other words people use.

While it was experienced as catastrophe—I did not mean to say that one would take the death of a loved one lightly, nor did I. In fact, these were the most painful invasions of my mind I have ever experienced. Still, there was replenishment to come, as well. The flow of life allows recovery.

Continuity is compelling if your mind is open to it. Trauma may not allow you to do that, however. Catastrophe may not permit you to flow forward; it may stop your mind right there. But there is something paradoxical about even traumatic paralysis and the natural fluidity that people have at their biological core.

So you are saying something quite optimistic, really, about human resilience.

Yes, but it is a very large challenge. It's not something that one casually succeeds in.

Are there discrete steps you experienced?

Well, there is always an interweaving. So while I may have experienced devastation, I had friends with whom I had ordinary conversations. And

I did eat my food as I would normally have eaten it. I did put my clothes on. I did read. So there are many things which go on in an interwoven way, which are built into our system. And to the extent that we can allow ourselves to incorporate those, we are able to restore the flow.

In the immediacy of a loss, I have thought things like, "How odd: The sky is still blue."

It seems incompatible . . . but one of the challenges in life is restoring that which seems incompatible into compatible. Sometimes people can't do it, and sometimes they do it partly and not as much as they would want, and sometimes it takes time. It can't happen at the snap of fingers. Fortunately for me, there were things going on which mattered to me, even though Miriam and Sarah had died.

I still had a son. I had friends. I needed to eat. I like walking. I like talking. I like tea. And I valued those. But if I didn't value them, and if my whole being was connected with the one trauma, it would have been a harder experience. In fact, over the years, I have recognized that some people have what I think of as a criteria cure: Only if such-and-such happens can I be okay. And usually, that can't happen. If your idea of restoration of life is that your dead mother smile at you, then you're doomed. Some people's thinking is not quite as disastrous as that, but they still have criteria: If such-and-such doesn't happen, nothing else matters.

One of my surprises about my hands becoming more and more gnarled is that I can accept the trade-off. They still work, so okay. They hurt, but okay.

Well, your thought process can help, but sometimes a thought process is not enough. You have to be able to replace the centrality of your hands and the devastation of their gnarledness with something else that is equally interesting and refreshing, equally nourishing. And one can do that through new relationships, new interests.

One of the things that I've been aware of, in relation to the question of dying—as I come closer and closer to that day—is that even though I know my remaining time is short, it still feels infinite. One of my thoughts about—let's call it the impossibility of dying, the impossibility of being up to dying—is that all my life I have felt that way about the next step. When I was in the fourth grade, I could not have imagined my doing algebra. When I got to the stage where I needed to do algebra, it was okay. And I could name five or six or seven different, forward-looking impossibilities that, when the time came, turned out to be doable. Life is filled with those sequences and you can see death as one of those with some confidence that when you get there, it would be just as impossible. Actually, it's quite possible. [Both laugh.]

One may even an innate gift for it.
There's something about having confidence—that when the time comes, you will be prepared—that you couldn't have had earlier.

When we spoke last time, you shared with me the story of going into surgery for your hip. And how you didn't review your life.
I tried, before going under anesthesia. I knew that coming out of it was likely, but at ninety-four, it was no "gimme," so I wanted to get some sense of my life. I didn't want my last moment to be going into anesthesia. And I tried to open my mind to the life I had lived. I couldn't do it.

Do you think that's because a life is too big?
That's where I was, where my mind was. I could not get to the context, the breadth of perspective of my life.

It is said that when you're in danger, your life flashes before you. Well, I flew thirty-five missions in the Second World War and I never had my life flash before me. I didn't care about my life. I cared about living; the idea of having perspective on my life was the last thing I cared about.

So you have the dilemma that there is a search for immediacy while our whole mindset is also geared toward context and perspective. And there's a continual clash between those two fundamentals of the brain, one fundamental being here now, immediacy, and the other being perspective: "What is my life about? What does my life mean? What kind of life have I lived? What do I belong to? What am I a part of?"

You are describing a task so large that I wonder if you think it's doable.
Well, it's not a sure win, but I think our whole being is geared toward

integrating immediacy and perspective. Figure-ground relationship, you might say, is fundamental. You can't see a tree, period. You can only see a tree that's on a spread of lawn or in a forest or in a picture. The tree always has a context. It's a given. Our minds don't allow a real separation between immediacy and perspective. They always have to coordinate with each other and be integrated. It's our biggest job in life, to be able to do those well. A lifetime—that's a big project, integrating all that, and human beings are fated to have to reckon with that complexity.

ERVING POLSTER, b. 1922, is a veteran teacher of gestalt therapy and has attracted students from all over the world to his training center in San Diego. He has authored six books, the most recent of which is *Beyond Therapy*. In it, he proposes the formation of congregations of people, exploring their lives together. These congregations would be driven by the innate need to survey life, illuminating the commonality and individuality of basic themes, such as home, ambition, and belonging.

Subjective Age: *I am astonished to find the number 94 next to my name. What it means is not clear to me but is surely a culturally important phenomenon. People repeatedly congratulate me. Like a lot of other things, though, age has more than one meaning. I think that basic human energy is ageless and content-free. From that standpoint, my attention is much the same to me now as it was when I was five or ten or fifty. But, that energy must join with content and from that standpoint, I am much different now than at any other age in my life. That is a remarkable storyline with all the continuity stories have.*
While I don't associate that sequence with a number, 94, I do associate it with a currently truncated future, to which I am adapting; to a greater isolation than ever from the daily assurance of connection and impact and forward movement. I am much more at home with the idea of dying, and, while I still don't want it, I am more confident that the trauma will be less than I previously imagined. In summation, though, my life is as it ever was: a mixture of great pleasure and a sense of interruption when either my health or wishes do not measure up. The bottom line is ambiguity, and I am quite at home with that as my human fate.

Epilogue

Elizabeth Bugental

This morning my husband and I had a conversation at the breakfast table. It began when he looked up from the paper to ask me how old he was, and progressed from there to all kinds of other questions about his life. I conjured up some memories for him, images and vignettes—his adult children, our daughter and her husband, our family and friends, his achievements, books he had written, wonderful celebrations in his honor, special moments between us, our travels—until it became clear that he was listening avidly to a tale about someone he didn't even know. I reached across the table to hold his hand as the tears ran down his cheeks, explaining to him, as I have many many times, that a stroke a year and a half ago had simply wiped out his past. He was quiet for awhile, bathed in grief. Then he looked up, the tears still standing in his eyes. "But I have you," he said, smiling. He sat a minute, struggled to his feet, dragging himself slowly on his walker into the living room and his favorite chair facing out the window into the garden.

When I came in a few minutes later and stood behind him looking out, my arms around his neck, he covered my hands with his. "I am out there naked in the sun and the wind," he said. "We have such a good life."

ELIZABETH BUGENTAL, b. 1926, was a writer and psychotherapist. While a nun in the Order of the Immaculate Heart of Mary, she earned a doctorate in Speech and Drama. In later life, she became an influential therapist with her husband, James Bugental, a pioneer of Existential-Humanist psychotherapy in the US. This essay was the introduction to her book *AgeSong: Meditations for Our Later Years*. Bugental died in 2009.

Copyrights

Author Index

About the Editor

Nan Narboe worked as a psychotherapist and trainer for forty years, and has since transitioned into consulting. Based in Portland, Oregon, she currently specializes in working with entrepreneurs and with people deciding what to do with the rest of their lives. The interplay between individual traits, chronological age, and developmental stage has been a lifelong fascination, the best part of which has been watching her daughter grow up. Nan co-founded L'Auberge, a five-course restaurant that presaged the "local food" movement, and Cascade Valley School, a democratic school inspired by the Sudbury model. She launched her writing apprenticeship at forty by attending the feminist workshop, Flight of the Mind, and sold her first piece a mere twenty-eight years later.